The Chippewa Landscape of Louise Erdrich

The Chippewa Landscape of Louise Erdrich

Edited by
Allan Chavkin

Afterword by
A. LaVonne Brown Ruoff

THE UNIVERSITY OF
ALABAMA PRESS
Tuscaloosa

1 2 3 4 5 6 7 8 9 • 06 05 04 03 02 01 00 99

∞
The paper on which this book is printed meets the minimum requirements of American National Standard for Information Science-Permanence of Paper for Printed Library Materials, ANSI Z39.48-1984.

Library of Congress Cataloging-in-Publication Data

The Chippewa landscape of Louise Erdrich / edited by Allan Chavkin.
p. cm.
Includes bibliographical references (p.) and index.

ISBN 0–8173–0942–X (alk. paper)
ISBN 0–8173–0955–1 (pbk. : alk. paper)
1. Erdrich, Louise—Criticism and interpretation. 2. Women and literature—United States—History—20th century. 3. Indians in literature. 4. Ojibwa Indians. I. Chavkin, Allan Richard, 1950–
PS3555.R42 Z63 1999
813′.54—ddc21

98–58015

British Library Cataloguing-in-Publication Data Available

For my parents and Laura

Contents

Acknowledgments

I would like to thank A. LaVonne Brown Ruoff, Nancy Grayson, Paul Cohen, Mark Busby, Angela Ingram, Fritz Oehlschlaeger, Nancy J. Peterson, John Blair, Robert Morace, Annette Van Dyke, John Purdy, Catherine Rainwater, Robert O'Connor, and Cynthia Lowenthal, and my wife and colleague Nancy for offering suggestions for improving this book. I also appreciate the financial support of the Office of Sponsored Projects of Southwest Texas State University for two Research Enhancement Grants. I am indebted to the National Endowment for the Humanities for a 1985 fellowship to work on another project on American literature but which also gave me time to read some of the work of Louise Erdrich. I owe thanks to the library staff of the university, who provided assistance numerous times. I am grateful to Copyeditor Michael Senecal, and to Senior Editor Curtis Clark, Director and Editor in Chief Nicole Mitchell, and the staff of The University of Alabama Press for their excellent advice.

Abbreviations

BP	*The Bingo Palace,* Louise Erdrich. New York: HarperCollins, 1994.
BQ	*The Beet Queen,* Louise Erdrich. New York: Holt, 1986.
LM	*Love Medicine: A Novel,* Louise Erdrich. New York: Holt, Rinehart & Winston, 1984.
LMN	*Love Medicine: New and Expanded Version,* Louise Erdrich. New York: Holt, 1993.
TBL	*Tales of Burning Love,* Louise Erdrich. New York: HarperCollins, 1996.
T	*Tracks,* Louise Erdrich. New York: Holt, 1988.

The Chippewa Landscape of Louise Erdrich

Introduction

ALLAN CHAVKIN

Often viewed as an outstanding practitioner of modern fiction, Louise Erdrich should be regarded as one of the country's most important writers. Her first novel, *Love Medicine* (1984, 1993), a collection of interconnected stories focusing on the lives of two Chippewa families, won several prizes, including the National Book Critics Circle Award. *The Beet Queen* (1986), *Tracks* (1988), *The Bingo Palace* (1994), and *Tales of Burning Love* (1996) also received critical acclaim and together with *Love Medicine* form an interlocking epic novel. With her husband Michael Dorris, Erdrich collaborated on the best-selling *The Crown of Columbus* (1991), which focuses on the theme of discovery. Erdrich also published two highly regarded volumes of poetry, *Jacklight* (1984) and *Baptism of Desire* (1989), and numerous stories in such periodicals as the *New Yorker, Harper's Magazine, Atlantic Monthly,* and *Paris Review.* Her book *The Blue Jay's Dance: A Birth Year* (1995) is a work of nonfiction consisting primarily of autobiographical recollections and meditations on nature and motherhood.

Although Erdrich has demonstrated her remarkable skill in several genres, it is for her fiction, especially her novels about the Chippewa, that she is renowned. Her brilliant, complex prose style and her unique vision are responsible for her immense critical and popular acclaim. In her novels she typically interweaves stories told by diverse narrators and chronicles different generations of Euro-American and American Indian characters. Her individualistic prose style includes the juxtaposition of the mundane and the fantastic, gritty realism and dreamlike hallucinations, the conversational and the lyrical, and existential bleakness and slapstick exuberance. Joyce Carol Oates has called her a "magical realist," but Erdrich doubts that the label best describes her, remarking to Allan Chavkin and Nancy Feyl Chavkin that "the events people pick out as magical don't seem unreal to me" (221). This yoking of the natural and the supernatural that one sees in her fiction and that is ascribed to the magical realism of the postmodernists probably has its origin in Erdrich's Chippewa heritage.

In fact, Erdrich's portrayal of the Chippewa is her greatest achievement and the source of much of the enthusiastic critical and popular attention directed toward her work. She depicts not only the tragedy of the dispossession and the suffering of the Indians but also their dignity and humor. In contrast to the ubiquitous stereotypes of Indians in film, television, and popular culture, she presents them in all their complexity and reveals their essential humanity.

Erdrich has become the country's most prominent writer of American Indian heritage, and she is one of only a very few American Indian writers who have found a large readership. It is perhaps surprising that her novels have sold impressively in Europe and the United States, because these books, with their multiple narrators, poetic language, experimental structures, and intricate blending of myth and realism, can be difficult. In fact, her departure from conventional realism and her deliberate artifice occasionally remind one of the abstruse metafiction of some postmodernist writers.

The purpose of this collection of previously unpublished essays is to remove some of the obstacles to understanding Erdrich's fiction and thereby enhance the reader's enjoyment and appreciation of her subtle art. Although the essays range widely in subject matter and approach, the tacit assumption of all of them is that Erdrich's American Indian heritage is at the foundation of her literary art. In fact, the critics in this volume focus upon the Chippewa aspects of Erdrich's art not only because that is the source of her greatest originality but also because it is the source of greatest difficulty for the vast majority of non-Indian readers unfamiliar with Chippewa myth, tradition, and culture. This concentration on the Chippewa aspects of her canon explains the emphasis in this volume upon certain works and the lack of emphasis upon or the omission of others.

In "Against All Odds: Games of Chance in the Novels of Louise Erdrich," John Purdy investigates the author's deliberate use of gambling scenes and the notion of luck and chance in her narrative cosmology. He suggests one way of understanding the linked novels of *Love Medicine, The Beet Queen, Tracks, The Bingo Palace,* and *Tales of Burning Love* is to see them as an exploration of the nature of chance and the efficacy of understanding the nature of possibility. Purdy examines the implications of Erdrich's preoccupation in her novels with chance and odd coincidences. Drawing upon ethnographic sources that address gambling in Chippewa culture, he observes that Indian gambling predates the European colonization of the New World. For the Chippewa in Erdrich's novels gambling can be a means of empowerment, of balancing out the ill effects of the modern world and compensating for the loss that has so dominated American Indian history. These novels explore the past and imaginatively dramatize the future. By understanding the suffering in the past and how individuals coped, one can understand the present. The novels imply that "loss need not be irrevocable; colonialism can be countered."

In "From Sacred Hoops to Bingo Palaces: Louise Erdrich's Carnivalesque Fiction," Robert A. Morace approaches Erdrich's work from a Bakhtinian perspective while being keenly aware that some American Indian novels might seem to be more dialogical than they actually are. He employs Bakhtin's theory of carnival, with particular emphasis on folk sources, disruptive/creative function, and attention to the body and discusses how the problem facing later carnivalesque works parallels the problem facing Erdrich as her American Indian fiction enters into a complex dialogue with the literary mainstream. His intricate analysis includes some important sociopolitical implications of Erdrich's carnivalesque art.

In "Life into Death, Death into Life: Hunting as Metaphor and Motive in *Love Medicine,*" Robert F. Gish emphasizes the historical importance of hunting in American Indian culture and literature; he also argues that it is central in contemporary American Indian fiction. Of course, contemporary writers often redefine and adapt the tradition to express their own vision. Gish reveals how much of the motives and metaphors of *Love Medicine* have their source in the polarities and associations of the hunter and the hunted. In fact, he shows how the sequence and linkage of the main "love stories" of the book are presented amid the contraries of hunter and hunted. The chapter "Wild Geese" and especially the titular chapter "Love Medicine" support his argument. Gish demonstrates how Erdrich's use of "expansive and reflexive image and symbol, her fine orchestration of pattern and rhythm whereby the paradoxes, the motives, and metaphors of hunting and the hunt, life into death, death into life, converge into the regenerative and reaffirming potency of *Love Medicine* to bring new life and insight to the reader through the clear and accurate aim of the artist—straight to the heart, mind, and soul of the waiting, wanting reader."

In "Vision and Revision in Louise Erdrich's *Love Medicine,*" I argue that the problem of the two versions of the novel has been ignored by critics. The existence of the two versions raises some important and puzzling questions. Which edition reveals Erdrich's "real intentions"? Which version is a better work of literary art? What motivated Erdrich to revise and republish her popular prize-winning novel? Using Jack Stillinger's theory of textual pluralism, I argue that those who have published on *Love Medicine* have not realized how the existence of the two versions of the novel complicates the critic's task. The existence of the two versions raises the question of what constitutes *Love Medicine,* a novel with a complex textual history that includes publication of parts of the book as short stories in periodicals before later incorporation in the novel. Is a work existing in multiple versions, such as *Love Medicine,* "a single version of the work or all the versions taken together?—and if it is all the versions taken together, is the work constituted by the *process* of its revisions, one after another, or by all the versions considered as existing simultaneously, as they might in a variorum edition giving a complete account of the successive readings?" (Stillinger v). Challenging the widely held assumption that the two editions of the novel are not fundamentally different, I focus upon the four new chapters and the new section of "The Beads" to reveal the key objectives underlying Erdrich's revised and expanded version.

In "Narrative and Ethos in Erdrich's 'A Wedge of Shade,'" William

J. Scheick applies an approach from art criticism that assesses the whole of a work in terms of a crucial part. Scheick uses Erdrich's "A Wedge of Shade," published in the *New Yorker,* in order to "atomize" her work and see the building blocks of her artistry and understand the ethos informing her fiction. This short story can stand on its own as an autonomous work of art, but it is also connected to Erdrich's linked novel sequence; it is, in short, "a well-crafted short story and an illuminating detail from Erdrich's larger project." In his analysis of the major tropes, Scheick reveals the antitheses of the story and "the antagonistic features and forces" inherent in nature, people, families, and culture. Implicit in the story is the assumption that in life there is some sacred mystery beyond human understanding. Scheick locates the source of this assumption in Chippewa culture and examines the circle, arc, and wedge references in the story and their association with Chippewa beliefs.

In "Of Vision Quests and Spirit Guardians: Female Power in the Novels of Louise Erdrich," Annette Van Dyke observes that historically Euro-Americans have seen American Indian women as stereotypes, usually as a "good Indian" or a "bad Indian." In both of these instances, the woman is subordinate to and dependent upon "her man." In contrast to Euro-Americans, however, American Indians regarded Indian women as powerful, as Paula Gunn Allen observes in her *Sacred Hoop: Recovering the Feminine in American Indian Traditions* (1986). As Van Dyke notes, Allen has pointed out that contemporary American Indian women vacillate between self-reliance and dependence and find themselves in a bicultural bind because of the "two hopelessly opposed cultural definitions of women." Van Dyke argues that Erdrich intends in her fiction to attempt to counter these stereotypes and the bicultural trap confronting American Indian women by presenting women who exemplify a "kind of power central to life on the reservation," what Erdrich regards as "transformational" sexual power. Van Dyke focuses on two pairs of mothers and daughters (Fleur/Lulu and Marie/Zelda) in order to reveal the women's power, a power that assumes a peculiarly sexual form for Chippewa women and that has its source in the Chippewa vision quest and spirit guardian. Despite having lost some knowledge of the traditional ways as a consequence of the influence of Euro-American culture and Catholicism, the female characters reveal this transformational power in various manifestations.

Catherine Rainwater begins "Ethnic Signs in Erdrich's *Tracks* and *The Bingo Palace*" with a deceptively simple question: "What makes a novel 'Native American'?" Is it the writer's ethnicity? Or is the content of the novel, more than the author's ethnicity, the decisive factor? Or is it something else? This question leads to an understanding of what constitutes an ethnic sign in literature, and Rainwater investigates the potential reader's experience of American Indian texts. She sees ethnic signs embedded in certain texts by Indian writers, including Erdrich, that function as a continual source of disruption and undermine a comfortable interpretive position for the reader. This may result in the reader's keen self-awareness of his or her role in text production and "the acts of world-making that texts imply." She demonstrates that the most ordinary sign might become ethnic in the social semiotic exchange of reading and that Erdrich's fiction implies an ethics of reading.

In "Indi'n Humor and Trickster Justice in *The Bingo Palace*," Nancy J. Peterson examines the novel within the contexts of postmodernism, the contemporary crisis in history, and the traditions of the Chippewa. While *Tracks* can be described as "a novel entirely haunted by historical dispossession" and tribal fragmentation, *The Bingo Palace* is very different in plot and tone. With slapstick humor and exuberant comedy, the later novel mitigates the tragic history presented in *Tracks* and presents a way of psychologically coping with the tragic past. Erdrich seems to be suggesting that readers should see Indians not as tragic victims but as complex people capable of laughter. Peterson argues that it is Erdrich's powerful intermixture of serious themes and comic laughter that has made "her vision of Native America so compelling." Using Erdrich's own comments on Indian humor and Kenneth Lincoln's theories in *Indi'n Humor: Bicultural Play in Native America* (1993), Peterson argues that the comedy at the heart of *The Bingo Palace* is an Indian humor that is inextricably related to the grim history of Native America. Lincoln's theory of Indian humor allows one to understand the "complex comic dynamics" of *The Bingo Palace* as well as the ways in which that novel "moves toward an unprecedented development—the emergence of a new kind of Indi'n humor rising out of triumphant laughter and (postmodern) trickster justice." Peterson explains how bingo operates in the novel as a postmodern strategy that enables the Indians to find a kind of trickster justice that serves as a compensation for historical dispossession.

In her "Afterword," A. LaVonne Brown Ruoff reminisces about her friendship with Louise Erdrich and evaluates her career. Ruoff knew Erdrich before she became a published writer and suggested possible revisions for early versions of the stories in *Love Medicine* and other works. Ruoff's recollections include much interesting information, such as the fact that the hilarious riot in "The Tomahawk Factory" of the revised *Love Medicine* was originally part of an unpublished novel called "Tracks," a manuscript quite different from the published novel of that title. Ruoff presents an explanation for Erdrich's great popularity and suggests what distinguishes her fiction from that of other writers. She also comments upon Erdrich's influence on other American Indian writers and her attitude about being placed in this ethnic category. She briefly evaluates Erdrich's works and the critical response to them.

I hope that this collection of original essays will illuminate the reader's understanding of Erdrich's unique vision of the human condition as it is expressed in her extraordinarily rich and profound fiction. The contributors to this volume examine her fiction from a variety of points of view and theoretical approaches that collectively allow the reader to see the many facets of her complex art. Erdrich is a prolific writer who still has many productive years ahead, and critics will continue to assess her influence and significance in the decades to come. But even at this relatively early stage it is clear that she has written some of the most significant American novels of the twentieth century and that her substantial body of work represents a permanent contribution to American literature.

Works Cited

Chavkin, Allan, and Nancy Feyl Chavkin, eds. *Conversations with Louise Erdrich and Michael Dorris.* Jackson: UP of Mississippi, 1994.

Stillinger, Jack. *Coleridge and Textual Instability: The Multiple Versions of the Major Poems.* New York: Oxford UP, 1994.

1

Against All Odds

Games of Chance in the Novels of Louise Erdrich

John Purdy

As their continued popularity attests, the novels of Louise Erdrich (Anishinabe) speak to readers in very personal ways. Despite their cultural and geographical specificity, the characters who people her pages are immensely recognizable to an audience comprised of many cultures: they exhibit all the frailties and strengths, the failures and triumphs one would expect for humans who face what we all—as individuals, as cultures, and as species—must face: change. In fact, change (the continuous, comparative revelation of a past and a desired future) is integral to human existence and experience, so it is quite understandable that it is also a concern, a subtext, in all Erdrich's novels. Moreover, the past, in particular the history of interaction between immigrant and indigenous peoples, is ever present in her stories, and that history figures prominently in the nature of the changes to be found in them; change can cut many ways, in any direction, as Erdrich's characters often learn. When they look to the future, they precipitate events—good or ill—that initiate the next episodes in their (hi)stories.

Some readers and critics have been quick to concentrate on the more dismal aspects of change in Erdrich's works. From the very beginning of her career as a novelist, in other words from the publication of *Love Medicine* in 1984, critics and reviewers alike have noted a sense of loss that informs her stories; this novel opens, after all, with the death of June

Kashpaw. Change, in this limited sense at least, is synonymous with death and, by extension it seems, the destruction of a way of life, a people. However, loss is only one factor in life's equation, one element in a balance one finds in her novels. Those who read only "victim" would no doubt round up Indians from offices, burn their casinos, and herd them back "where they belong" around the dance fires and teepees of the silver screen. For the essentialist reader, in other words, Erdrich's novels remain enigmatic.

The past is important for us all, and Erdrich makes this apparent in the lives of her characters. All her novels are intricately concerned with what has happened previously, but, more significantly, they are the imaginative dramatization of an abiding concern for the future. The four that have been called, and appear to have been originally conceived of as, a tetralogy—*Love Medicine, The Beet Queen, Tracks,* and *The Bingo Palace*—move from the 1980s to the earlier part of the century and finally into the 1990s. The latest addition, *Tales of Burning Love,* extends this chronology to the present. Going back, it seems, can enlighten the present and the future as well. In other words, by understanding the stories of how loss came about and what individuals did to deal with it, one can better address contemporary events, some of which may prove equally threatening. Furthermore, the novels suggest that loss need not be irrevocable; colonialism can be countered.

The publication of *The Bingo Palace* in 1994 revealed how pervasive Erdrich's concern for empowerment had been in her earlier works. Consider the title itself, in light of issues in "Indian Country" immediately surrounding its publication. Articles in all the country's major newspapers, debates in Congress and its various committees and subcommittees, television news broadcasts, and radio talk shows featuring the quintessential opportunist Donald Trump focused upon one curious issue: Indian gambling. The furor that this issue generates is at once understandable and ominous. For Native nations, the potential for the generation of large sums of capital carries with it the potential for self-sufficiency and therefore self-determination, but with this potential also comes the threat of reprisal and loss. To put it succinctly, social gambling in its current usage does not simply mean gambling in a social setting, but in actuality the engagement of two societies and the juxtaposing of two conflicting views of the future. Which society (Euro- or Native American), should have the funds and therefore the final say in what will be? Like gamblers poised over the poker table, Native nations face off against the federal government and individual states, and at stake are future generations.[1] This confrontation is a recurring motif, another locus of colonial tension, but also transformation, in Erdrich's novels, including *Tales of Burning Love.*

Indigenous cultures, like all others, have always had an inherent interest, a tradition, in gambling. Long before the first European tried his luck on this continent, players participated in the stick game, the bone game or any number of analogous games throughout the land. Today, at powwows, at gatherings of numerous varieties, and—more to our purpose here—in every Native literary canon, gambling can be found.

Fundamentally, all "games of chance" are games of change and power over it, and "Indian gaming" recognizes and celebrates that basic reality. But, as the scene with Lyman in Reno in *The Bingo Palace* reveals, Erdrich recognizes that there are many ways to engage in the game. In fact, one way of reading her novels is to consider them an exploration of the nature of chance as it engages the history of colonialism in this hemisphere, and more specifically, as a thesis on the efficacy of understanding the nature of possibility, of cusp, and employing it to one's advantage. Using this reading, one may discern a moral embedded in her stories, structured by events hinged on apparent chance. Clearly, Erdrich's fiction is, as Anishinabe author Gerald Vizenor so aptly encapsulates in his title for a book of literary criticism, a Narrative Chance in which events reveal that probability is, like beauty, in the eye of the beholder, and power is in the future of the gambler with a good heart, a love medicine.

To apprehend this thesis at work, one must of course examine Erdrich's overt use of gambling scenes, which are crucial, pivotal events in the long story of the central families of the Turtle Mountain Chippewa as depicted in the novels. These punctuate the history and colonialism, the chances and changes, within which the families are situated. By considering these scenes in conjunction, as they evolve through the novels, one better comprehends the intricate nature of the narrative cosmology Erdrich constructs, while recognizing those elements of it that seem stable from generation to generation. One of these elements is "luck." Consider her first published novel.

Love Medicine

From the very outset, the concept of luck is prominent in *Love Medicine,* both its originally published version and its more recent, expanded edition. In the very first pages it is brought immediately to the foreground, as June Kashpaw walks down a street of Williston, North Dakota, killing time before her bus leaves for home. Her walk is cut short when she decides to turn from the sidewalk into a bar to join a man who has caught her attention; when she enters, she finds him eating Easter eggs, and when he pays for their drinks, she notes his "good-sized wad of money."[2] Why does she decide to stay with him, miss her bus, and therefore precipitate the events that are to follow in her story? "That roll helped [her make the decision]. But what was more important, she had a feeling. The eggs were lucky" (*LMN* 3).

Like our own, June's life is presented as a series of chance encounters, or more accurately put from the point of view of a storyteller, a series of episodes in which characters make choices that—from an audience's point of view—may or may not seem logical or rational at the moment. As events unfold, we need points of reference to enlighten what is actually happening and what it signifies. For June, as she gambles for the possibility of love, intuition and her belief in luck are referential; they determine her play.[3] She takes a chance, and Erdrich's canon pivots on this type of action. It is hardly coincidental that June's play is tied as well to economics and exploitation: the flute end of colonialism suggested by the oil worker's (Jack Mauser's) "roll."

There are other events in the novel that are equally suggestive, for instance the scene in which Marie and Nector meet in 1934. Here, the unlikely love triangle that motivates and informs many of the subsequent events in the novel takes shape.

In the preceding chapter, we have witnessed the creation of "Saint

Marie." The young Marie Lazarre, by her own admission as she tells her story in retrospect, is both ignorant and ambitious, and she perceives the Catholic church as her sole means of salvation and success: a salvation that is described and defined in terms of social class and monetary reward. She wishes to be worshiped by those who ignore her, who do not value her and therefore undermine her attempts to construct a sense of personal power and fulfilling identity. In short, as her self-definition attests, she wants to be "above" the Euro-Americans who hold the positions of power in the church and therefore over the community, and part of her claim is based upon her small amount of "Indian blood" (*LMN* 43). She wants "to rise above" that blood and, with sainthood, be adorned in gold and precious colors, and the nuns "would have to stoop down off their high horse to kiss" her toes (*LMN* 43).

As she comes down the hill at chapter's end, however, her hopes, paradoxically, have been dashed and realized: the nuns have indeed knelt and worshiped her, but she will never possess the keys to the riches or power held by Sister Leopolda. In her gamble for empowerment she has lost one "hand" and won another. At this moment of transformation she meets Nector, who trudges up the hill to sell to the nuns the geese he and his brother Eli have killed. As he tells us his story in retrospect, he emphasizes the wonder and immediacy of the encounter, for he has committed himself to Lulu Nanapush and is reveling in what the future holds for the two young lovers. However, this chance encounter on the hill alters that future dramatically, not only for the three but also for subsequent generations of several families. In a scene in which logic and reason—"the odds"—do not prevail, we have the quintessential ambiguity of an Erdrich confrontation. Neither of the two players wants to be involved with the other; however, they marry, have children, and spend the rest of their lives joined. Later in the book Nector describes the ways this and other happenings work: this "is where events loop around and tangle . . . " (*LMN* 128).

Indeed. But why does this event evolve as it does, against all the odds? Read from the perspective of the history revealed in the other novels, in particular *Tracks,* it is even more unlikely.[4] The two young people represent warring factions within the community; she is thought to be a

Lazarre, "the youngest daughter of a family of horse-thieving drunks" (*LMN* 62). The Lazarres and the Kashpaws have a long-standing enmity stemming from financial conflict: the struggle to delineate and maintain "family" lands during the catastrophic era of the General Allotment Act. However, there is more involved. For the Kashpaws, the Lazarres seem to be the "wave of the future" and thus represent the potential loss of family lands, but also the family itself: clan, culture, and community. This conflict, then, is also about survival.

There is yet another element of the event that is enlightened by a reading of *Tracks:* Marie is fresh from a game of chance with her own mother, Sister Leopolda (nee Pauline Puyat). Either wittingly or unwittingly, Marie has severed herself from her adoptive and her biological families and the change they represent; in the text of *Love Medicine,* that renunciation is reiterated when she turns her dogs loose on the Lazarre woman (her "mother"), who brings June to her to raise. In any event, as she meets Nector on the hill above town, she has lost the bright future offered by sainthood in the church, an orphan once more at the mercy of chance. Her crafting of a future using Nector is certainly understandable in this context, but it also represents the "recapturing" of a generation from families pulled into the potential degeneration of a new, alien sense of good fortune.

And there is one final, very subtle element of chance in the encounter: the geese strapped to Nector's wrists. The section is entitled "Wild Geese," after all, and they represent an "external," non-human force at work in the event. As Nector and Marie wrestle, bringing the moment to a physical crisis/cusp, Nector's movements are impaired. "I lose my balance and pitch over. The geese pull me down" (*LMN* 63). He and Marie exchange insults and taunts, and then he pulls her to the ground as well, and the "geese are to my advantage now; their weight on my arms helps to pin her; their dead wings flap around us; their necks loll, and their black eyes stare, frozen" (*LMN* 64). What ensues is a sexual game, at least from Nector's point of view, and he loses: "I know that when I take my hand away [from her mouth] the girl will smile, because I have been beaten at what I started on this hill. And sure enough, when I take my hand away she growls" (*LMN* 65). The lack of a smile, characteristically enough, reveals Marie's strength in adversity and her anger at the physical assault she has had to endure, but it also—taken in light of Nector's comments and subsequent events—emphasizes that she has, indeed, won.[5] And, as we learn later in the text, the geese, who mate for life and who Lipsha sees as the epitome of "staying power," had their own influence in the outcome of the game. As the event concludes, the "dead birds feel impossibly heavy" and he drops them to the ground (*LMN* 66).

As reader/voyeur, we have the objective distance and information necessary to contextualize the event and construct waves of meaning from it. The fictional agents of that meaning—Marie and Nector—are not afforded that power, and neither are we in "real life." In the midst of any situation, we may feel empowered, only to find that it was not actually so; conversely, we may feel we have lost control, only to find that our best interests prevail, that we "win." The concept of chance is based upon such experiential evidence, yet each culture's conceptualization may be based upon very different experiences, histories, and cosmologies. In Marie and Nector's case, their meeting at first reads as purely coincidental, yet there remains a persistent, nagging implication that other forces impinge on it. Only by reading it referentially, by investigating its inherent dynamic as enlightened by history and the beliefs it engenders, can one comprehend the event's significance in a definition of "chance."

But what of an event in which characters actively, deliberately engage the element of chance and thereby precipitate change? There are many such events in Erdrich's works, yet their outcomes are never determined by completely random forces. For the sake of brevity, I will address only those most prominent, and therefore—perhaps—most significant.

In the final pages, in Lipsha's section entitled "Crossing the Water" (which is preceded in the new edition with a chapter entitled "Lyman's Luck," a title clearly tied to those in *The Bingo Palace*), we find the crucial scene in which Lipsha and his father, Gerry Nanapush, play poker with June's other son, King. Here, their familial tie is revealed by Lipsha's mere marking of the cards in the deck; Gerry recognizes his mother's "signature" on the cards, since he has acquired it himself. King does not. She, of course, learned it from her family, the Pillagers, and old Nanapush, the elder trickster. This ability to manipulate chance, then, is tied in *Love*

Medicine directly to family and all that comes with it: clan definitions, character connections, and knowledge of power. This power of lineage is exerted to control events, and therefore the future, and it is as ethereal, mysterious, and significant as the slight tick of the heart that Gerry seemingly imparts to Lipsha.

In this gambling scene, as elsewhere, luck is manipulated by those with insider knowledge who wish to reverse the ill effects of life in a colonial society. As a result of the game, father and son meet (both figuratively and literally), win, and escape. Using June's car, won by the manipulation of apparently random draws of the cards—in other words, King's perception of chance—Gerry escapes the police. Using the slight tick of the heart won from his "chance" meeting with his father, Lipsha escapes the army. The correlation is revealing. The seemingly disempowered victims have "turned the tables" and rewritten the "inescapable" outcome of events. In this one encounter, long-standing foes—King, army, and police—lose.

The novel ends in circular fashion; for the moment, however, there is a sense of closure in a game won. Lipsha, driving "June's car," stops on a bridge that marks the edge of the reservation and, looking down into the waters below, has a revelation. Throughout his life he had considered himself a loser, the discarded son of a woman who did not love him. Here, he realizes that he "was lucky she turned [him] over to Grandma Kashpaw," for King has suffered far more (*LMN* 367). This personal revelation of loss and gain is framed by an even more poignant one that is tied directly to the land, and the water with which it has contended for all time.[6] "It's a dark, thick, twisting river. The bed is deep and narrow. I thought of June. The water played in whorls beneath me or flexed over sunken cars" (*LMN* 366).

This image—the water metaphor so prominent in Erdrich's works—is fully descriptive of how fortune is constructed in all her narratives. First, it employs a shifting perspective and hierarchy, moving from the preposition "beneath" to "over." Second, it describes the nature of life, and therefore reorients our perception of chance. The current at first view seems chaotic and ever-changing, but of course it is not: good fortune comes in whorls and graces, and goes and returns, moved by numerous forces in a perceptible but also a non-linear fashion. The general flow remains in the same direction, of course, but with myriad variations of directions and encumbrances along its course. Third, it connects with death, the potential for ultimate loss. Earlier, Henry Jr. has lost his possibility for an afterlife of any comfort when he drowns himself, a tragic thing for an Anishinabe, as Lulu and Lyman tell us; immediately, Lyman sends Henry's car into the same swollen river, perhaps to make the death seem accidental. Also, but probably not finally, it calls to mind the Anishinabe Road of the Dead, described elsewhere in Erdrich's novels, where the dead encounter yet another test of their lives. If they have not lived a good one, they will fall from the log bridge they must cross into the afterlife and into a river where they will be lost forever. This is not a cheerful future. Lipsha, however (like June in the book's opening), crosses and returns home. Both have controlled chance and therefore mitigated loss. It is no small matter that June returns in *The Bingo Palace* to bring Lipsha some winning bingo tickets and to reclaim her car. The game does not always end with death.

The Beet Queen

The novel published next in the series, *The Beet Queen,* carries the "chance encounter," or more accurately the encounter with chance, even further. In fact, taken as a whole, the novel can be said to hang solely on chance, or to be structured by some very questionable coincidences. This stylistic device continues in the latest novel, *Tales of Burning Love,* where it becomes almost unacceptably overbearing. While this may reflect an intensification of Erdrich's fascination with issues of chance and luck, the question becomes: at what point does a preoccupation with this topic begin to affect adversely the audience's reading?

Left destitute after the untimely death of her married lover, Adelaide Adare is faced with a bleak and foreboding future, and when the opportunity to exert power over that future arises—in the guise of a young barnstormer with an available plane—she takes it. Unfortunately, her act leaves her three young children to sort out their own ways of survival. After their mother flies away, Karl and Mary turn to their aunt, but as they walk down yet another North Dakota street on their way "home" to her, Karl chances under a tree whose white, fragrant blossoms turn him aside from this one, set goal. Like June and Adelaide, he makes a seemingly impulsive decision that shapes much of what follows, a decision based upon a seemingly coincidental run-in with a blossoming tree. Of course, this is a literary illusion.

The novel is full of odd coincidences that imply a pattern of interconnectedness: Mary's best friend conceives a baby when Karl suddenly re-materializes to visit Wallace Pheff, an acquaintance of Mary's who happens to meet Karl at a convention in Minneapolis. With Karl, he has had his first homosexual experience. Karl and Celestine's daughter, Dot, conceives her own child with Gerry Nanapush in *Love Medicine,* and Karl is saved by Fleur Pillager when he jumps from a moving train and is injured. The coincidences compound, on and on, until the grand finale when Dot impulsively jumps into a plane and disappears, echoing her grandmother's desertion, while Mary's cousin is discovered dead in her truck by Dot's recently returned father, and Adelaide's missing third child arrives, after all these years, to try to find his siblings. What are the odds?

Obviously they are not good. The complete reliance on seemingly contrived coincidence may seem a bit much, but if one looks at it in the context of the other works, then it makes a certain sense. Considered as imaginative chronicles of the history of Turtle Mountain in this century, they chart an obvious alteration in the landscape and investigate the fundamental essence of that change. They dramatize "the reservation" as it evolved over time, and what it signifies for the individual identities not only of those who live on it, but also of the "newcomers" with whom they interact. Just as Lipsha explained in *Love Medicine,* the land now holds two cultures' gods, and therefore two perceptions of what the future holds and how it will unfold.

There is a distinct difference between the encounters with chance found in the *Love Medicine* and *Tracks* and those in *The Beet Queen.* The first two novels present characters who identify—to varying degrees—as Chippewa; the latter is comprised of characters who primarily identify as Euro-American. Taken together, we have the various ancestries of the author. The distinction in their world views lies in the culturally defined ways in which they deal with "chance." For instance, when Pheff returns from Minneapolis, he stops along the road at a popular lovers' lane. He is alone, trying to sort out his recent experiences with Karl; immediately he is startled by a police officer and, embarrassed and feeling guilty, he tries to explain his presence and thereby fumbles upon a lie that becomes the future of Argus, North Dakota: he tells the officer that he has been considering the sugar beet and all its potential for their community. In other words, the characters, here, are moved about by chance like puppets, and, once moved, they, in common phraseology, play the hand that is dealt them. The responses to adversity are clearly delineated. One can become aggressive (as we see in the poker scene in *Tracks*) or attempt to bluff one's way through (as with Wallace). The reaction to loss is simply to work harder to overcome it and to ensure success (as with Mary), or else one may lapse into an internal, a created and isolated, reality (like Karl or Sita). In *Love Medicine* and elsewhere, other alternatives are posited through the interactions of the Anishinabe characters; Lipsha determines what hands are dealt in the crucial card game.

Another way of conceiving of the difference is to consider the apparent lack of a crucial attachment to place for most of the characters in *The Beet Queen,* all of whom are immigrants. Even Celestine and her relatives come from the reservation to the north. Like the sugar beet itself, they are imported alterations to the landscape; like Argus, they are revisions of place who attempt to play out their tentative fortunes in a land of extremes. Perhaps the greatest irony of the characters is that they seem to be completely self-motivated—motivated by a concern for self—yet they are wholly lacking in the power of self-determination: they do not determine their own fates. Instead, they accommodate what chance throws their way, and in this way they are completely powerless, despite their apparent self-control. Once deserted by Karl, Mary eases into the secure monotony of a lifelong place in Kozka's Meats. Karl wanders the country drifting from job to job with little or no concern for the future, and he ends his life with nothing one could consider a satisfying legacy. Although Mary plays at predicting what will be—using her deck of fortune-telling cards—she is, like her fellow immigrants, moved about by forces beyond her comprehension. It seems that without this generations-long attachment to place, one's good fortune is ephemeral, one's ill fortune unbearable.

However, Sister Leopolda (*née* Pauline Puyat) is in Argus as well, and if there is a quality that defines her character it is her unflappable certainty in her ability to direct the future. She emerges from the Anishinabe community, of course, but she also brings the immigrant ideology to the foreground in that community. In fact, when she describes one of the formative events in her life, she lapses not into a Native telling but into one that reflects the idea of fate derived in Europe over long centuries. As she attends the death of Mary Pepewas, she behaves like one of the Fates of old: "Perhaps, hand over hand, I could have drawn her back to shore, but I saw very clearly that she wanted to be gone. . . . That is why I put my fingers in the air between us, and I cut where the rope was frayed down to string" (*T* 68). In this construction only the gods have control over the future, and humans are relegated to the role of supplicants moved by the whims of those gods. This is where two cultural orientations touch, but they ultimately hinge in different ways when we consider the degree of characters' control over that future. Pauline was raised in the same culture as her daughter Marie, who also wished to become a saint. Their lives, however, take very different trails.

Tracks

Of the first three novels, *Tracks* makes the most prominent use of gambling scenes. Interestingly, this was the first novel composed in the opening tetralogy. There are numerous card games, games of guile between Nanapush and the Morrisseys, Pauline's manipulation of Sophie and Eli, and so on, but three events of confrontation and cusp seem most prominent for one's understanding of chance as defined in Erdrich's works: the series of poker games at Kozka's Meats, its sequel in the next world, and the "stick game" at book's end. All have Fleur Pillager as the main player.

Fleur's time in Argus is alluded to in *The Beet Queen,* where the life of Dutch James intersects both Fleur's and Celestine's, Dot's mother. Pauline, who is to become Leopolda, is there as well: later as a nun teaching school when Mary, on an icy slide, smashes her face into the ice to produce what people perceive as the face of Christ. First, however, in *Tracks,* Pauline visits Argus as a young person who, with Russell, acts as our witness to the poker game between Fleur, Dutch, Lily, and Tor.

The game lasts for days, and as Pauline tells the story of it we find—at least in her mind and telling—that there is little element of chance in it. From the outset Fleur is in complete control of the other players' perception of chance. Ironically, she seems the least likely person to be graced with "luck": she is a woman, a "squaw," and poor. There is no power in that combination for the colonized, nor from those who conceive of themselves as possessors of all power: white male "pioneers" with expertise at "making their own luck." However, as the game progresses and they fail to win her money immediately, they look for an advantage, a way of ensuring success, which they seem to gain when Tor sees Fleur's hand shake at a crucial moment. His conclusion is logical, and wrong: "Well, we know one thing . . . the squaw can't bluff" (*T* 20). Despite their supposed advantage, Fleur wins exactly a dollar every night, "no more and no less, too consistent for luck" (*T* 21). The event comes to a cusp when the men pool their resources to join in league against her for one last game of poker, winner take all, and the stratagem seems to work for Fleur "played unevenly, as if chance were all she had" (*T* 23). But it is not, of course, and when all their money is in the pot and the game rides upon the turning of one card, she wins.

When luck does not smile, aggression is an acceptable alternative for these players. They beat and rape her—at least Pauline believes they do—and the moment of empowerment is lost. But it is lost only for a moment. The next day, a tornado—the Western epitome of whimsical, inexplicable chance—sweeps into Argus, sending the men into the freezer of the meat plant. As the storm screams around Pauline and Russell, whom the men have left to its mercy, the wind "at last spoke plain" (*T* 27). Pauline and Russell drop the large, locking bar down on the outside of the door, sealing the men's fate. Russell runs away with "a peaceful look of complicit satisfaction" (*T* 28). Against all odds, tossed about like Dorothy in *The Wizard of Oz,* neither is injured. "Whimsical, random chance" is a construction of one's perception; this storm is moved by will. Fleur wins again.

Fleur ultimately returns to her home and pays the annual fee for the Pillager lands. She also gives birth to Lulu, whose parentage the community debates. Is she the offspring of a rape or of Misshepeshu? In any event, she is the child of a new generation, one that brings families like the Pillagers, Nanapushes, and Kashpaws together, so the card game and Fleur's return have had a profound effect in the community. Out of it comes an equally profound revelation for Pauline, who has become a nun and thus an agent of colonization:

> Power travels in the bloodlines, handed out before birth. It comes down through the hands, which in the Pillagers are strong and knotted, big, spidery and rough, with sensitive fingertips good at dealing cards. It comes through the eyes, too, belligerent, darkest brown, the eyes of those in the bear clan, impolite as they gaze directly at a person. (*T* 31)

Although Pauline's reliability as a narrator has been contested, her insight here is reiterated by other characters, including Nanapush and the community at large, for which the fear and respect for Fleur is ubiquitous. Her power over chance and her bear clan affiliation are demonstrated time and time again.

The card game in Argus has a close counterpart later in the novel, once again with Pauline as narrator/participant.[7] Here, Pauline and Fleur travel to the land of the dead where they encounter once more the players from Argus. Now, however, rather than play for dollars and cents, they play for life itself: the lives of Lulu and Fleur's premature baby. In other words, they play for the next generation of Fleur's people, for the future. The older generation has already been lost as the result of the incursion of Europeans; disease has decimated the powerful families, and those who survive question what the future will hold. Fleur loses the first hand and therefore the baby. The next hand, for Lulu, she wins—tellingly—with five queens (against the representative kings and jacks of the others). Even in the land of the dead, she is not powerless, it seems, to circumvent the plans of the pioneers.[8]

However, her inability to save her newly born child shakes Fleur's confidence. In the ensuing power plays within the community, she "loses" her lands as well; the lumberjacks continue to encircle and encroach upon the lake that is her center. All seems lost; the odds are not good; yet, when the moment comes and the "inescapable" destiny, "the fate," of colonial domination seems assured, Erdrich once again withholds the easy dismissal of power, the simplistic nod to the inevitability of loss. As the loggers drive their wagons in to cut the last trees, Fleur's influence is once more felt. Nanapush describes the scene, and in that description there appears a veiled reference to gambling. As in Argus, the winds rise. "I heard the waves begin to slap with light insistence against the shore. I knew the shifting of breeze, the turn of the weather, was at hand. I heard the low murmur of the voices of the gamblers in the woods" (*T* 222).

Anyone who has watched the stick game or any of its numerous analogs recognizes that gambling in some traditions is not simply a game of one completely isolated player against another. Instead it is one group of players against another group, with one individual focusing the play while others sing, chant, drum, or verbally spar in the background. This final scene is interestingly similar to that model, with Fleur the focal point of resistance to the encroachment of foreign ideas of "resources" and land use while her ancestors murmur in the background. She does not lose as much as she folds her hand without showing her cards, waiting for the next hand. She deflates her adversaries' victory by sawing through the trees herself, and with the help of the wind the trees fall like sticks in a game. Fleur walks away in control, undefeated. At the very least, the other team has developed a great deal of respect for her power, and so has the reader.

With the publication of *The Bingo Palace,* the nature of that power is given further elaboration, its conclusion resonating with the motif first found in the conclusion of *Tracks.* Fleur has won her land on the lake back in a poker game with its "owner," and that land will support a tribal casino. What is seemingly lost in one story is regained through another.

The Bingo Palace

The title of the latest novel in the series speaks for itself. Once more gambling becomes a central aspect of events in the text. Here, however, the element of "chance" is most clearly defined: it is indeed "in the eye (and the actions) of the beholder." Erdrich delineates two distinct modes or types of gambling, much as the previous novels delineated two distinct conceptualizations of "randomness," "chance," or "chaos" for that matter. Understandably, the ways in which these types of gaming work are found in the behavior of characters; together, Lipsha and Lyman dramatize the attractions, and the ill effects, of engaging in games of chance with the wrong attitude, or without the proper "luck," and the nature of empowerment in gambling is defined in their two central chapters: "Lipsha's Luck" and "Lyman's Luck."[9] The resulting concept of gambling is a telling blend of culturally determined means and motivations.

Lipsha's luck is tied directly to the past: to the power in his hands, passed down to him through the bloodlines, as Pauline has noted. It is connected in his chapter to an ancient, invaluable ceremonial pipe that is also passed to him, the chapter beginning with Marie giving it to him. Nector had been its holder, and now Lipsha has been chosen to assume that duty. Interestingly, it becomes a point of contention between Lipsha and Lyman, who considers Lipsha a lost cause and therefore believes that only he should be the holder of such an important tribal pipe and therefore in control of the future. Thus begins a game of power, much like the one they play for the affection of Shawnee Ray Toose.

"Lipsha's Luck" ends with Shawnee and Lipsha on a date, driving across the medicine line, the border, into Canada, and "here's where it started, that little wrinkle in destiny which [Lipsha] somehow came to believe that Zelda might have arranged" (*BP* 32). The border guard—quintessential agent of colonial power—searches their car, June's car, and finds one seed, ostensibly a marijuana seed. The search continues and he finds the pipe. He confronts Lipsha with it and with Zelda's annual gift to him, a pemmican fruitcake wrapped in foil. Of course, the guards draw the wrong conclusions: that they are hashish and a pipe for smoking it. Lipsha and Shawnee are detained, and as the scene concludes, in slow motion, the guard connects the pipe bowl and stem, something that should only be done at certain times and places and then only ceremonially by the pipe's holder. He carries it off, also in the wrong way, slowly lowering it until its eagle feather touches the ground. The effect on the future is catastrophic.

The next chapter is entitled "Transportation." In the context of this discussion, it records the transporting away of Lipsha's luck, but it also marks the initiating point of its return through the lessons he learns from its loss. It opens with a direct transition to the eagle feather touching the floor:

> WHEN I THINK OF ALL THE UNCERTAINTIES TO FOLLOW, the collisions with truth and disaster, I want to dive, to touch and lift that broad feather. . . . And yet, as there is no retreating from the moment, the only art left to me is understanding how I can accept the consequence. For the backwardness, the wrongness, the brush of heaven to the ground in dust, is part of our human nature. Especially mine, it appears. (*BP* 37)

Although each chapter in the novel begins with the first line all in capital letters, here they have an added emphasis. Uncertainty, chance, is tied directly to the event of the feather touching the ground, and to Lipsha's luck, which has suddenly turned bad. The implication is that luck can render uncertainty predictable, and luck is tied to heritage, to the power inherent in the pipe, but more significantly to the obligations one has to performing duties to them both, to doing them responsibly. There are many external forces that work upon luck, evidently. Moreover, the passage undermines that certainty with a telling comment about human nature: we are prone to shirk, neglect, be turned aside. How one deals with that realization, and the adversity such actions bring, creates character, and it is an "art" based upon belief and faith in a power that—at times—is less than apparent.

Later in the chapter, the external forces that affect individual lives appear, as June. Alone in the bingo palace long after everyone has left, Lipsha sees her. "Now I always told myself before that there was a good side to ghosts. My reasoning goes along on the base of the following *uncertainties:* Beyond this world, is there another? . . . A ghost could answer the basic question, at least, as to whether there is anything besides the world I know, the things I touch. If I see a ghost, possibilities will open" (*BP* 53, emphasis added). Of course, he is seeing one; the question and answer appear simultaneously, and possibilities are opened as the primal uncertainty of life is resolved. June brings him a book of bingo tickets; when she leaves, she takes "her" car.[10] The epistemological significance of this event for Erdrich's character is telling: there is a future beyond this life, and it can have a direct effect upon the present, if one knows how to engage it.

His education continues as he uses the tickets to win the bingo van, the top prize in Lyman's bingo palace, for which people have played for five months. The process Lipsha goes through—the choices he makes and the "lucky" occurrences he has—is revealing. In abbreviated form, it runs like this. He observes the ways that his grandmother, Lulu, plays bingo: "All business, that's Lulu. And business pays" (*BP* 62). He follows her model and becomes one-minded in his pursuit of the van, with a slight and significant variation upon Lulu's: "To get the van, I have to shake hands with greed. I get unprincipled" (*BP* 64). In other words, he employs the "touch," the healing power he has been graced with and which, when wrongly used in *Love Medicine,* kills Nector. He begins to charge money for his healing services: "But I do not realize I will have to give up my healing source once I start charging for my service" (*BP* 64). Finally, using only one of June's cards, which he lost but then miraculously found again, he wins the van, then loses it immediately. In a scene strongly reminiscent of Fleur's poker playing in Argus in *Tracks,* several Anglos, led by a man he argued with earlier, kidnap him, humiliate him, then dump him at Russell Kashpaw's to get an equally humiliating tattoo to commemorate their revenge and their power over him. They destroy the van, and the lesson is obvious. Although he has been granted the ability to manipulate events by some force external to his character, Lipsha has not won the van in the right way: he plays for self. "For the backwardness, the wrongness, the brush of heaven to the ground in dust, is part of our human nature." As a result, his apparent winnings are ephemeral, the lesson momentous.

Russell releases him, and Lipsha tells the story of how he came to be there, tied and awaiting his unwanted tattoo. He tells of the van, and Russell understands: "That's an unusual piece of good fortune." Lipsha is curious: "Have you ever had any? Any good fortune?" The answer is equally curious, given Russell's history, as depicted in *The Beet Queen;* he is a veteran of several wars who has been wounded so often that he is left horribly scarred. From his wheelchair, he answers: "All the time" (*BP* 82). Luck, it seems, has many sides and is not always physically apparent in those who possess it, as the "loser" Lipsha signifies. As Russell shows him his book of tattoos, Lipsha finds the falling-star design that he saw the night of his mother's visit and later as a sign that the time was right for him to win the van. He has Russell tattoo it in the only appropriate place for a descendant of the Pillagers: on his hand. The van is gone, for it was not the end product anticipated by the bingo tickets, only a vehicle to it. Lipsha has gained something unexpected and much more valuable: an understanding of his own nature and the ways that it is shaped by both his own volition and by forces external to his character.

"Lyman's Luck" immediately follows this lesson in appropriate ways to engage chance. It extends the "greed" and "unprincipled" concepts Lipsha first exposes, and it is revealing that Lyman's encounter with Western concepts of gambling take place in Reno, Nevada, "the biggest little city in the world," whose reputation was built on its gambling mystique. It is also revealing that he travels to Reno to participate in an Indian Gaming Conference. What we see emerge is hardly Indian gaming in the sense Erdrich has constructed it. Gain and loss are tentative measures of any game of chance, but Lyman's losses in Reno are molded by a Western model; he plays for self, and thus only the house can win.[11] Here we are privy to the workings of an addiction based in an overpowering desire for monetary reward and personal power through employing one's luck.

Throughout Lyman's ordeal in Reno, we find an understated implication that he has been through all this before, that he has felt the attraction to gambling, is now cognizant of its power, and is attempting to overcome the desire to succumb. He is of course unsuccessful, in part because he is not at home, where as the manager of "the house" he has the power. Instead, the whole environment of Reno is dedicated to undermining one's attempts to rationalize and therefore resist: the casino's trappings induce a "dreamlike" effect; the immediate reality—time, connections to others, physical movement—is subdued. He sits down at a blackjack table and wins. As he takes his chips to the cashier to collect his winnings and leave the casino, he is drawn aside by his sense of luck again. In a description strongly imaged by automaton qualities, Erdrich makes her point: "His features were a mask. His outside expression was fixed, serene, but beneath that, on the real face that was hidden, he could feel his look of bewildered dread" (*BP* 92). This is a moment of powerlessness, but before he can sit at another table a man "accidentally" bumps into him, scattering his chips and gathering his willpower. For the moment he is saved. Here, in a town carved from the desert by the desire for gain, he moves like a puppet; he moves like the European immigrants to Argus.

Later, in his room, he awakes. "It was two A.M. when he woke, starting into clarity, his brain on and humming like a machine connected to that money" (*BP* 92). He returns to the game, wins nearly three thousand dollars, then he "started losing his way in a muddy sluice of sloppy plays, and he got desperate. His luck turned unpredictable and he played on, but the momentum had died" (*BP* 93). And so has his "luck." He loses not only his winnings but all he has brought with him as well as the tribe's Bureau of Indian Affairs loan. In a last degradation, he pawns Nector's pipe for a few hundred more, only to lose. In a scene interestingly reminiscent of Lipsha on the bridge after he has won June's car in *Love Medicine,* Lyman walks to a bridge and briefly contemplates drowning himself, but the Truckee River is too shallow. He is far removed from his world, and he has no control.

There are several revealing elements to this event. First, Lyman is lucky, but I suggest that luck here has nothing to do with random chance. Second, when he succumbs to the attraction of the place and the chance for easy winnings—easy money—he loses his power. His adversary, the player/dealer on the other side of the table, is empowered. Lyman can no longer direct probability. Third, the sense of power Erdrich exposes here is based upon the idea of predictability. In fact, his loss of power is described in those terms: "His luck turned unpredictable." Predictability is based upon knowledge, most assuredly. One must know the odds, but there is more to it than that alone. If randomness is taken out of the game, perhaps through power and knowledge, predictability is assured. This is what Lipsha does in his poker game with Gerry and King in *Love Medicine.* In *Tracks* Fleur's co-workers feel that they remove it when they believe that "the squaw can't bluff." They are of course sadly mistaken.

Power resides in vision, in an awareness that events are not based upon random chance but upon recurrent movements and motifs that swirl in recognizable patterns. In this model, this recognition allows one to predict, to improve the odds, and sometimes to win. Moreover, the ability to predict is tied equally to an understanding of oneself—one's nature, but also one's family and history—and human nature as revealed in the stories of the long history of life on this continent. In recent times, those stories include Europeans and colonialism.

The lessons in these two chapters are echoed throughout the life stories of others; the chapters of the book are named after the major characters, each with a "Luck" attached. Moreover, once again Fleur plays cards for her land, lost for a time in the concluding events of *Tracks,* and wins it back. But in Lipsha's odd vision quest one finds an even more emphatic statement of value, situated within the complex matrix of the Anishinabe present. Here the future of all the community is central.

Once again Lyman and Lipsha are tied; they both go on vision quests at the same place and time. Lyman, of course, successfully completes his on schedule and in ways following the tradition. Lipsha, of course, emerges from his still wondering what he has experienced, and, of course, he appears a complete failure to the community. His "helper," it appears, is a skunk. Humiliated, smelling so badly that no one will approach him, he returns home in defeat. This is Erdrich: just when one appears to have lost everything, the last card is turned. Vision comes in unlikely packages, for character and reader alike. Later the skunk returns with a common refrain: "This ain't real estate" (*BP* 218). The enigmatic statement is punctuated with Lipsha's vision of the future. (The title of the chapter is "A Little Vision," an equally enigmatic statement and perhaps a plea for people to employ a little vision for the future.)[12]

In the first segment of his vision, Lipsha sees the casino that Lyman is to build. Lipsha sees its construction, which requires bulldozers and the hauling of lake stones into the woods; each detail is significant and reflects the potentially destructive nature of change, of "development," which alters the landscape dramatically. But one also sees "revenue falling out of the sky. . . . Easy money, easy flow. No sweat. No bother" (*BP* 219). The casino provides the means to ensure the future; it will be built, however, on Pillager land. Just as in *Love Medicine* where Nector's factory requires the land upon which Lulu's house rests, this will require Fleur's. The casino will be situated on the spot where she played her game at the end of *Tracks* and where she is living once again, the place where the influence of Misshepeshu is the strongest. In the next segment of his vision, Lipsha feels the money in his hands; in such a place, a Pillager could not lose. And then the skunk delivers his final message, the moral we must consider: "Luck don't stick when you sell it." And there we have it again.

The next day, Lipsha's "little vision" carries us further. Since he knows the future of this place and the integral place gambling will hold, he shows us that such complex issues are never clear-cut: "it's more or less a gray area of tense negotiations. It's not completely one way or another, traditional against bingo. You have to stay alive to keep your tradition alive and working. Everybody knows bingo money is not based on solid ground" (*BP* 221). This ain't real estate, indeed. He also realizes that Lyman's plan has Fleur's blessing, perhaps her influence. She is, after all, a Pillager gambler who recognizes that Lyman may be the one "who can use the luck that temporary loopholes in the law bring to Indians for higher causes, steady advances" (*BP* 221). After all, she has engaged in immigrant games of chance to maintain her lands and assure the life of the next generation. Now, Lyman's plan offers the chance for the whole community.

The concluding pages of the novel are beautifully poetic. Here, Fleur walks off into legend, but like June, who appears at times to influence the lives of other characters, she is never very distant:

> We believe she follows our hands with her underwater eyes as we deal the cards on green baize, as we drown our past in love of chance, as our money collects, as we set fires and make personal wars over what to do with its weight, as we go forward into our unsteady hopes. (*BP* 274)

It is a wonderfully fit epilogue for the stories in the first four novels, perhaps even an equally fit introduction to a whole cycle of novels to explore the ever-changing nature of those hopes. It also reiterates Lipsha's "gray area of tense negotiation," in which the Lymans handle the "house" and thus the revenue flows home to the rez., and the Lipshas remind us what the house is built upon and thus keep the luck alive; it depicts losers turned winners, if they remember the true stakes for which they play; and together with the portrayal of gambling from the previous works, it underscores the necessity for an equally compelling memory of "solid ground," in both the figurative sense of belonging and identity but also in the literal sense of place and home. What could be construed as a powerful tone of nostalgia is in fact an intricate plea for the future, one that holds the past sacred but that is not consumed its history of loss, nor by the individual conflicts that are not isolated events in the lives of one generation but connected intricately to the long story of life on this continent.

> It's a dark, thick, twisting river. The bed is deep and narrow. . . . The water played in whorls beneath me or flexed over sunken cars. . . . I'd heard that this river was the last of an ancient ocean, miles deep, that once had covered the Dakotas and solved all our problems. It was easy to still imagine us beneath them vast unreasonable waves, but the truth is we live on dry land. . . . The morning was clear. A good road led on. So there was nothing to do but cross the water, and bring her home. (*LMN* 367)

Tales of Burning Love

The fifth novel connects with the others. Here Jack Mauser is presented; he is the man June spent her last few hours with in Williston. Like her, he is part Anishinabe; unlike her, he has spent very little time on the reservation, growing up in another cultural milieu. He has also had to live with her death, since he failed to follow her into the stormy night that claimed her. As a result, he has been married four times, the last time to Dot, the daughter of Karl and Celestine. In other words, this novel brings the various cultural orientations introduced in the earlier novels into a kinship. They become relative. Significantly, Sister Leopolda dies in the first pages.

The overt references to chance and luck abound. The night of

Leopolda's death, Jack and his first wife hide in her room in the convent after witnessing the nun's departure, and he tells Eleanore of his recent marriage to Dot: "Turned out she's part Chippewa too. Coincidence or sign? . . . Do you think it's a sign, that maybe I'm supposed to do something. Identify?" (*TBL* 59). Much like Lipsha's interrogation of an afterlife when visited by June, Jack searches for a meaning that transcends the individual human life. Later, on the evening of Jack's funeral, the three wives who attended go to the casino where his other ex-wife works. In a paragraph describing the game of blackjack, Erdrich encapsulates a description of human society and its interaction with the luck life brings. It is in a way a description of life itself:

> Blackjack is an unenlightened game that fools and drunks play well but never win, not in the long run, through mesmerized evenings. In the course of a night, a table of strangers betting idly together can turn passionate about one another's welfare, or resentful because of some irrational habit of mind. People's faults glare. Players sitting elbow to elbow close ranks against newcomers, sometimes, if their entry breaks a streak of hopeful wins. They mentally kick out a player whose dour caution brings bad luck, and draw close to someone else who wins with no letup on the averages. (*TBL* 169)

Such is life in the "mainstream." One hundred pages later, Marlis, the blackjack dealing ex, extends the commentary: "You like percentages? . . . Try these. You're born. Hey sucker, welcome to the casino! Just remember, the house always wins in the end" (*TBL* 269). Enigmatic if viewed from the narrow confines of her cynicism in this one context, this can also be a revelatory insight about the powerfully positive nature of life if viewed from a perspective that transcends a concern for one's individual well-being. With whom does one identify: sucker or house? Lyman, in Reno, is a sucker. Lyman, the casino builder, may be more.

And there is the other end of life. As Jack searches through the whiteout of a horrible plains blizzard for his son, unwittingly kidnapped by Gerry and Lipsha (as described in *The Bingo Palace*), he calls forth the image of the Anishinabe Road of the Dead, as always a significant allusive element in Erdrich's novels. He leaves the warm cab of his snowplow and walks into a sugar beet field to investigate a mound he takes for the car containing his son, realizing that if he misses it he will "go straight west, on into the other world of the Ojibwa dead where skeletons gambled, throwing and concealing human wristbones. He saw their arms rise and toss, but he lunged ahead anyway" (*TBL* 384). He is lost in the storm, but continues. "He walked in a big circle and then a small one and smaller, concentric, following June. It took him all night to get back where he started" (*TBL* 385). He returns changed, though, and he also finds his son and Lipsha, against all odds. The story has come full circle as well. Jack's walk ties directly to June's in *Love Medicine,* but here he walks into the possibility of a fulfilling, a meaningful future, one that is tied to Lyman's (Fleur's) casino. Jack will build it, and his return to the reservation to do so is conveyed in terms of survival:

> Jack rocked the baby, half dreamily, his heart both lifting and sinking. . . . Now he would be part of the biggest temporary concept yet—the thrill of instant money. The power of house odds. The security of eventual small-time petty loss. Nothing new. . . . He had the sense of a swift undertow, pulling from beneath the glazed Formica table, tugging. Home. (*TBL* 408)

The connection of games of chance to home, and the water metaphor that describes one's attraction to it, is a consistent motif in Erdrich's fiction. In each of her novels, the line between "suckers" and those who understand the true nature of chance is clearly drawn. However, as we find in the stories of so many of her characters, including the central one of Lipsha, knowledge does not always ensure power over one's future. It only helps.

As a narrative device, however, this interrogation of the concepts of chance, coincidence, fortune, fate, and luck is central. The questions her characters ask, as they fumble through their lives attempting to understand the "true" meaning of events and plot out a future, are the questions all humankind has asked and will continue to ask. They are, therefore, a point of convergence for all cultures: a recognizable common ground as we search for meaning. In the characters of Nanapush and

Fleur, as well as some of their descendants, however, we find an intriguing negotiation of culturally defined ways of answering those questions. We would be lucky to understand the lessons they learn from such a negotiation, and the nature of their winnings on the card table of history.

Notes

I am indebted to Paula Gunn Allen for the idea for this essay. Although we discussed gambling in other contexts, the connection to Erdrich's texts seems interestingly provocative.

1. It is interesting to consider Gerald Vizenor's (Anishinabe) stories in this context, particularly the scene in *Darkness in Saint Louis Bearheart* where the pilgrims face The Evil Gambler who has grown up on the nation's Interstates, and the short story "The Moccasin Game" in which the people face the wiindigoo who wants to win their children.

2. I will refer solely to the new edition of *Love Medicine.* Since its publication almost coincides with the publication of *The Bingo Palace,* it is therefore a revised conceptualization, in a way, of the whole early tetralogy. With the publication of *Tales of Burning Love,* June's story and the subsequent nature of "chance" have been extended dramatically.

3. Furthermore, in her story, and indeed in the stories of all Erdrich's characters, we find a fundamental questioning of our immediate readings of events: is there such a thing as chance, coincidence, destiny? A contrived plot? If one considers these questions in an historical context, they lead to one other: is the continuation of colonial domination of Indigenous communities inevitable; is it "meant to be?" If one believes so, the communities—and in this one instance June—become tragic victims, their "fate" inescapable. Obviously, for someone at a gambling table playing for the future of generations, this question is central; the working out of an answer becomes a test of knowledge and faith.

4. It is interesting to note that, in a televised interview with Paul Bailey for BBC, Erdrich revealed that *Tracks* was written first, as early as 1980. Gambling is central to the text, as I discuss later. To have it play such an overt role so early in Erdrich's fiction lends further support to its centrality not only in *Love Medicine* but also in the less obvious *The Beet Queen.*

5. There is a significant revision of this scene in the later edition. In it the sexual act is not "consummated." In other words, they do not fully complete sexual intercourse, although Nector understands that Marie thinks they have, because he has touched her with his hand as he rolls around on top of

her. (He later hides his "shame" with the geese.) It is an interesting revision, for it raises several issues as well as strengthens Nector's character, in a way. For our purposes here, it highlights the nature of the power game they have just played. Since they have not consummated the act, she cannot be pregnant with Nector's child and he could, quite easily, walk away; however, he does not. He has lost, and he pays his bets.

6. It is interesting to note in this context the Latin roots of the words *rival* and *river* and their variations: for example *rivus* for "stream."

7. In an interesting narrative ploy, Erdrich calls to question any attempt to dismiss this event as the mere dream of an unreliable narrator. Later we find that Lulu's shoes return to the narrative in such a way that the veracity of the land of the dead scene is reinforced.

8. The nature of the afterlife Pauline describes is curious. It is obviously not exclusionary for the Europeans are here. Also, unlike Argus, here Pauline is visible. The disfigured, dismembered people she sees reflect her own vision of reality, bleak as it is.

9. Luck in gambling is synonymous with luck in other aspects of life, and vice versa. Although it may be a bit too playful to suggest it, this luck may also relate to success in a literary sense. In fact, it is interesting to review the various inscriptions to the five novels, each of which includes Michael Dorris, Erdrich's spouse/collaborator. Those in the last three published novels are particularly interesting: in *Tracks,* "Michael, / The story comes up different / every time and has no ending / but always begins with you"; in *The Bingo Palace,* "To Michael, / U R lucky 4 me"; and in *Tales of Burning Love* "To Michael" followed by a heart symbol and Q, a heart and J—the queen and jack of hearts.

10. Tellingly, Lipsha outlines the road of the dead, as June has walked it to return to him. Once again the road is found in her novels, and once again it is tied to gambling. Here, Lipsha takes the return as a sign of her concern for him, or at least of the importance of what she is conveying. Her potential concern is, of course, qualified by June's reclaiming her car.

11. In terms of the water metaphor Erdrich employs at the conclusion of *Love Medicine,* the (cash) flow always remains the same: toward the house. One needs to recognize this reality and play in those eddies where flow direction changes, in the whorls, and turn the current to one's benefit like Fleur does in Argus. However, one may also turn the flow to one's benefit over the long term, and thus the Indian casino is born.

12. Erdrich's use of English is wonderfully playful at times. Here, "real" could mean reality; "estate" evokes the legal sense, of something that is left for future generations. The phrase could be read as the casino ain't nothing real

(substantial) to leave for the next generations. There are other possibilities, such as Fleur's land is not for "sale."

Work Cited

Dorris, Michael, and Louise Erdrich. "Louise Erdrich and Michael Dorris with Paul Bailey." *The Rolland Collection.* Videocassette. Northbrook, IL: ICA Video, 1989.

2

From Sacred Hoops to Bingo Palaces

Louise Erdrich's Carnivalesque Fiction

Robert A. Morace

In her influential and controversial study of "the feminine in American Indian traditions," Paula Gunn Allen posits Native American gynocracy as a largely silenced but still viable, indeed preferable, alternative to Euro-American patriarchy. Although she tends to idealize and dehistoricize the former, her analysis of essential differences between the gynocratic and the patriarchal is both stimulating and persuasive. Especially forceful is her discussion of the various means used to effect "the social transformation from egalitarian gynecentric systems to hierarchical, patriarchal" ones (40–42). Allen astutely, albeit polemically, attributes this transformation and its result, the "physical and cultural genocide of American Indian tribes," to "patriarchal fear of gynocracy." Far from proving the limitations of her lesbian-feminist approach, Allen's claim, while extreme, nonetheless underscores the great strength and usefulness of her work in that she attends to the constellation of aesthetic, economic, and sociopolitical values that inhere in each of the two antithetical systems. In what follows, I want to consider Louise Erdrich's fiction in light of those values by translating Allen's formulations into Bakhtinian terms. More specifically, I want to read Erdrich's fiction in the context of Bakhtin's theory of carnival, showing the ways in which her use of carnivalizing techniques supports the communal, egalitarian values that, according to Allen, characterize traditional Native American culture and thereby offer an alternative to, a decrowning double of, the nominally democratic but in fact deeply hierarchical and, by comparison, monologic Euro-American culture to which the contemporary Native American writer is inextricably and unavoidably connected.

I am not, of course, the first to see the relevance of Bakhtin's theories to Native American literature in general and Erdrich's fiction in particular. Nor am I unmindful of the fact that, as Arnold Krupat has warned, certain Native American novels may appear far more dialogical than they actually are: Silko's *Storyteller,* for example, with its "unabashed commitment to Pueblo ways as a reference point" (65). Bakhtin figures glancingly throughout Kenneth Lincoln's lengthy study of "Indian humor," though not, surprisingly enough, in his Erdrich chapter, which draws instead on Frye's theory of comedy in *Anatomy of Criticism.* Louis Owens employs Bakhtin more extensively in virtually every chapter of his comprehensive study of "the American Indian novel" except the one devoted to Erdrich. Joni Adamson Clarke makes more pointed use of Bakhtin (via Kristeva) in her reading of *Tracks* as a "doubly transgressive" novel, and Daniel Cornell rightly notes that "much of the comic humor in [this] novel involves [the] representation of the most serious conflicts through the material level of bodily functions, which is characteristic of the carnivalesque nature of the trickster" (60). The implications of the connection between carnival and trickster[1] become especially significant in light of the point Erdrich has repeatedly made in interviews concerning the ability of Native American readers to recognize and respond to the humor in her work that non–Native American readers often miss.

Before going on to discuss the specific ways it manifests itself in each of Erdrich's five novels, I want to consider Bakhtin's carnival theory in relation to a number of more general aspects of her work. The appropriateness of Bakhtin's theory to Erdrich's fiction begins with a certain similarity in their backgrounds. In Erdrich's case this entails her "mixed blood"/multicultural heritage and upbringing, considered in the broadest sense to include Native American and Euro-American (French and German), Chippewa and Catholic, North Dakota and New England, Turtle Mountain Reservation and Johns Hopkins Writing Seminars, as well as her belonging to a marginalized group while occupying a privileged position both within that group and outside it. Similarly, Bakhtin's "extraordinary sensitivity to the immense plurality of experience" (Holquist, "Introduction," DI xv), his defining the utterance as "a very complex and multi-faceted system of relations" (Bakhtin, SG 124), and his preoccupation with thresholds, border areas, and points of intersection derive in large measure from his early experiences in the multicultural and heteroglot cities of Vilnius and Odessa (Clark and Holquist 21–27). Encyclopedic, multi-styled and multi-form, carnival, as well as carnivalization ("the transposition of carnival into the language of literature"), is one such point of intersection. During carnival the "hierarchical structure" of monologic authority gives way to "organic unity," "joyful relativity," and "free and familiar contact among people." These "carnivalistic mesalliances" point to the essential dualism of life; they bring together not only individuals from different social groups but birth and death, the sacred and the profane, high and low, past and present, wisdom and foolishness: all the comic joinings which evoke the laughter that Bakhtin associates with "the people's unofficial truth" (PDP 107–9, 119, 122–23, 135; R 90, 407–8, 434, 454).

Related to this laughter and central to Bakhtin's conception of carnival is the grotesque and its literary counterpart, grotesque realism, whose chief characteristics are exaggeration, associated with "fertility, growth . . . abundance," and degradation, a positive force which "transfer[s] to the material level . . . all that is high, spiritual, ideal, abstract" (R 19). Often overlooked in discussions of Bakhtin's theory of carnival and in danger of being forgotten entirely as critics follow Morson and Emerson's lead and begin to emphasize the less subversive aspects of his writings is Bakhtin's situating Rabelaisian grotesque realism at a specific, indeed crucial point in time, one of considerable relevance to Allen's analysis of Native American culture. Grotesque realism occurs at a typically Bakhtinian "crossroads" where "the folk culture of humor" (and the oral tradition on which it is based), just then beginning its decline, intersects with "the bourgeois conception of the completed atomized being," just then, along with printing and the novel, coming into existence. Unlike the "atomized" individual, "the grotesque body is not separated from the world" but "open" to it; thus grotesque realism's emphasis on those bodily points at which self and world intersect: mouth, anus, genitals (R 24–26). Bakhtin's "explosive politics of the body" implies a set of utopian communalist ideals similar to the ones Allen posits at the heart of Native American culture.[2] These ideals are embodied, as it were, not only in carnival but in language as Bakhtin conceives it, which is to say along similarly social/communal lines, as an "ecosystem" rather than a "prison house," in which meaning is not individually possessed but arrived at as the result of "co-creation" and "creative understanding" (Clark and Holquist 227, 12).

In much the same way that Erdrich's multicultural background may have led her (as it led Bakhtin), however indirectly, to the carnivalesque, it may have also contributed to her and her late husband Michael Dorris's "virtually unprecedented collaboration" (Chavkin 84). Erdrich's initial resistance to this collaboration and the interest, indeed the surprise, even dismay implied in the frequency with which the topic has come up in reviews and interviews, suggest that for many collaboration is an unnatural act. In a way, perhaps it is. This is after all not only a word burdened with negative connotations of betrayal, but one whose most literal meaning and deepest essence is so inimical to American individualism and the economic system and aesthetic principles it serves. As Bakhtin points out, "Capitalism created the conditions for a special type of inescapably solitary consciousness" (PDP 288). Collaboration stands in opposition to the modern Euro-American obsession with "solitary consciousness," both as subject/hero and as author (the Romantic genius transformed into owner of her or his text/work). It is wholly consistent with (even if not identical to) Dorris's and Allen's depictions of Native American "cooperation" and with Bakhtin's repeated emphasis on carnival's foundation in folk culture, the oral tradition, and communal values. This is not to say that Erdrich's Native American-ness led her to accept the joys of collaboration (which Dorris attributed to nothing more than their being able to work well together; interview with Hertha Wong in Chavkin 36). I argue only that her complex and hybridized upbringing may have helped sensitize her to collaboration and, further, that this collaboration, which many have judged odd and unprecedented, bears some relation to the communal/collaborative style and values of Erdrich's carnivalesque novels.

(There is, of course, considerable irony in the fact that the book in which Erdrich and Dorris acknowledge their collaboration most directly, *The Crown of Columbus,* through the device of legal co-authorship, is the one in which this collaboration proved least successful in all but financial terms.)

The collaboration issue is related, albeit indirectly, to two other points of critical debate. One has to do with an at times obsessive interest in establishing the genealogy of Erdrich's characters. Whether intended as a preface to the Danish edition, as a teaching aid in college classes, as a navigational device for reviewers, or as the subject of critical inquiry, the subtext of this interest remains the same: a commitment to carefully defined genealogical and chronological lines and limits that make Erdrich's fiction seem far more conventional and less carnivalesque than it actually is. (This is accomplished in part by substituting patriarchal lines of descent for matriarchal clans and in part by putting her work in the shadow of García Márquez's exuberant but now already canonized *One Hundred Years of Solitude,* its excesses already tamed and therefore made familiar; cf. Malcolm Cowley's chronological ordering of *The Portable Faulkner,* with its appendix, "1699–1945: The Compsons.") The second issue has to do with a different kind of genealogical enterprise: critics' efforts to define the precise nature of Erdrich's work in terms of Western literary taxonomy. The question as to whether her books are actually novels or (only?) collections of short stories is interesting, but only as a question, and even then only as one in a series. Should the books be read in the order published, the order conceived, or the order of their plots? Does the New and Expanded Version of *Love Medicine* supplant or supplement the original (old and reduced?) edition? Does the former, which is of course the later, share in the many honors and awards won by the latter, which is to say the earlier? *Love Medicine* spills over, all unknowingly, into *The Beet Queen,* eventually giving birth to a trilogy, the original manuscript version of *Tracks* compressed into the short story "Fleur," in turn expanded to novel length, taking the story back as far as Erdrich has (as yet) been willing to go, only to have trilogy become quartet, then quintet, taking the story ahead as far as Erdrich has as yet gone, perhaps will go.

Erdrich's books are novels in the capacious but nonetheless immensely useful Bakhtinian sense of the word in that each comprises "a diversity of social speech types and a diversity of individual voices artistically arranged" (DI 262). This diversity is the result as well as the reflection of a "verbal and semantic decentering of the world, a certain linguistic homelessness of literary consciousness" (DI 367) not unlike Lukacs' view of the novel as a reflection of "transcendental homelessness." No less pertinent to our reading of Erdrich's fiction is Bakhtin's belief that every utterance is a rejoinder in search of a response (DI 279) and therefore part of "an unfinalized dialogue" (PDP 32). In Erdrich's case this is a principle at work both within individual novels (most obviously *Tracks*) and between them—so much so that we can say of the entire but still incomplete body of her published work what Bakhtin said of Dostoevsky's *Crime and Punishment*, "from the very beginning a certain stable semantic multiplicity exists, with unchanging content, and all that occurs within it is a rearrangement of accents" (PDP 240). As Erdrich explained to the Chavkins, "There is no reason to think of publication as a final process. I think of it as temporary storage. . . . Perhaps short pieces become more connected, more resonant, within the context of a novel, and then again, I miss how as short stories these pieces once stood alone. I'm not so thrifty about the work that I do this on purpose, it is just that the novels consume the short pieces while at the same time the pieces suggest additions to the novel" (232). Asked a little later whether her "writing forms an organic whole," Erdrich offers this Rabelaisian response: "more like a compost pile" (240). Arrangement and rearrangement, contextualization and isolation, thrift and excess, expansion and contraction, creating and consuming, compost and construct, novel and story: all play their parts in Erdrich's effort to explain through a Gargantuan relay of (carnivalized/mixed) metaphors a *body* of work that proves at once repetitive and unfinalized, in fact unfinalizable. Let me qualify now what I said a bit earlier when I called Erdrich's books "novels" according to Bakhtin's definition, by referring to the distinction Bakhtin makes in *Art and Answerability* between "compositional" and "architectonic" forms, the one being merely structural (e.g., novel, drama) in its orientation, the other essentially (and more importantly) axiological (268–70). It is precisely the axiological dimension of Erdrich's carnivalesque fiction that has been largely misunderstood and misrepresented.

Catherine Rainwater approaches this issue from a broadly semiotic perspective in what is clearly the most important, detailed, and stimulating study of what reading Erdrich's fiction is actually like for most readers. *Love Medicine,* she contends, situates the reader between two "conflicting codes," one Western, the other Native American, which compete "for domination of narrativity." Rainwater may be a bit too optimistic in her assessment of the reader's final "empowerment," but her account has certainly empowered others, including Owens and Bak. My own debt to Rainwater is considerable, but I believe that her semiotic approach can only gain from attending more closely to the limitations, axiologically considered, of the ways critics and reviewers have responded to Erdrich's work, particularly her endings, in terms of survival and affirmation (Catt and Owens), homecoming and redemption (Gleason), "wholeness" and "transcendence" (Hanson), and "the redemptive oneness which reconciles painful polarities and dissolves alienation" (Crabtree). Equally telling is the language frequently used to describe Erdrich's achievement, a language that often comes perilously close to kitsch. According to Lincoln, for example, "The ends of the stories [in *Love Medicine*] rise up off the page, soar through the reader's mind, and hang etched and limpid against a canvas of blank space" (234). Even Bak, in an otherwise restrained and intelligent essay, seems to lose hold of his critical senses in describing *The Beet Queen* in terms of its "searing realism" and "graceful lyricism," the "wondrous magic of lingering tribal lore and the equally wondrous capacity for endurance and survival" (146). This is not to say that Erdrich's endings do not seem to invite such readings and such language, only that critics are mistaken in placing so much emphasis on them. To give them (the endings and their admiring critics) the final word is yet another way to make the novels seem more conventional than they are and thus to control the spirit of carnival, at once subversive and regenerative, which is always "hostile to any sort of conclusive conclusion" (Bakhtin, PDP 165).[3] In the pages that follow I will address what I consider the most important carnivalesque features of Erdrich's novels. I intend my discussion of each of the five to be representative rather than exhaustive. Rather than rehearse the complete repertoire of carnivalesque elements at play in each novel, I accent those I feel are most important to a particular work while counting on the reader to recognize the presence and relative significance of other elements discussed elsewhere in the essay. My interest throughout is in the axiological implications of Erdrich's carnivalesque fiction.

In *Love Medicine,* Erdrich's description of Lyman sitting "in his bunkerlike office," wielding enormous if arbitrary power, does not so much polemically critique as comically decrown the process by which Euro-Americans effected the "transformation from egalitarian gynecentric systems to hierarchical, patriarchal" ones (Allen 40–42). The novel as a whole conforms to even as it contemporizes Allen's point concerning traditional tribal literature's "tendency to distribute value evenly among various elements, providing a model or pattern for egalitarian structuring of society as well as literature" (240). Thus the novel's emphasis on points of intersection of various kinds and at all levels: Lulu "just at the edge of slim" (*LMN* 62), Zelda "living just at the edge of the reservation" (*LMN* 12), Marie having "a son on either side of the line" (*LMN* 19), mixed blood, half-brothers, and the like. Geographical, political, and biological points of intersection such as these are fairly obvious. Others, less apparent but no less important and pervasive, include the rhetorical, as in Lipsha's non-sequitur, "I never really done much with my life. I never had a television" (*LMN* 230), and the generic.

Although done less insistently and self-consciously than in the works of postmodern writers such as Barth and Coover, *Love Medicine* incorporates a vast array of inserted (often parodied) forms and modes of address. There are Indian jokes, letters, IRS forms, factory directions, "Red English," slapstick comedy, cartoon-like scenes, a painting, and, in Lipsha, the vernacular idiom of Huck Finn, including many Huck-like verbal slips (e.g., "Lulu Lamartine's little blue tweety bird, a paraclete, I'd guess you'd call it," *LMN* 243). There is a mixing and matching of "spoken" and written discourse, first and third person, past and present tense. Repetition plays a conspicuous role, underscoring the novel as the intersection of various centrifugal and centripetal forces, with each repetition constituting a Bakhtinian reaccenting rather than a simple reenactment or corrective reinterpretation. In its very structure, *Love Medicine* calls attention to the communal nature of storytelling and to the communal need for story. Though clearly dispersed, even attenuated, more the reader's construct than a distinct narrative presence, this communal voice is preferable to both Lyman's pronouncements and Zelda's "royal we" (*LMN* 8) on the one hand, and a reductive relativizing and fragmenting of narrative voice on the other.

In much the same way and in much the same spirit that it exposes the pretensions of the will to monological power, the novel works itself out against (or in dialogue with) "white time" and white space to create its own distinctive chronotope (Bakhtin's term for the "inseparability of time and space," "the intrinsic connectedness of temporal and spatial relationships . . . artistically expressed in literature," DI 84). It is important to note in this regard that the disorientation—or reorientation—that one experiences in reading Erdrich's fiction has little to do with the spatial disorientation that, as Jameson has pointed out, characterizes the various postmodern arts. Erdrich's chronotope more closely resembles, both in its sources and its effects, the premodern. As Bakhtin notes in "The Folkloric Bases of the Rabelaisian Chronotope," this premodern (and pre-class) time is collective, productive, "tensed toward the future," inclusive and unified (the human and the natural are one), and "profoundly spatial and concrete," though marked as well by one negative feature, a "cyclicity" which precludes the "becoming" that Bakhtin so highly prizes in Rabelais and in the modern novel (DI 209–10). In *Love Medicine,* as in all of Erdrich's fiction, the past is physically present, the distant near at hand, the legendary alive here and now. Against the progression of years (which figure only in chapter titles), and other temporal markers, e.g., "one week later," "on Thursday," common in realistic fiction but rare in Erdrich (aside from chapter headings), we find the coexistence of different generations and the passage not of years so much as of seasons, of cycles of drought and flood (*Beet Queen*), abundance and starvation (*Tracks*), and of space saturated with time and characters who possess the "startling ability to see time in space," to discern, that is, "the fullness of time" (SG 31, 41).

"All through my life I never did believe in human measurement," Lulu says. "Numbers, time, inches, feet. All are just ploys for cutting nature down to size" (*LMN* 281). The spatio-temporal palimpsest that Bakhtin found in Goethe offers a Romantic alternative to the reductive forms of human measurement that Lulu rejects. Another, equally important and far more pervasive, is Rabelaisian grotesque realism and grotesque humor. The grotesquerie ranges from simple exaggeration to exuberant distortion, from Marie's looking as "weathered and massive as a statue roughed out of rock" and Henry Lamartine's carrying enough shrapnel deep inside him . . . to set off the metal detector at the airport" to Albertine's description of Gerry Nanapush, a description as outsized as Gerry himself and, appropriately enough, far too long to be quoted here (*LMN* 204–5). The grotesquerie is as much situational (a matter of plot) as descriptive. Virtually every aspect of Nector's affair with Lulu (one for which the qualifier "adulterous" seems beside the point) is charged with the grotesque, from its inception in the delivery and distribution of "seventeen tons of surplus butter on the hottest day of '52" to the literally fiery end to this tale of burning love in which Nector plays the part of a Chippewa Charlie Chaplin.

The Rabelaisian spirit also manifests itself in the pervasive references to food and sex. The egg which Andy peels for June in the novel's opening section may be conventionally symbolic, but the pies and other foods that follow serve to anchor the text to a decidedly physical world that includes beer and wine, "shit," and "vomit" (*LMN* 263). Sex serves the same end. June's sexual freedom is transformed into the language of grotesque realism in Lulu's numerous children, none of them her husband Henry's "in the factual sense." If Lulu is part earth mother, part strumpet, as Malcolm Jones contends (Chavkin 7), then Marie is the Old Lady Who Lived in the Shoe with her similarly numerous but mainly adopted children. Frequently the references to food and sex intersect. Andy's down vest rubs June "like an enormous tongue" (*LMN* 5); Nector and Lulu cover each other with surplus butter; and Moses licks, sips, and tastes Lulu, whom Nanapush had earlier warned, "Come winter, you'll eat him up" (*LMN* 75). More ambivalently, we see the very young Lulu feeding and exploring the body of the dead man (Napoleon Morrissey) she finds in the woods.

The interconnectedness of sex and food is most extensively and perversely rendered in the relationship between Marie and Sister Leopolda. The nun, thin from fasting and a version of the witch from "Hansel and

Gretel," holds the keys not to A. J. Cronin's Kingdom but instead to the convent's larder. Marie is initially drawn to her and the Catholicism she grotesquely represents out of shame deriving from her Indian blood and metonymically focused on her body. Her dislike (distaste?) for the "low comparisons" that characterize Indian life lead her to the "top of the highest hill" where she first imagines her victory in decidedly ambivalent terms, closer to Polanski's *Repulsion* than to Rabelais:

> I was rippling gold. My breasts were bare and my nipples flashed and winked. Diamonds tipped them. I could walk through panes of glass. I could walk through windows. She was at my feet, swallowing the glass after each step I took. I broke through another and another. The glass she swallowed ground and cut until her starved insides were only a subtle dust. And then she was only a black rag that flapped off, snagging on a bobwire, hung there for an age, and finally rotted into the breeze.
>
> I saw this, mouth hanging open, gazing off into the flagged boughs of trees.
>
> "Get up!" she cried. "Stop dreaming. It is time to bake." (*LMN* 54)

Paulo Medeiros discusses their relationship in terms of the psychological significance of Marie's eating disorder. In literature as in life, Medeiros points out, eating disorders "present the stage for a conflict grounded on desire and power in which the individual process of identity formation clashes with and rebels against traditional notions of what constitutes a human being" (12). Good as it is, Medeiros' reading proves doubly limited: first because it approaches the relationship as figured in the attenuated form of a "story," "Saint Marie," in a collection rather than a chapter in a novel; and second because in focusing on the "story's" psychological content, it overlooks the comic aspect which, while more pronounced in Marie's later life, is nonetheless present in "Saint Marie," where it takes a different and more grotesque form. Not unseriously but not humorlessly either, she devotes much of that later life to food (just as Lulu devotes much of hers to sex): growing and canning fruits and vegetables, comically obsessive potato peeling, etc. Significantly, when she goes off to visit Leopolda, whom she mistakenly believes is dying, she goes not to say goodbye or make amends but instead to offer her body (and that of her daughter) as visible, or rather, given the darkness of Leopolda's room, tangible proof that she "had not been living on wafers of God's flesh but the fruit of man" (*LMN* 148), including the jar of crabapples she brings with her: an afterthought serving as an alibi in the form of a gift. Marie's subsequent struggle (for a spoon) with a now "shrivelled" Leopolda, "frail as a dead plant," her arms "thin as ropes," suggests more than lingering psychological insecurity, as Medeiros' reading would have us believe. The struggle is comic, even farcical, and as such accentuates what the "story's" climax (Leopolda's scalding and piercing Marie's flesh) and denouement (Marie's playing on the nuns' credulity and on Leopolda's fear of exposure) already imply, albeit more ambiguously and ambivalently.[4] Here we see that typically carnivalesque bonding of opposites which manifests itself throughout Erdrich's novel, first in June's Easter death, then in the Punch and Judy scene in which King nearly kills his wife Lynette, in Marie's recalling the time the children played at hanging June, in Henry's drowning with its "My boots are filling with water" punchline, in Gordie's drunkenly believing that the doe he has hit with his car and later killed with a tire iron is his wife June returned from the dead (a shaggy dog, or doe, story that gets funnier and funnier only to end in madness), and similarly Nector's choking to death at the end of a long chain of jokes, tricks, and comic substitutions.

The most important difference between *Love Medicine* and *The Beet Queen* is not that the latter deals almost exclusively with characters who are not Native Americans. Rather, it is the way *Beet Queen* highlights its essential carnivalesque nature. Incorporating a number of fairground scenes (the Orphans' Picnic) and climaxing with a modern day carnival (carnival, Bakhtin would say, in its reduced form), Erdrich implies what another, less ambivalently Catholic writer, Flannery O'Connor, said outright about her own grotesque fiction, that "for the near blind, you have to write large." In addition to the carnivals themselves, we find a proliferation of decrowning doubles, inserted forms, and gender (as well as genre) bending. Instead of merely mentioning food, Erdrich offers a meat market, a restaurant, an entire town devoted to growing, processing, and shipping sugar beets, which, like a single gigantic organism, ingests everything it needs and evacuates everything it produces along the same passage, first railroad, later highway. For all the appearance of tidy chronological order (chapters by year, parts by decade), it is excess not orderliness that triumphs, most graphically in QUEEN WALLACETTE written in Gargantuan letters by order of the carnival's organizer, also the beet queen's literal deliverer and namesake, closet homosexual, and whilom lover of the mixed-blood, box-shaped queen's absentee biological father, Karl Adare. To say, as Louis Owens does, picking up on the image of a "delicate" spider's web on page 176, that "all [the novel's] relationships are terribly frail," is to miss or at least misrepresent both the novel's exuberance and its heterogeneity, figured in everything from the naming of the town after the hundred-eyed giant charged with guarding the heifer to Fleur's making "her living by peddling whatever came her way to sell" (*BQ* 50), Celestine's putting in her soup whatever happens to be at hand, and Mary's oddly concocted Jell-O salad.

Between the scenes of abandonment with which it opens and the complementary and rather conventional scenes of redemption with which it closes, *The Beet Queen* is a tour de force of comic grotesquerie. In one scene, Karl, looking like he just stepped out of Nathanael West's *Miss Lonelyhearts,* has sex with Celestine, whom he first mistakes for his own sister, Mary, then for his cousin, Sita. During intercourse Celestine ponders the considerable difference between sex as described in the novels she has read and sex as she experiences it for the first time with Karl. Afterwards, as she makes a post-coital pot of coffee, he opens up his traveling case, sets up his display board, and mechanically switches from none-too-seductive sex spiel to equally ineffective sales pitch for a set of cheap knives (one of the many items Karl will attempt to sell during the course of the novel). Scenes of comic grotesquerie such as this one prove the norm, not the exception, in a novel in which the characters' jokes often backfire (e.g., Wallace Pfef's revenge on Mary—getting her drunk—at Dot's birthday party), but Erdrich's do not. Mary's comically paranoid fear of killer robots (Cold War paranoia typical of the time, reinforced by sci-fi films like *Invasion of the Body Snatchers*), becomes flesh when her absurdly thin, robot-like brother arrives on the scene. A lovesick cop named Lovchik, who has pulled Mary over for speeding, believes himself spurned yet again when Sita fails to respond to or even acknowledge his greeting. Sita, however, does not respond because she cannot; she's dead, propped up in Mary's car (fortunately air-conditioned) because, as Mary has rightly surmised, on the day of the Sugar Beet festival even the undertaker will be at the parade, the same parade—joke leading to joke—in which Sita will soon participate, the result of a wrong turn on Mary's part.

The excessiveness also evidences itself in the novel's language (see, for example, *BQ* 302–9) and in both the range and number of comically inserted forms, from baptisms and ordinations to postcards and letters, résumés and sales pitches, crime stories and romantic novels. Seen against a backdrop of reduced but not entirely debunked magic (Mary's palmistry, yarrow sticks, tarot deck, ouija board, mind reading), the excessiveness includes an abundance of decrowning doubles: the bland Pfef as Fisher King; bisexual Karl Adare, alternately devil and deliverer; Wallacette become Dot, the tight-skirted juvenile delinquent turned shot-putter and reluctant, resentful Beet Queen; Celestine's parody of Mary's version of a Jell-O salad; permutating lovers' triangles; Mary's pronouncing like "pez" the "chez" in Chez Sita, the name of her faux French restaurant, its grand opening nearly spoiled when the chef is stricken with food poisoning but saved when Russell, Mary, and Celestine, pressed into service, offer up the usual fare under unusual names and at inflated prices to a local clientele that dupes itself into believing it is getting the real thing. And then there is Russell, who may have been intended and certainly may be read as a comic version of another returning vet, Tayo in Silko's *Ceremony.*[5]

The ambivalent nature of carnival humor is particularly evident in and important to Erdrich's handling of Sita, who tries to be all that carnival excessiveness is not. Early in the novel she finds herself doubly displaced, first in a variation on the sibling rivalry theme and, slightly later, in a muted version of a same-sex lover's triangle. Having failed in her attempt to use her newly pubescent body to win back Celestine's affection, Sita becomes increasingly private and possessive. Even as she uses her body for economic advantage, working as a model for a small-town department store, she punishes herself physically in order to exert a measure of control over a world of carnival excess. Her efforts to keep herself looking attractive leave her looking starved, or as Mary puts it, "stuffed and preserved." And her two childless marriages suggest an aversion to sex (or heterosexual sex) underlying her desire to remain sexually appealing. Her pretensions to regal status are exposed first at a Minneapolis department store, where the salesperson treats her as a hick, then at the grand opening of her "French" restaurant, and lastly in her, or rather her corpse's, looking "imperial and stern" as she, or it, becomes part of the Beet Festival parade. Her plot takes her from meat market to department store (and modeling, another kind of meat market) to restaurant to marriage (to a state food inspector) to obsession with pure food and finally to living alone on virtually no food at all, not even the boxes of candy Lovchik gives her but she never opens, only the prescription pills she hordes, parsimoniously doling out one at a time until her suicidal binge.

Sita controls not only what she puts into her mouth but what she allows out, as the reader first learns in one of the novel's funniest scenes. Sita silently watches as the chairs on which her husband and her cousin Karl are sitting sink deeper and deeper into the wet backyard soil, until they are eventually swallowed up, at least in what the reader only now realizes is Sita's disturbed mind. Later still, Sita will deny herself speech altogether and be committed to a mental hospital where she soon achieves a partial cure when her roommate claims to be a cannibal who has eaten her entire family, right down to the youngest grandchild. It is a revelation that seems no less effective than comically grotesque and contextually apt. Given that she is just as parsimonious with words as she is with pills, food, and sex, Sita's last *spoken* words, to Mary and Celestine after her cousin has accidentally hit her on the head with a brick, prove no less appropriate: "You'll eat shit with the chickens someday." Sita's words connect her to the world outside herself, most directly to those whom she addresses but also to her father, for these are not "her" words at all, but his, or rather theirs. And though addressed to Mary and Celestine, they apply just as well to Sita, returning her to the bodily stratum she has tried so hard to deny.

Tracks, the first of Erdrich's novels to be drafted but the third to be published, and then only after extensive reworking, develops the opposition between the carnivalesque and all that Sita represents in still starker terms. Far from signaling a turning away from carnival excess, Erdrich's use here of dual rather than multiple storytellers focuses attention on certain narrative features that help bring the novel's deeply carnivalesque nature into even sharper focus. One is Bakhtin's point that "Who speaks and under what conditions he speaks . . . determines the word's actual meaning" (DI 401). Another is the difference between explanation, requiring "only one consciousness, one subject," and understanding, requiring at least two (SG 111). Finally, *Tracks* enables us to see in Pauline's character and narration a version of the abject hero. For Michael Andre Bernstein, not the first to fault Bakhtin for defining carnival in unreservedly positive terms, "the abject hero is condemned to dialogue, since his consciousness is an echo chamber of incompatible desires and prohibitions. . . . The essence of abjection is to occupy, as it were, the logically impossible space created by the intersection of the servile and the satanic" (222). As descendant as well as precursor of both Marie and Sita, Pauline proves one of fiction's most powerfully rendered abject heroes, worthy successor to Dostoevsky's Underground Man.

Obsessed by the ugliness that she believes makes her invisible to others (a reflection, as it were, of another of the Underground Man's offspring, Ralph Ellison's Invisible Man), Pauline becomes a voyeur, a nonparticipant, barely living and even then only vicariously. She is "midwife" to death, alternately "death's bony whore," her discourse a troubling mix of restraint and desire, revenge and righteousness, exaltation and shame. Her names suggest her perverted nature, the one a reminder of a misogynist saint (his loathing for women transformed into her self-loathing), the other (from *Love Medicine*) an echo of Leopold von Sacher-Masoch and index of her masochistic (and later sadistic) personality. Because "names tell stories, or half stories, if only we listen" (Erdrich, "Names" 132), it is not surprising that Pauline recoils from an Indian community ministered to by a Father Damien. Rather than risk contamination/contagion, she attempts to seal herself, her body, off, becoming in the process withdrawn, self-contained, repressed, perverse, "white." We see this in the way she responds to Fleur's cries as Fleur is being gang-raped: covering her ears, closing her eyes, shutting her mouth. And we see it in her interest in the statue of the Virgin, which she calls "perfect," meaning, one assumes, perfectly impervious and imperturbable and therefore powerful. Against its frozen timeless smile, *Tracks* posits Lulu's mocking laughter directed at everyone and "everything," nuns and priests included, and Fleur's "rich, knowing laugh, an invitation full of sadness and pleasure I could not help but join" (*T* 214).

The speaker here is the trickster/sage Nanapush, who directs much of his sexual and scatological banter at Pauline, who tries as best she can to deny all bodily functions and desires. "Stealing food like a weasel, listening with open ears" (*T* 52), Nanapush is, as Pauline is not, both receptive and responsive. In his life as in his narrative, food, sex, and storytelling all play their equally important, interconnected, undeniable parts. He has survived, like Fleur, the consumption that has eaten away at the tribe, is opposed to whites "nibbling" at Indian land (hoping soon to swallow it whole at auction), and envies Margaret her strong teeth. He is "moved" by the taste of the heart of the moose Eli has killed to keep them from starving but disgusted by the merely representational value of "the sacred bloody lump that the blue-robed woman [the Virgin] held in the awful picture that Margaret kept nailed to her wall" (*T* 51). When Pauline tells him in stylized biblical fashion, "I shall not live by bread alone," Nanapush, playing the part of uncomprehending, literal-minded carnival fool, tells her, only half-mockingly, I suspect, "There is meat, good stew!" (*T* 199).

Pauline's narration takes the form of a diatribe, "(a conversation with an absent interlocutor), confessional in nature and saturated with hidden polemic" (PDP 154). Like the Underground Man, Pauline's self-imposed isolation necessitates her playing the parts of both addresser and addressee, and not only of her own silently "spoken" narrative but of "His" as well, this "He" being at times God and at times the Devil. The most notable exception—her telling Margaret and Nanapush what happened to Fleur in Argus—only proves the general rule governing her narration, for not only is Pauline "possessed" by God, Satan, and her psychological demons; she is possessive. Although the telling/sharing of her story does her good, she gives up her story only reluctantly and then only partially. "The truth, or some version of it," has to be "pulled" from her (*T* 65). Her possessiveness in this and nearly all matters inverts Fleur's situation at the time of the rape, her "curses in the old language" which Pauline hears but does not heed, and Russell's situation at the time of the tornado, his cries which the three men who raped Fleur and who have now taken shelter in the meat locker presumably hear but do not heed. Two will freeze to death, and the third suffer frostbite so severe that pieces of his body begin falling off, the morally monstrous transformed into carnival freak (leper) that the townspeople "pay" to see, a dish of food the price of their admission. Metaphorically, Pauline shares—as literally she may have sealed—his fate.

Nanapush's narration takes a very different form (oral and communal rather than novelistic and psychological) and is rendered in a very different style (multi-toned and "Native American"). Intended to make Lulu understand why her mother Fleur left her behind, it is at once narrow in its focus on a single, identifiable, physically present addressee yet expansive in its scope, making clear that Fleur's story can only be understood as part of a larger tribal narrative. Where Pauline is reluctant, secretive, possessive, self-contained, and self-centered, Nanapush is responsive, open, sharing, free, and adaptable—willing to incorporate Lulu's (implied) responses in his telling. His narration foregrounds the generating and performance contexts of Native American oral literature and, to some extent, given Lulu's unfamiliarity with her family history, the reception context as well (see Allen, *Studies* 33–34). His storytelling is linked to another oral activity, eating (his "tongue tingl[es] for the last word" and needs to be "oiled by strong tea, lard and bread," *T* 48, 7). Equally important, his narration is communal not only in scope but in origin and purpose. The story he tells is, as he freely acknowledges, as dependent on the stories others (especially women) have told him as they are on events he himself has witnessed. Moreover, his story can work its medicine only if addressed to a community of listeners; thus one reason he tells Lulu "his" story, which is also hers and Fleur's and the tribe's, is to "convince your mother and your father to visit me. I'd bring the old times back!" (*T* 210).

Even as it looks ahead in order to look back, the double ending of Nanapush's story, which is also the ending of the novel, seems not so much lyrical (as Bak and others have claimed) as problematic, despite its García Márquez-like brilliance (García Márquez being another writer with important links to oral/folk culture and the carnival tradition). Lulu's homecoming, complementing Fleur's leave-taking one page/several years before, opens onto the future but in a troubling way. Compared to a "fierce dry wind," it connects *Tracks* not only to *One Hundred Years of Solitude,* with its cyclonic wind that wipes both the Buendias and Macondo from the face of the earth, but also to the tornado whose appearance early in the novel seems less meteorological than magical, avenging Fleur's rape, and to the similarly supernatural wind that enables Fleur to complete her final act of defiance. Foretold in Nanapush's dream (*T* 127), Fleur's wind takes the form of a decrowning double, a grotesque parody of the logging industry that has come to dispossess the last of the Pillagers and all she represents. Fleur's wind supplants, but only momentarily/narratively, the "wind from the east, bringing exile in a storm of government papers" that began blowing twelve years, 220 pages before, that continues to blow at the time of Nanapush's telling (by now "a blizzard of legal forms," *T* 225) and that will continue to rain down papers at least figuratively made from the very trees felled by Fleur herself at novel's end. For all Erdrich's "soaring lyricism" and Fleur's special effects and Nanapush's storytelling skills, it is beginning to look like Dorothy was right, that we're not in Kansas any more, and not in Oz either—the Wizard exposed, his power gone with the wind—but back in north central North Dakota on the verge of Erdrich's most topical novel.

Like Lulu's apartment in the senior citizens' building, Fleur's house on a reservation allotment is filled with official papers—tangible proof in *The Bingo Palace* of the storm of government paperwork mentioned in *Tracks.* The papers that seem so appropriate in the context of Lulu's modern surroundings and position as tribal leader (proof that *Track*'s wizard had not lost all his formidable powers), appear quite differently in Fleur's more primitive dwelling, less official, more functional, reduced in importance if not in size in a world that includes animal skins and Fleur's spirit rocks, the "ones that she always talked to" (*T* 45). More than a "graphic" reminder of the victory of Euro-American written culture over the Native American oral tradition, of values that are legally inscribed rather than communally shared, the papers suggest a much greater attentiveness on Erdrich's part than in any of her earlier fiction to the increasingly intertextual dimension of all contemporary cultures, Native American included, which enables her to create here in pastiche shades the verbal equivalent of Shawnee Ray's colorful ribbon shirts.

Despite its leisurely opening, with its oddly intersecting echoes of Faulkner's "A Rose for Emily" and Cheever's *The Wapshot Chronicle, The Bingo Palace* alludes to a vast array of intertextual references and contemporary media, from Xerox copies of wanted posters to radio news, television documentaries, video cassettes, animated cartoons (television's *Roadrunner* and film's *Dumbo*), Indian jokes and in-jokes (Zelda's "tale of burning love," Lipsha's claiming it was the "heat of [Nector's] attraction" that set Lulu's house on fire), black humor (when Lipsha asks Fleur whether the Pillagers would take him back, she replies, "Why not? There's none of us left," *BP* 133). There is Chaplinesque comedy (Lipsha as lover with his pants around his ankles), a food fight that recalls the slapstick-inspired family feud that brings the factory, rather than the house, down in *Love Medicine,* a car chase reminiscent of *Raising Arizona,* right down to escaped prisoner and inadvertent kidnapping, chapter endings that parody suspense novels, adaptations of traditional Catholic and Native American forms and rituals (credo, litany, vision quest), and a perfectly pitched send-up of social worker "Vicki Koob's trained and cataloging gaze" (*BP* 175).

The novel's intertextuality is most clearly foregrounded in Lipsha. In "between" in various senses (jobs, identities, etc.), he has the fullest and most diverse array of discourses from which to chose, and while this multiplicity certainly and positively frees him from the kind of monological certainty and presumptuousness that characterizes Vicki Koob, it possesses its own negative feature, insofar as it evidences, however comically, the extent of Lipsha's cultural and "linguistic homelessness." This is especially evident when, awaking on an Astroturf rug in the sweat lodge, he mentally replays Jimi Hendrix recordings, reviews "all the *Godfather* series," and rereads the Dune trilogy and *Moby Dick* (*BP* 198). Throughout the novel, Lipsha's discourse is self-consciously drawn from a similarly wide range of contemporary cultural sources: Alger Hiss's denial of ever having been a member of the Communist Party ("I am not now, and nor have I ever been, interested in visiting here [Matchimanito Lake]," *BP*

133), a Henry Roth novel ("Call it sleep," *BP* 98), the Persian Gulf War ("the mother of all skunks," *BP* 200), and name brands (he is proud to be "related to the reservation's biggest cheese" even though he thinks of Lyman as "a big, bland Velveeta," *BP* 15). When all else fails, he looks for guidance in a Gideon's Bible, less perhaps for its wisdom than for its metonymic association with Shawnee Ray. Lost in a Dantean dark wood and speaking in his updated Huck Finn idiom (as in the "and nor" above), Lipsha substitutes the tangle of intertextual references for the interconnectedness of tribal relations. In his repetitions we sense both a "longing for other human voices" (*BP* 199) and a Bakhtinian difference, at times a diminution of power (e.g., in his using Fleur's words to keep Zelda at bay), even resentment (in a simple "How are you?" he hears echoes of every "How" spoken by every "Indian" in every Hollywood western, *BP* 31).

The bingo palace, or palaces, the rather shabby, relatively small-scale one Lyman already owns and the far grander resort he envisions during his ruinous trip to Reno and plans to build partly on Pillager land, are Lipsha's intertextuality writ large. The place where people go to satisfy their hungers (*BP* 42), the bingo palace provides meager fare, only the illusion of sustenance. "If you are what you eat, I will live forever," Lipsha says of the foods he has been consuming at Lyman's bar, the beer nuts and beef jerky laced with chemical preservatives (*BP* 63). "The big casino . . . the luck place, the money-maker scheme that will build day cares, endow scholarships, cure the ills of addiction of which it is a cause" (*BP* 190) is, of course, related to traditional Native American culture (cf. Fleur's card playing here and in *Tracks*) and to carnival, but in a decidedly reduced form (cf. Bakhtin's view of the irony of modern literature as a form of reduced laughter, only distantly and feebly connected to its roots in folk culture). The bingo palace seems more closely related to the newly opened tribal mall than to either Bakhtinian carnival or tribal culture, closer to entrepreneurial spirit than decrowning double, and thus not an alternative to but an extension of monologic capitalism and all it represents aesthetically and axiologically. Lipsha understands that "You have to stay alive to keep your tradition alive and working. . . . And yet I can't help wonder, now that I know the high and the low of bingo life, if we're going in the wrong direction, arms flung wide, too eager" (*BP* 221). Here the voice of Huck Finn intersects with that of a wised-up yet nonetheless wistful Nick Carraway at the end of *The Great Gatsby* as he contemplates Gatsby's all too American belief "in the green light, the orgiastic future." Lipsha has good reason to be skeptical. Recall (from *Love Medicine*) Lyman's earlier effort to save the tribe: Anishinabe Enterprises, devoted to the mass production of "traditional Ojibwa items" for the tourist trade.

The Bingo Palace is Erdrich's most topical novel and, perhaps for that reason, her least carnivalesque. Despite its titular link to the carnival tradition, the novel is far more firmly rooted in the ongoing debate between Native Americans and state governments on the one hand and progressives and traditionals within individual tribes on the other. This topicality may have been inevitable given the attention Erdrich pays to Native American history in *Tracks* (1988), her collaborating with her husband on *The Broken Cord* (1989), Dorris's highly personal yet socially charged study of Fetal Alcohol Syndrome, and finally their co-authoring *The Crown of Columbus* (1991), which, while perhaps not written for the quincentenary "celebration" of Columbus's discovery of America, was certainly read and reviewed in that politically revisionist context. Whatever its causes and uses, the effect of this pervasive topicality in *The Bingo Palace* (ranging from the gambling debate and American Indian Movement at one extreme to secondhand smoke at the other) is to limit rather than increase its carnivalesque power. Instead of subversion, we find the monological urge to finalize, to explain, as in the transformation of what had been June's richly ambivalent sexual freedom into simple causality, mere grist for the mill of an Oprah or a Donahue: one more instance of a child sexually abused by an adult, in this case, her mother's boyfriend. The "community voice" that is so subtle and yet so significant a part of the earlier fiction appears here in similarly reduced form. Like the novel's and especially Lipsha's intertextuality, it is more self-consciously deployed. Indeed it hardly seems communal at all, representing only a segment of the tribal community and none of the novel's major characters.

In this reduced communal voice, as in the novel as a whole, we discern a sense of limits which the earlier fiction seemed so much better able to transgress. In *The Bingo Palace,* the carnival spirit resembles the reservation that "was once six times bigger" and that Lulu is now trying to "reclaim" (*BP* 29). The "old lines, old places, old grounds of the long dead Pillagers" have been replaced by this novel's emphasis on boundaries of all kinds, from border checkpoints and jurisdiction disputes to questions of ownership and real estate against which Lipsha's love of open space seems merely nostalgic. As a result, the lyricism of the novel's double ending seems all too consistent with what precedes it. In the first, Lulu, the tribal leader turned trickster, gives up her spike heels and low-cut dresses for full tribal regalia, playing first the fool (for the police who have come to question her about Gerry's whereabouts) and then the woman warrior (for the TV cameras). In the second Fleur goes off, leaving the novel, or rather the story, completely open-ended but in a decidedly mechanical way, as if counting its options, looking ahead to its own sequel, the unfinalizability of the carnivalesque dialogical novel turned into a mere plot device. Fleur presumably (but not necessarily) goes off to die, giving up her life so that Lipsha and the infant, stranded in a snowstorm (to die, like June), can come back, if not from death then from near death, if not in this novel, then in the next one. Fleur dies (if she dies), passing her power on to her daughter Lulu and making it possible for Fleur or her spirit to return to tease "us" with a word unsaid, a word that she knows but "we" do not.

That possibility, like the possibility of Lipsha's and the baby's being saved, of Lyman saving the tribe by "somehow wangl[ing] his way out of the great Native apocalypse" (*BP* 197), of Shawnee Ray getting her college degree while raising her son and keeping more than one Native American tradition alive, and of the communal voice cheerfully joining Lulu in her made for TV war whoop as if this were *Sing Along with Mitch,* tugs at the strings of "our" heart, a heart that, once upon a time, not so long ago, Nanapush would have cooked and eaten. Possibilities may proliferate, but *The Bingo Palace* is no Garden of Forking Paths. Unlike *Tracks,* a much "darker," more elegiac but also more exuberant, carnivalesque novel, *The Bingo Palace* is doubly, deceptively light. Its vision is bright but substanceless: disembodied, literally decarnivalized. As a whole the novel appears as if made in the image of its male characters—as powerless as

Lipsha, as "pasteurized" as Lyman, as suddenly and dismayingly "small" as the once Gargantuan Gerry Nanapush—and as such serves as the inverse measure of Erdrich's carnivalesque art and achievement.

Does this diminishment "represent" a temporary aberration on Erdrich's part, or a new direction? Does it reflect her understandable ambivalence concerning the high cost Native Americans must pay in cultural capital in order to improve their economic situation, or does it only "write large" the lyricism and transcendent vision already present in the earlier work and remarked on so approvingly by so many reviewers and critics? Perhaps *The Bingo Palace* only brings to light that which the earlier, more carnivalesque works seemed better able to disguise, that the role carnival plays in modern times is not to liberate but, instead, as Stallybrass and White argue, to allow us to indulge ourselves in that which we define ourselves against. "It would be wrong," they contend, "to associate the exhilarating sense of freedom which transgression affords with any necessary or automatic political progressiveness. Often it is a powerful ritual or symbolic practice whereby the dominant squanders its symbolic capital so as to get in touch with the fields of desire which it denied itself as the price paid for its political power" (201). Theirs is a conclusion that, while it does not invalidate what I have written above (even Bakhtin thought of carnival as a "temporary liberation" only, R 10), does call it into question, offering, as it were, a decrowning and disturbing but by no means final word on the sociopolitical implications of Erdrich's carnivalesque art and its reception. Indeed, as Terry Eagleton has more recently and, I believe, more accurately pointed out, "The current North American fetishism of the body, all the way from Jane Fonda to Michel Foucault, is at once a precious advance on a fleshless politics and, in the manner of the Freudian fetish, a standing in for something elusively absent" ("Discourse").

Unlike *The Bingo Palace, Tales of Burning Love* is more firmly, and comically, grounded in the realm of the carnivalesque body. It is, in fact, Erdrich's most physical and sensuously gratifying novel. Every aspect of its world, from the weather to the pouring of concrete and the laying of asphalt, possesses its own physical density and weight. The characters do not merely "live and breathe"; they see, smell, hear, touch, and taste. They devour so many whole pizzas, loaves of freshly baked bread, bags of Halloween candy, and double breakfasts as to make Sister Leopolda's rumored "replication of the marvel of the loaves and fishes during one lean winter, when a bowl of custard kept in the convent refrigerator was filled and refilled over the course of many nights" (*TBL* 48) seem more mundane than miraculous. The novel's characters are intensely physical beings, narratively embodied both as feeding, copulating wholes and fragmented parts ("forgiving hands," "wise ass"), given to pleasure but just as often subject to physical pain (toothache, childbirth, old age, freezing temperatures, burning flames, crushing weight, violent blows).

The novel possesses a certain physicality of its own, fully formed and rounded off on the one hand, porous and interconnected on the other. The snowstorms that figure so importantly in its opening section and latter half, although thirteen years apart, form a circle that complements the novel's complicated but essentially linear progression. The snowstorms also link Erdrich's fifth novel to the beginning of her first (June Morrissey's death) and the ending of her fourth (Lipsha and the baby stranded in the same blizzard that figures even more prominently in *Tales of Burning Love*). This latest novel not only alludes to and supplements these and other earlier fictions; it continues the work of fleshing out characters and situations, extending families as it extends story, combining a typically postmodern interest in literary recycling and an organic approach to earlier material. This "compost" (*TBL* 273) includes not just Erdrich's own work but a host of less incestuously, more conventionally intertextual materials ranging from Boccaccio's *Decameron* and Chaucer's *Canterbury Tales* at one extreme, through the comical linking of food and sex in the movie version of *Tom Jones,* to radio bulletins and tabloid headlines at the other.

This range of intertextual reference is just one of the ways the novel incorporates extremes and excesses of various kinds. These include the rhythm of feast and famine evident in Leopolda's miracle of the custard bowl, which repeats itself throughout the novel with not only food ("Some days [Eleanor ate] nothing but steamed broccoli and brown rice and other days a wallow of corn chips, ice cream, dark imported beers," *TBL* 447), but sex, money, weather, and more. There are droughts and blizzards; a day when the temperature drops forty degrees in two hours; Jack Mauser's five marriages, $500 shopping spree, and five thousand square foot house; his second wife Eleanor's numerous lovers; Dot's habit of buying food by the case, never the box or can, and her plans for opening a Super Pumper–style gas station; Marlis's shopping and drinking binges; and Sister Leopolda's more than ripe old age and extreme frailty ("108 years old, so light and ancient that her bones could barely support the garments of her habit"). Erdrich's scaling back Eleanor's advanced degrees from two Ph.D.'s (and an arrest record) in the short-story version of "Night Prayer" (1991, where she is called Isabel) to two MA's in the novel serves, in this regard, as a small concession to the merely plausible in a work that so often and so effortlessly crosses back and forth between grotesque realism and the more conventional kind.

The novel's comic grotesquerie manifests itself in other, similarly carnivalesque forms. One is the way the characters are individually, often cartoonishly described. Dot, for example, is "tall and board-square, with long arms and big knuckles. Her face is rawboned, fierce and almost masculine in its edges and planes." Marlis on the other hand "had an eye-focusing quality, matched a swimsuit-calendar ideal, her smile was a fast print film that invited instant response. . . . Starvation, peroxide, and manic devotion to the cause of herself had transformed Marlis, born plain, into a stare-gathering creation" (*TBL* 166). Another is the way in which virtually all the characters exist as points at which opposites intersect. Marlis is "bipolar" and "has the problems of any bright woman trapped in a dumb job" and a bimbo's body, according to Candice Pantamounty, formerly Jack's third (and least sexually inclined) wife and dentist, more recently Marlis's protector and ardent lover. Eleanor is petite, brainy, sexually voracious, and temporarily living in a convent (ostensibly doing research rather than penance). Jack's doubleness is even more apparent. A proto-male on the one hand, a scarecrow/straw man (or woman) on the other, at one point disguised as the Virgin Mary and at another made more "other" still when Marlis ties him up, plucks his eyebrows, waxes his legs, and jams his feet into high-heel shoes in order to teach Jack a lesson, that "it hurts to be a girl." Jack proves as divided as his workshop (neat on one side, messy on the other) and his land (half-developed, half in collateral), thoughtful one minute, dismayingly thoughtless the next; alienated from his Native American heritage (willing to subdivide the land) yet strangely if tenuously connected too (in his roles as trickster, healer, and visionary).

Important as the divisions within characters are, they pale by comparison to the differences, as well as animosity, that exists between Jack's four surviving wives.

> Each woman had seen the others as usurpers and killers, as thieves, as sluts driven by the same lusts that she treasured as sublime in her own heart, but despised emanating from any other source. They had boiled their hatred to a dense jam, enriched and condensed it over years. Nothing could contain it now, even the curved metal walls and breath-sealed windows of the car. Ripe fury had escaped and it was delicious. Hot, wholesome, filling. (*TBL* 199)

Stranded together in the blizzard, the four cooperate in order to survive, sharing the only food available (candy) while alternately telling their individual tales of burning love in order to stay awake and thus alive. As Eleanor later learns from Sister Leopolda in what is either a religious vision or a hypothermia-induced hallucination, "You and your sisters are blind women touching the vast body of the elephant, each describing the oddness beneath the surface of her hands" (*TBL* 370). Whereas the individual stories in effect fragment Jack ("forgiving hands" and "wise ass"), communal storytelling puts him back together again. In this sense, their collective narration plays a variation on the theme introduced by Eleanor. "In Plato's theory of our loss of innocence, we search for our other half. We are one body cut off from itself, rolling wild, a wheel of longing for the other sex. I often believed that with Jack I had found the other half of my wheel, the match, all of my body's missing pieces" (*TBL* 250). Eleanor and Jack's reuniting at novel's end—one of the many happy endings in Erdrich's self-consciously fairy tale-like conclusion (Dot's contentment and determination, Candice and Marlis's lesbian parenting of Jack's son, Lyman's enlisting, or forcing, Jack's participation in the construction of his Bingo Palace, for example)—proves Plato right, and more besides. The novel situates pairings such as Jack and Eleanor's within a larger context in which they appear less as self-contained, self-sufficient units than as nodes in a network of communal relationships, ties that even if they do not tightly bind do lightly connect. These tenuous connections appear all the more important in a novel that, even as it revels in carnivalesque excess, underscores the individual's precarious situation. Not only do so many of the characters find themselves alone; most are, or appear to be, their parents', or single parent's, sole offspring. The novel that abounds with comic disguises, mishaps, even deaths also abounds with rescues and resurrections. Most of the latter are the result of collective rather than individual effort and are generally figured in female terms, the role of women in the novel being at once remarkably understated and grotesquely overdetermined.

Although overtly Erdrich's least political book, *Tales of Burning Love* is arguably her most open (and of course her longest). This openness, which is certainly worth reading in the context of the New American Puritanism in general and the "debate" on family values in particular, manifests itself in various ways. There are, for example, the permutating yet strangely stable (and stabilizing) sexual and family relationships; the comically conflicting, complementary cast of characters; the exuberant as well as farcical depiction of the joys of sex and excess; and the alternating succession of enthusiasm and irony that is one of the hallmarks of the grotesque. Using these means (and others) to incorporate, embody, and carnivalize the "elusively absent," *Tales of Burning Love* succeeds to the extent that we can say of it, and the rest of Erdrich's carnivalesque fiction, what the novel says of one of its own characters, town undertaker and fool for love Lawrence Schlick: that "familiarity with death had connected him to all of life" (*TBL* 252).[6]

Notes

1. Mary Dearborn's point, in *Pocahontas's Daughters,* is especially apropos here: "It is this link between the trickster and language that I want to emphasize here, rather than the trickster figure himself or herself. . . . Ethnic women's fiction presents few trickster characters. Rather, the notion of ethnic female

authorship often hinges on the notion of playing a trick within language, of subverting authority while seemingly endorsing it" (28). I will return to the subversion/endorsement question later.

2. "It is striking that the most successful attempts to apply Bakhtin *tout court* focus upon cultures which still have a strong repertoire of carnivalesque practices, such as Latin America, or upon literatures produced in a colonial or neo-colonial context where the political difference between the dominant and the subordinate is particularly charged" (11). Stallybrass and White are correct, but why the condescending *"tout court"*? Bakhtin has considerable relevance to the study of these cultures, as much as these cultures do to the study of Bakhtin, as this essay everywhere implies though nowhere directly argues.

3. Bakhtin explains the apparent discrepancy between "the fundamental open-endedness of the polyphonic novel" and Dostoevsky's "conventionally literary, conventionally monologic" endings in terms of the necessary discrepancy between "the fundamental open-endedness of the characters and dialogue and the *external . . . completedness* of every individual novel" (PDP 39).

4. Leopolda will finally (and comically) die at age 108, apparently of heart failure, in "Night Prayer," when the ex-husband of a forty-year-old novice with two Ph.D.'s and an arrest record jokingly bows down from his hiding place, the pedestal formerly occupied by a statue of the Virgin, to answer her prayer (to end her earthly life). A bolt of lightning will later reduce Leopolda's shriveled body to ashes that the wind will blow into the honeysuckle to mix with the pollen before a priest can arrive on the scene to verify the "miracle." Erdrich's habit of recycling materials adds to the comic grotesquerie by bringing Leopolda back from the dead, as it were, to suffer the same fate a second time in *Tales of Burning Love.*

5. Against Erdrich's comic carnivalizings, compare Silko's more-Native-American-than-thou (and error-prone) review of *The Beet Queen.*

6. In Erdrich's most recent short fiction, "Satan: Hijacker of a Planet," one finds a similar emphasis on the senses and juxtaposition of sex and death, as well as visions, but visions of an intensely physical kind, rendered in terms of sights and sounds, smells and touches, featuring food and drink no less than mountains and rivers.

Works Cited

Allen, Paula Gunn. *The Sacred Hoop: Recovering the Feminine in Native American Traditions.* Boston: Beacon, 1986. Cited as "Allen."

———, ed. *Studies in American Indian Literature: Critical Essays and Course Designs.* New York: MLA, 1983. Cited as "*Studies.*"

Bak, Hans. "Towards a Native American 'Realism': The Amphibious Fiction of Louise Erdrich." *Neo-Realism in Contemporary American Fiction.* Ed. Kristiaan Versluys. Amsterdam: Rodopi, 1992. 145–70.

Bakhtin, Mikhail. *Art and Answerability: Early Philosophical Essays.* Trans. Vadim Liapunov. Ed. Michael Holquist and Vadim Liapunov. Austin: U of Texas P, 1990.

———. *The Dialogic Imagination: Four Essays.* Trans. Caryl Emerson and Michael Holquist. Ed. Michael Holquist. Austin: U of Texas P, 1981. Cited as "DI."

———. *Problems of Dostoevsky's Poetics.* Trans. and ed. Caryl Emerson. Minneapolis: U of Minnesota P, 1984. Cited as "PDP."

———. *Rabelais and His World.* Trans. Helene Iswolsky. Bloomington: Indiana UP, 1984. Cited as "R."

———. *Speech Genres and Other Late Essays.* Trans. Vern W. McGee. Ed. Caryl Emerson and Michael Holquist. Austin: U of Texas P, 1986. Cited as "SG."

Bernstein, Michael Andre. "The Poetics of Resentment." *Rethinking Bakhtin: Extensions and Challenges.* Ed. Gary Saul Morson and Caryl Emerson. Evanston: Northwestern UP, 1989. 197–223.

Catt, Catherine M. "Ancient Myth in Modern America: The Trickster in the Fiction of Louise Erdrich." *Platte Valley Review* 19.1 (Winter 1991): 71–81.

Chavkin, Allan, and Nancy Feyl Chavkin, eds. *Conversations with Louise Erdrich and Michael Dorris.* Jackson: UP of Mississippi, 1994.

Clark, Katerina, and Michael Holquist. *Mikhail Bakhtin.* Cambridge: Belknap-Harvard UP, 1984.

Clarke, Joni Adamson. "Why Bears Are Good To Think and Theory Doesn't Have To Be Murder: Transformation and Oral Tradition in Louise Erdrich's *Tracks.*" *Studies in American Indian Literatures* 4.1 (Spring 1992): 28–48.

Cornell, Daniel. "Woman Looking: Revis(ion)ing Pauline's Subject Position in Louise Erdrich's *Tracks.*" *Studies in American Indian Literatures* 4.1 (Spring 1992): 49–64.

Crabtree, Claire. "Salvific Oneness and the Fragmented Self in Louise Erdrich's *Love Medicine.*" *Contemporary Native American Cultural Issues: Proceedings from the Native American Studies Conference at Lake Superior State University.* Sault Ste. Marie: Lake Superior State UP, 1991. 49–56.

Dearborn, Mary V. *Pocahontas's Daughters: Gender and Ethnicity in American Culture.* New York: Oxford UP, 1986.

Eagleton, Terry. "Discourse and Discos: Theory in the Space Between Culture and Capitalism." *Times Literary Supplement* 15 July 1994: 3–4. Cited as "Discourse."

———. *Walter Benjamin: or, Towards a Revolutionary Criticism.* London: Verso, 1981.

Erdrich, Louise. "The Names of Women." *Granta* 41 (Autumn 1992): 131–38.

———. "Night Prayer." *Granta* 38 (Winter 1991): 195–222.

———. "Satan: Hijacker of a Planet." *Atlantic Monthly* August 1997: 64–68.

Gleason, William. "'Her Laugh and Ace': The Function of Humor in Louise Erdrich's *Love Medicine.*" *American Indian Culture and Research Journal* 11.3 (1987): 51–73.

Hanson, Elizabeth. *Forever There: Race and Gender in Contemporary American Fiction.* New York: Lang, 1989.

Holquist, Michael. "Introduction." Bakhtin, DI xv–xxxiv.

Jameson, Fredric. *Postmodernism, or, The Cultural Logic of Late Capitalism.* Durham: Duke UP, 1991.

Krupat, Arnold. "Post-Structuralism and Oral Literature." *Recovering the Word: Essays in Native American Literature.* Ed. Brian Swann and Arnold Krupat. Berkeley: U of California P, 1987. 113–28.

Lincoln, Kenneth. *Indi'n Humor: Bicultural Play in Native American.* New York: Oxford UP, 1993.

Medeiros, Paulo. "Cannibalism and Starvation: The Parameters of Eating Disorders in Literature." *Disorderly Eaters: Texts in Self-Empowerment.* Ed. Lillian R. Furst and Peter W. Graham. University Park: Pennsylvania State UP, 1992.

Morson, Gary Saul, and Caryl Emerson. *Mikhail Bakhtin: Creation of a Poetics.* Stanford: Stanford UP, 1990.

Owens, Louis. *Other Destinies: Understanding the American Indian Novel.* Norman: U of Oklahoma P, 1992.

Rainwater, Catherine. "Reading Between Worlds: Narrativity in the Fiction of Louise Erdrich." *American Literature* 62.3 (1990): 405–22.

Silko, Leslie. "Here's an Odd Artifact from the Fairy-Tale Shelf." *Impact/Albuquerque Journal* 8 October 1986: 10–11.

Stallybrass, Peter, and Allon White. *The Politics and Poetics of Transgression.* Ithaca: Cornell UP, 1986.

3

Life into Death, Death into Life

Hunting as Metaphor and Motive in *Love Medicine*

ROBERT F. GISH

> Now therefore take, I pray thee, thy weapons, thy quiver and thy bow, and go out to the field, and take me some venison; And make me savory meat, such as I love, and bring it to me, that I may eat; that my soul may bless thee before I die.
>
> Genesis 27:3–4
>
> Now, watch me, *ungilisi,* grandson,
> as I prepare this deer
> which the Great Spirit has given to us.
>
> Geary Hobson, "Deer Hunting"

Contemporary American Indian fiction relies consistently on hunting and the role and character of the hunter. Such a preponderance of attention to hunting by Indian authors is only natural since American Indian literature in all its forms, oral and written, mythic and historical, reflects indigenous and aboriginal cultures—societies almost always linked closely to the land, to sustenance from it and to cultural identity reciprocal with it, especially with fishing and hunting. (Notwithstanding the differing injury or death awaiting the prey, hunting is regarded here as also generally subsuming trapping in that traps and snares are inevitably set in an act of hunting.)[1]

Part of the "story" and many of the plots of contemporary American Indian fiction involve how hunting as an indigenous and primal act affects and interacts (psychologically and in overt behavior) with modern urban cultures wherein hunting, for the most part, is either ignored or, if acknowledged, championed as New Age shamanism or condemned as atavistic and only dimly remembered in the controlling technological and scientific modern world. In sum, if hunting is acknowledged today it is usually perceived reductively and condescendingly by self-perceived "civilized" readers, as blood sport or murder. And some zealots who know animals mainly as pets clamor stridently for animal "rights" in protest of the crass huntsman—Indian or non-Indian characters, real or fictive, regarded with the same abhorrence directed to medical researchers who experiment on dogs and monkeys.

Of course, the metaphor of the hunt and the real and attributed motives for hunting go much beyond American Indian literature, and much beyond the individual or cultural human hunter/killer of animals. The ironies and implications of life as hunt, of hunter becoming hunted, of killing to live, of animal life transformed through food and sustenance, resurrected and regenerated through death, of the sacred and ceremonial initiations of the hunt, and of the more profane rituals of self-quests, genealogical hunts, man hunts, job hunts, house/home hunts, investment hunts—all such "hunts" are recognized in the activities and lexicons of modern life.

It is, however, predominately American Indian authors who interpret, redefine, and focus the more fundamental metaphors and motives of hunting, not just for traditional and adaptive Indian peoples but for modern, non-Indian metaphorical hunters. These authors, like Isaac's sincere fatherly request and instruction to Esau, seek to bless us with their soul-felt fictions of the hunt.

Because the hunt and its plots and players are everywhere in life and in literature, it is thus worthwhile to comment on the imaginative and creative resource that hunting provides to Indian authors. This is especially true in a work such as *Love Medicine*—a novel that in its themes and structures, plots and patterns, in its own motive and metaphor positions the centrality of the hunt in the essential act of writing and reading, of author and reader on the hunt in and beyond the worded ways of the "hunting stories" in this half-century family saga for the affirmation of love over hate, life over death—the affirmation of art and of humanity which the novel provides.[2]

The heart of hunting as motive and metaphor in *Love Medicine* is found in the chapter "Wild Geese" and in the especially important titular chapter, "Love Medicine." Surrounding and supporting these two central hunting chapters are expansive and reflexive images and motifs—at once naturalistic and romantic, tragic and comic—which deal with human death and life in relation to animals and their hunting. Moreover, the crucial connection between the first chapter, "The World's Greatest Fishermen," and the eleventh chapter, "Crown of Thorns," demonstrates surrealistically but convincingly the hunter/hunted, animal/human convergence.

The plots (or subplots) of these two key sets of chapters and their imagistic and thematic undergirding throughout the novel work to secure its controlling metaphor: erotic and familial love, the power and "love medicine" of characters facing life's temporal and transcendent transmutations, not so much like players on a stage but like hunters and hunted, acceding to the ironies and paradoxes of the hunt—life into death, and death into life, hunting as crucifixion and resurrection. The purpose here, then, is to demonstrate how much of the motive and metaphor, the sequence and linkage of the "love stories" of Nector Kashpaw and Marie Lazarre, of June Morrissey and Gordie Kashpaw are established amidst the polarities and associations of hunter/hunted, the crucified and the resurrected.

Eli Kashpaw, twin brother to Nector Kashpaw (with certain affiliations and likenesses to the biblical hunter Esau and his deceptive brother, Jacob, and like Erdrich's legendary medicine man, Old Man Pillager, and grandpa Kashpaw's mother, old Rushes Bear), haunts the peripheries of the novel as a representative of the older and more obscure traditional Cree (and Chippewa) mythic ways known in the novel's present mostly through the nuances and glimmerings of family scripts, and by the more central characters in the novel such as Nector Kashpaw. As seen in his own account of the seductions of Marie Lazarre, of her "trapping" of him, Nector plays the dual role of hunter and hunted. Lipsha, although not the hunter his uncles are, does have the "touch," the gift of healing—or so he wants desperately to believe in his own hunt for his identity, and for the identity of his parents. In this motive he becomes a more metaphorical hunter.

In such a richly reflexive and recursive novel as *Love Medicine,* the fated capture and metaphorical sexual "snaring" and "killing" of Nector in "Wild Geese" is both anticipated in earlier and remembered in later-portions of the novel. Not just hunting imagery but bird and waterfowl, duck and geese, deer and fox, skunk and gopher descriptions and associations rise and fall rhythmically, build and diminish in architectonic pattern and counterpoint. It is clear that metaphorically, through Erdrich's use of "objective correlatives," Nector and Marie are made to be the human, metaphorical counterparts to wild geese. Similarly, June and Eli, but especially June, are portrayed as deer, wild eaters of pine sap and nibblers of buds.

Through the two dead geese tied to Nector's wrists, the killing and "death" of sexual orgasm (as associated in the metaphorical correspondences of Renaissance and Courtly Love literature particularly) occurs in reflexive association with the first death dramatized in the novel (the death of June Kashpaw, Lipsha's mother)—the love medicines of the novel work their way. And since *Love Medicine* is not a strictly linear novel, rather at once synchronic and diachronic, this death of June, preceded, perhaps precipitated by another instance of "hunter/hunted" figurative death in intercourse, the associations of that seminal scene (in two senses of the word) serves to impregnate, to germinate the "Wild Geese" chapter and its sequel chapter, "Love Medicine." June too sought, partook of, and bequeathed her own special love potion. Thus her promiscuous Williston "boomtown" love(s) and death—narrated comparatively more objectively, more cosmically (in third person), informs all of the prior and subsequent prescriptions and doses (i.e., chapters) of love medicine(s) in the novel.

June's death and mourning, described in the chapter "The World's

Greatest Fishermen," reflect the ironic scrawl on Lipsha's half brother's, King's, hat and point toward discussions at June's wake, and elsewhere in the novel, that the world's greatest fishermen, like the world's greatest hunters, are long removed from the older more authentic and triumphant traditional times of Cree/Chippewa elders and ancestors. Eli, not as old as Pillager and Rushes Bear, though acclaimed by the family as "the greatest hunter" (30), when the reader first meets him, is old and wizened, and a man of diminished appetites. Although Eli is a semi-modern hunter who relies on a gun and shells, albeit sparingly, he is still the nearest link to the old ways, the old hunters, and is complimented as such: " 'Only real old-time Indians know deer good enough to snare,' Gordie said to us. 'Your Uncle Eli's a real old-timer' " (*LM* 28).

June grew up roaming the woods with Eli and both shared a wildness common to older times and animal affinity. Marie notes the commonality: "Sometimes I thought she was more like Eli. The woods were in June, after all, just like in him, and maybe more. She had sucked on pine sap and grazed grass and nipped buds like a deer" (*LM* 65). And, somewhat ironically, given her snaring and monitoring of Nector, Marie has more use for Eli than his more dissolute (and deceiving) brother, Nector, with his predilections for pool halls and home-brewed wine. In his quietness, in his ways with children, and especially in his lessons for June, Eli impressed Marie:

> Spring and summer, when the furs were thin, we'd see more of Eli around home. He lived in a mud-chink bachelor shack on the other end of the land. He was a nothing and-nowhere person, not a husband match for any woman, but I had to like him. Eli drank but he never lost his head. He rarely spoke. Sometimes we sat in a room all evening, hardly talking, although he spoke easy with the children. I'd overhear. He had a soft hushed voice, like he was stalking something very near. He'd showed them how to carve, how to listen for the proper birdcall, how to whistle on their own fingers like a flute. He taught June. (*LM* 69)

Marie asserts that, in her own special wildness, it was probably June who taught Eli. But she confesses that Eli's abilities as a hunter went beyond stalking and luring game. He knew the old ways, and the old songs, hunting songs, haunting siren songs, which could even attract the likes of her:

> They [Eli and June] went into the woods with their snares and never came home empty-handed. They went to the sloughs to shoot mudhens and brought home a bag of the tiny, black greasy birds. Nector was rarely home then. He worked late or sneaked to gamble. We'd roast the birds and make a high pile of their twig bones in the middle of the table. Eli would sing his songs. Wild unholy songs. Cree songs that made you lonely. Hunting songs used to attract deer or women. He wasn't shy when he sang them. I had to keep to my mending. (*LM* 69)

June, a child of nine when taken in by Marie, goes to live with Eli soon after, lured to him and the wild and the attractions embedded in Eli's songs, by "pine sap and grasses." June, as an abandoned child, intuits that there is more love, more caring in life in the wild with Eli than even with Marie and all of her adoptive, motherly ways. June's material and spiritual legacy to Marie—although not necessarily intended as such—is the string of beads, a misappropriated rosary hung on her to ward off the devil, the spirits that the debauched Morrisseys attributed to be inside her. When touching those beads Marie feels small stones rolled and grinded aimlessly by the lake waves until they disappear. It is an image of submergence first encountered by the reader in the account of June's death, along with other images of birds and wildness that come to be associated with her in her death and its aftermath, especially the howling animal madness, the punishment, the crucifixion and "crown of thorns" it brings on her one-time husband, Gordie Kashpaw.

If Marie sees no real kindness in June's symbolic, abandoned rosary beads, June's death brings a special kind of crucifixion and damnation to Gordie and a faith-shaking sense of life's angst to the tragicomic, clarinet-playing nun, Sister Mary Martin de Porres, who tries, briefly but devotedly, to assuage him in his deluded and delirious confession that he has murdered his wife, murdered June. Here, in the "Crown of Thorns" chapter, June's resurrection becomes a haunting into madness, leaving Gordie, a kind of Indian Lear, howling beyond the Edenic orchards and pines, amidst the grass and woods behind the convent, hunter become the hunted, predator become prey to the hounds of heaven: "She [Sister Mary Martin] followed him, calling now, into the apple trees but lost him there, and all that morning, while they waited for the orderlies and the tribal police to come with cuffs and litters and a court order, they heard him crying like a drowned person, howling in the open fields" (188).

Gordie comes to such straits of madness and mistaken reckoning in drunken grief and guilt for his beating and abuse of June when they were married—failed Golden Gloves boxer turning his fists on the wrong, wifely opponent. One month after her death "the morning before Easter Sunday," Gordie begins drinking. He visits Eli who, in an action with reflexive imagery associated with June's death, offers him an egg that he cannot eat. From drinking beer at Eli's, Gordie walks home (with more reflexive imagery from June's stark and similarly inebriated fateful walk into the snow), where he calls his cousin Royce for some quarts of homebrewed wine.

After hours or days of drinking filled with regrets and reminiscence, he calls out June's name in a drunken love song—the violation of a taboo that frightens him and sets the stage in his mind for June's ghostly reappearance: "Her name burst from him. He wanted to take it back as soon as he said it. Never, never, ever call the dead by their names, Grandma said. They might answer. Gordie knew this. Now he felt very uneasy. Worse than before" (177).

Soon June does answer. While Gordie is trying to evade her by shaving, June's face appears at the window and when he runs to the kitchen she pounds at the window in anger. He turns on all the lights then overloads the circuits by plugging in the toaster and there in the darkness of the house she enters, stalking him room to room, coming for him, tearing the sheets off the bed, arranging the perfume bottles. Gordie, in a panic, runs to his car and guns it into the night for a five-mile escape into town and the hope of another bottle. But he hits a deer and, thinking the hide would be worth a bottle of booze and unable to open the car trunk, he drags the deer, a doe, into the back seat. And Erdrich continues reflexively to re-create the inside of the truck where June has sex with the "mud-engineer," Andy, a heater-infused cab which she leaves only to walk to her frozen death (and resurrection). Here, however, in a Malibu Chevy June is resurrected in Gordie's mind as a stunned rather than dead deer that stares its way into his very soul in the terror of the visage he now sees in the rear-view mirror:

> Her look was black and endless and melting pure. She looked through him. She saw into the troubled thrashing woods of him, a rattling thicket of bones. She saw how he'd woven his own crown of thorns. She saw how although he was not worthy he'd jammed this relief on his brow. Her eyes stared into some hidden place but blocked him out. Flat black. He did not understand what he was going to do. He bent, out of her gaze, and groped beneath the front seat for the tire iron, a flat-edged crowbar thick as a child's wrist. (*LM* 180)

Gordie then concludes, in total emotional and mental breakdown, that he has not just bludgeoned a deer, he has killed his wife, June, and that leads him to seek the help, and to offer the confession, rendered with flourishes of black comedy, which only heighten the poignancy of events. For Sister Mary Martin, thinking she will see the corpse of Gordie's wife, sees what he sees and finds herself in strange communion in the back seat of the Malibu with the dead deer, involved, like Gordie, like June, (like her own great Savior, the Greatest Fisherman) with humanity's suffering and the relentless, inevitable pursuit of mortality, of being born into death with only the promise of life after death to light and lighten the way.

June's death one week before Easter Sunday becomes even more significant in light of Gordie's crazed "crucifixion" and Mary Martin's comic but gruesomely serious catharsis (epiphany). June dies with a ticket home in her possession. In the literal sense she never makes it home, not to the home and family which the rest of the novel "resurrects" for the reader, as the times and places and family members are revealed across time, almost as if June, transcendent and resurrected herself through the techniques of fiction, is somehow able to see simultaneously with the reader. That she is transcendent and resurrected, that she does make it home—to a more heavenly albeit imaginatively fictive home (novel as heaven)—is clear in her walk into but over the frozen, numbing snowscape of the Dakota plains. Gordie too makes a walk, an escape across a similar landscape; however, he never makes it home (novel as hell) in the same sense that June does. Her life is in a sense her ticket "home." She walks, doe-like, deer-like at first, then Christ-like:

> By now it was unclear whether she was more drunk or more sober than she'd ever been in her life.
>
> . . . Even when it started to snow she did not lose her sense of direction. Her feet grew numb, but she did not worry about the distance. The heavy winds couldn't blow her off course. She continued. Even when her heart clenched and her skin turned crackling cold it didn't matter, because the pure and naked part of her went on.
>
> The snow fell deeper that Easter than it had in forty years, but June walked over it like water and came home. (*LM* 5–6)

Much of the reflexive imagery of June's brief time with Andy, the "down-vested mud engineer" clusters around some of the geese and waterfowl imagery that takes full control in "The Wild Geese" and "Love Medicine" chapters. Perhaps it is not too farfetched to suggest, also, that subliminally there is something of the myth of Leda and the Swan at work as well. Admittedly, mud engineers are not mud-hens, and geese are not swans, but the consensual "rape" of June by Andy in the truck, and the mutual "seduction-rape" of Nector and Marie as youths and the later old-age, manipulated seductions (with the misguided assistance of Lipsha's goose heart/turkey heart aphrodisiac) suggest, at least to this reader, such anthropomorphic and mythic, metaphorical correspondences. The predominance of Easter eggs, their repeated peeling and eating, the mention of turtles, robins, and reptiles in Erdrich's rendering of June's final hours all reinforce the significance and function of the wild geese and deer at the top of the novel's evolving hierarchical bestiary.

"Wild Geese" and "Love Medicine," as narratives of the love relationship of Nector Kashpaw and Marie Lazarre, are linked together, fittingly, by images of the hunt and of a pair of geese. The dead geese, shot by Nector and his brother, Eli, and taken into town to sell by Nector, are more than literally tied to Nector's wrists. Just as geese, unique in relation to more promiscuous waterfowl, mate for life, Nector and Marie are destined to remain paired early and late in their marriage of tribulation and trial. Despite Nector's lifelong attraction for Lulu Nanapush and their love dalliances, a relationship that makes them a wild pair of lovers as well, Nector chooses not to leave Marie. The "love medicine," songs and potions with which Lipsha and Eli claim some special touch, some special knowledge, alternately work and don't work their ways on the Marie-Nector-Lulu lover's triangle. Eli and Marie have their moments of lustful attraction, but, as alluded to above, Marie keeps to her knitting.

Erdrich, in beginning "Wild Geese" with mention of Eli's hunting prowess, sets the tensions of the novel again along the lines of the hunt not just for animals but for a mate. The results of the hunt mean different things for each brother as they turn death into commodity and diverse pleasure. Nector narrates the story of Marie's snaring of him on what turns out to be a not-so-ordinary departure from the weekly, Esau-Jacob ritualized divided labor of the hunt:

> On Friday mornings, I go down to the sloughs with my brother Eli and wait for the birds to land. We have built ourselves a little blind. Eli has second sense and an aim I cannot match, but he is shy and doesn't like to talk. In this way it is a good partnership. Because I got sent to school, I am the one who always walks into town and sells what we shoot. I get the price from the Sisters, who cook for the priests, and then I come home and split the money in half. Eli usually takes his bottle off into the woods, while I go into town, to the fiddle dance, and spark the girls. (*LM* 57)

This particular day Marie Lazarre, running frantic and wounded from her gothic and frightening encounter with Sister Leopolda at the Sacred Heart Convent, collides with Nector. He is thinking amorously about, "aiming" for, Lulu Nanapush but hits (and gets hit by) Marie. It is an errant errand for Nector, albeit fateful, but Marie (injured and "winged" herself) wings Nector as surely as a blast of birdshot. The "sacred heart" image, too, is a significant and expansive/reflexive "heart" image which carries over not just to the affairs of the heart of "Wild Geese" but the actual goose heart Lipsha tries to isolate and prepare as an aphrodisiac for the continuing struggle of wills of Nector and Marie.

Nector thinks of Lulu in hunting terms, singling her out (e.g., "I have already decided that Lulu Nanapush is the one," *LM* 58), and taking what he sees as difficult aim (e.g., "She is small, yet she will never be an armful or an eyeful because I'll never get a bead on her," *LM* 58). But Nector, among such lustful thoughts and aims, becomes prey to another's "aiming," to Marie who is also described in shooting terminology: "Because I am standing there, lost on the empty road, half drowned in the charms of Lulu, I never see Marie Lazarre barrel down" (*LM* 58).

Nector, contributing to his own snaring, insists that Marie slow down, and he essentially stops her, thinking she is on the lam from stealing some of the convent's silver. The geese tied to Nector's wrists hit upon Marie's hips and she resists his hold. Her tears cause him to let loose of her twisted, injured arm. Erdrich describes the release, again, in hunting terms: "So I let up for a moment. She moves away from me. But it is just to take aim. Her brown eyes glaze over like a wounded mink's, hurt but still fighting vicious" (*LM* 59). She charges him and then they are on the ground exchanging insults about person and family. Then the dead geese assist in the ensuing "rape"; Marie suddenly (like Leda) engulfed by wings, attracted to and yet repulsed by another kind of feathered gore (glory): "The geese are to my advantage now [says Nector]; their weight on my arms helps pin her; their dead wings flap around us; their necks loll, and their black eyes stare, frozen. . . . Her eyes are tense and wild, animal eyes. My neck chills" (*LM* 60). Then the control shifts and Marie, in effect, catches and holds Nector with her own sexual power, her breasts like soft bullets grazing him, arousing him:

> I stiffen like I am shocked. It hits me then I am lying full length across a woman, not a girl. Her breasts graze my chest, soft and pointed. I cannot help but lower myself the slightest bit to feel them better. And then I am caught. I give way. I cannot help myself, because, to my everlasting wonder, Marie is all tight plush acceptance, graceful movements, little jabs that lead me underneath her skirt where she is slick, warm, silk. (*LM* 60–61)

Marie, described in colors of black (her skirt) and white (her pillowcase-wrapped hand), is associated with both a wild Canada goose and a crow (her "crow's rasp" voice and her alleged meanness). Nector, feeling like a "stupid fish" with failing breath, holds the two dead geese (analogical fig leaves) in front of him to hide his Adam-like sense of guilt and shame. And once Nector sees the painful wound in Marie's hand (resulting from her, in effect, crucifixion by the sadistic Sister Leopolda in the convent), a shot shoots through his own hand and he drops the geese and gives them to Marie, gifts of atonement and commiseration for her to take home to roast and eat—gifts for her sustenance and resurrection. Nector, holding Marie's fevered hand, views her, attends to her mercifully in a manner akin to putting a wounded animal out of its misery:

> I'm not ashamed, but there are some times this happens: alone in the woods, checking the trapline, I find a wounded animal that hasn't died well, or worse, it's still living, so that I have to put it out of its misery. Sometimes it's just a big bird I only winged. When I do what I have to do, my throat swells closed sometimes. I touch the suffering bodies like they were killed saints I should handle with gentle reverence.
>
> This is how I take Marie's hand. This is how I hold her wounded hand in my hand. (*LM* 62)

June too is associated reflexively with Nector and Marie through the imagery of the dead geese, their necks in leather bands. Once in childhood Gordie and Aurelia had "a rope around her neck and looped over a tree" (*LM* 20), and her dead but resurrected image abides throughout not just in Gordie's mind but also in the reader's.

At June's wake the men discuss (both truths and lies) all the animals they have killed—from skunks to fox—and including a discourse on how to skin and boil a skunk by Eli, the old hunter and last man on the reservation that could snare a deer. June's son, King (Lipsha's half-brother and killer of "gooks" when in the Marines), also boasts, in the tradition of hunting tall tales, of killing a fox with bow and arrow and hitting it right in "that little black hole underneath a fox's tail" (*LM* 29). When challenged, King tells what he jokingly proposes as a truer hunting story: "I heard of this guy once who put his arrow through a fox then left it thrash around in the bush until he thought it was dead. He went in there after it. You know what he found? That fox had chewed the arrow off either side of its body and it was gone" (*LM* 30).

No longer a clan of true hunters, the men nevertheless still rely on hunting stories, remnants of more purposeful accounts and more authentic deeds, to bring some perspective on June's death, on the death in life and life in death known to the hunter.

A year after June's death and nearly fifty years after Marie Lazarre snared Nector Kashpaw, another traditional ritual is resurrected in an attempt to rekindle the love of Marie and Nector. Like Eli, Nector's grandson, Lipsha Morrissey, has "the touch" of the old ones, of the old ways. In his case it is the touch of healing: "I got the touch. It's a thing you got to be born with. I got secrets in my hands that nobody ever knew to ask. . . . The medicine flows out of me" (*LM* 190).

Nector, in his second childhood, stands in the woods and cries out—primal cries to be sure, albeit for different reasons than Gordie's howling because of June's death. Nector also reverts to his old ways of making visits to see Lulu, "to have his candy" (*LM* 191). It is Marie, out of enduring jealousy and love, who enlists Lipsha to put the touch on Nector to make him stay home. Lipsha, although angry at the injustices done to Indian peoples generally and to June and Gordie more specifically, consents to "cure" Nector in the hope of bringing some greater happiness to his grandparents in their old age.

It is Marie who mentions the possibility of love medicine to Lipsha and although he knows such remedies are an old Chippewa specialty he doesn't particularly want to visit Old Man Pillager for a refresher course in the recipes. Hunting for the best remedy, Lipsha realizes that hunting itself will provide the appropriate means. Erdrich's way of providing this solution for Lipsha is through patterning and extending her earlier use of geese as objective correlatives for Marie and for Nector. Lipsha's realization of how to proceed is, again, abetted by Marie:

> Well I got it. If it hadn't been the early fall of the year, I never would have got it. But I was sitting underneath a tree one day down near the school just watching people's feet go by when something tells me, look up! So I look up, and I see two honkers, Canada geese,

> the kind with little masks on their faces, a bird what mates for life. I see them flying right over my head naturally preparing to land in some slough on the reservation, which they certainly won't get off of alive.
>
> It hits me, anyway. Them geese, they mate for life. And I think to myself, just what if I went out and got a pair? And just what if I fed some part—say the goose heart—of the female to Grandma and Grandpa ate the other heart? Wouldn't that work? Maybe it's all invisible, and then maybe again it's magic. Love is a stony road. We know that for sure. If it's true that the higher feelings of devotion get lodged in the heart like people say, then we'd be home free. If not, eating goose heart couldn't harm nobody anyway. I thought it was worth my effort, and Grandma Kashpaw thought so, too. She had always known a good idea when she heard one. She borrowed me Grandpa's gun. (*LM* 200)

It is because of this motive that Lipsha becomes a hunter. And the reader is back once again in the times a half-century earlier when Nector and Eli hunted for geese and when Nector first encountered Marie on a literal "stony road of love," with two dead geese tied to his wrists, and a lifetime's weight of marriage.

Lipsha takes his grandpa's gun, goes to a slough, improvises a blind, and sits and waits among the rushes, patiently watching the herons hunt for their own prey. Erdrich's description of Lipsha's moment of truth as a hunter ends in anticlimax and disappointment:

> I was still hunkered in the slough. It was passing late into the afternoon and still no honkers had touched down. Now I don't need to tell you that the waiting did not get to me, it was the chill. The rushes was very soft, but damp. I was getting cold and debating to leave, when they landed. Two geese swimming here and there as big as life, looking deep into each other's little pinhole eyes. Just the ones I was looking for. So I lifted Grandpa's gun to my shoulder and I aimed perfectly, and blam! Blam! I delivered two accurate shots. But the thing is, them shots missed. I couldn't hardly believe it. Whether it was that the stock had warped or the barrel got bent someways, I don't quite know, but anyway them geese flown off into the dim sky, and Lipsha Morrissey was left there in the rushes with evening fallen and his two cold hands empty. He had before him just

> the prospect of another day of bone-cracking chill in them rushes, and the thought of it got him depressed. (*LM* 202)

Lipsha is depressed not only because he misses two "accurate" shots but because the two geese, described as devoted, eye-gazing lovers, emphasize his own aloneness. But he rallies and rationalizes that store birds would work just as well. He buys two frozen turkeys. And it is this violation, what he calls an "evil shortcut," which causes his love medicine to backfire. It isn't the love medicine itself, he tries to convince himself, that counts—rather it is the faith in the cure which brings results. He compounds his error by asking a priest to bless the two hearts which he wraps in a clean handkerchief. He is referred to the same Sister Martin who took Gordie's confessional and prayed him all the way into the hospital in Bismarck. Like Jacob's lies and deceptions about his own hunting to Isaac, Lipsha first tells Sister Mary Martin that the turkey hearts are intended for the statue of Saint Kateri, and failing to convince her of that motive leads her to believe they are love charms for himself. And when she tells him he doesn't need such assistance, he leaves, reaching into a cup of holy water and blessing the turkey hearts himself. Such an act, such a poignantly comedic scene brings new, extended, and ironic meaning to the name of the "Sacred Heart Convent."

Lipsha can't watch the spectacle of Grandma Marie eating the turkey heart raw and then trying to trick Grandpa Nector into eating it on doctor's orders to enrich his blood. But the comedy increases and when Nector taunts Marie by rolling the heart around in his mouth and then displaying it on his tongue, she gets up and slugs him between the shoulders to make him swallow it. The comedy turns blacker when Nector chokes—and dies.

Then in a wonderfully reflexive moment, Marie, rushing back to Nector, stumbles and falls to the floor too. The circle is full and complete. Now they are both prey to the throes of death rather than young lust and love—life into death, death into life. Lipsha passes out—reviving to see the regret in Marie's eyes that she too has been resurrected from her near death by the Senior Citizen staff. Lipsha shares the guilt for his grandfather's death with Marie at the funeral.

The resurrection theme continues, however, and in a way recursive and reflexive to June's return to haunt Gordie, Nector returns to invite Marie to follow him, as Marie explains it to her grandson: "'It's the love medicine, my Lipsha,' she said. 'It was stronger than we thought. He came back even after death to claim me to his side'" (212).

Then the true love medicine of the novel works its own conjuring way and Erdrich gives Lipsha the heart and courage to tell his grandmother the truth—that the love medicine was a fake, and that it was true love which brought Nector back to Marie to allow him to tell her how he loved her. In her love and appreciation of Lipsha's confession and his own state of hunting for his parentage and for love, Marie gives him June's rosary beads which hang on her bedpost. And just as Nector had once held Marie's wounded hand, Marie holds Lipsha's hand in utter love:

> She took the beads off the bedpost, where she kept them to say at night, and she told me to put out my hand. When I did this, she shut the beads inside of my fist and held them there a long minute, tight, so my hand hurt. I almost cried when she did this. I don't really know why. Tears shot up behind my eyelids, and yet it was nothing. I didn't understand, except her hand was so strong, squeezing mine. (*LM* 214)

The reader understands. Erdrich's wondrous techniques of utilizing expansive and reflexive image and symbol, her fine orchestration of pattern and rhythm whereby the paradoxes, the motives and metaphors of hunting and the hunt, life into death, death into life, converge into the regenerative and reaffirming potency of *Love Medicine* to bring new life and insight to the reader through the clear and accurate aim of the artist—straight to the heart, mind, and soul of the waiting, wanting reader.

Notes

1. See my related essays on hunting and American Indian literature: "Rights Gone Wrong: Indigenous Hunting Rights in Contemporary American Indian Fiction" and "Ironies of Consent: Hunting and Heroism in *The Surrounded.*" See also my book *Songs of My Hunter Heart: A Western Kinship;* Mar-

shall, *On Behalf of the Wolf and the First Peoples;* and Hobson, *The Remembered Earth: An Anthology of Contemporary Native American Literature,* 90–108.

2. I use the original publication of *Love Medicine* (1984) instead of the new and expanded 1993 version because I consider the original publication to be a better novel than the revised one and a good example of "less as more."

Works Cited

Gish, Robert F. "Ironies of Consent: Hunting and Heroism in *The Surrounded.*" *The Legacy of D'Arcy McNickle.* Ed. John Purdy. Norman: U of Oklahoma P, 1996. 102–14.

——. "Rights Gone Wrong: Indigenous Hunting Rights in Contemporary American Indian Fiction." *North Dakota Quarterly* 61.4 (Fall 1994): 11–25.

——. *Songs of My Hunter Heart: A Western Kinship.* Albuquerque: U of New Mexico P, 1992.

Hobson, Geary, ed. *The Remembered Earth: An Anthology of Contemporary Native American Literature.* Albuquerque: U of New Mexico P, 1979. 90–108.

Marshall, Joseph, III. *On Behalf of the Wolf and the First Peoples.* Santa Fe: Red Crane Books, 1996.

4

Vision and Revision in Louise Erdrich's *Love Medicine*

Allan Chavkin

Love Medicine (1984) made Louise Erdrich famous almost overnight. This novel prompted an unusual amount of critical attention, won the National Book Critics Circle Award, and has since become a work frequently anthologized and taught in college. Yet in 1993 Erdrich published the novel again after revising it, adding four new chapters and a new section that became the second part of "The Beads," and resequencing the chapters; the title page of the book was changed from *Love Medicine: A Novel* to *Love Medicine: New and Expanded Version.* Although occasionally writers have revised and "corrected" published books, there have been very few instances in which a major modern novel has been so substantially revised and expanded as *Love Medicine* was.

If *Love Medicine* is a collection of stories, as Gene Lyons in a review in *Newsweek* insists, the importance of Erdrich's publishing a new edition of her book would be less problematical than if it were a novel. Adding a few more stories to a collection would not result in the kinds of critical problems that occur when adding new parts to a novel; on the other hand, if *Love Medicine* is an integral work, the addition of the new chapters should influence one's reading of the entire book. Hertha Wong, who sees *Love Medicine* as a short-story sequence, challenged Erdrich and Michael Dorris, her collaborator on *Love Medicine,* to defend their claim that it was a novel. "It's a novel in that it all moves toward a resolution," Erdrich responded, and Dorris quickly added, "It has a large vision that no one of the stories approaches." After Erdrich stated that she was not worried about the issue, Dorris then elaborated upon why they regarded the book as a novel:

> If it had been a collection of short stories, it would have been very different. . . . we went through the entire manuscript. We wove in all the changes and resolutions and threads to tie them [the stories] all together. By the time readers get half way through the book, it should be clear to them that this is not an unrelated, or even a related, set of short stories, but parts of a large scheme. (Wong, "An Interview" 47)

In an interview with Malcolm Jones, Erdrich stated that while she knew she would have been able to write the plot as a traditional novel, she decided to use an experimental but legitimate novelistic form of interrelated stories because it was "something I have always loved reading" (4).

Love Medicine should be regarded as an experimental novel unified by a variety of methods. Focusing on several interconnected Chippewa families over three generations, *Love Medicine* tells the story not of a central protagonist but of a reservation community in northern North Dakota. Helen Jaskoski explains the structure of the novel as "a complex series of . . . tales, interlocking through recurrence of character and event and through variation of point of view" (59). The original *Love Medicine* consists of fourteen chapters narrated by seven first-person narrators and a third-person omniscient narrator. The first chapter begins in 1981, and with the second chapter Erdrich shifts the story back in time to 1934, whereupon the book progresses in its fragmented narrative to 1984.[1] On the first page of the chapters Erdrich indicates the year and, if the story is not being told by the omniscient narrator, the name of the first-person narrator. Erdrich also unifies *Love Medicine* by the inclusion of a common regional setting, repeated images (especially water), recurring themes, repetition of events narrated from different perspectives by different people, and humor (Wong, "Louise Erdrich's *Love Medicine*" 170–87). As critics have observed and Erdrich has acknowledged, not only has Faulkner with his interrelated stories and interweaving divergent points of view been a major influence, but also American Indian oral tradition with the "storyteller's use of repetition, recurrent development, and associational structure" (Wong, "Louise Erdrich's *Love Medicine*" 172).[2] In fact, in her interview with Malcolm Jones, Erdrich stated that the novel was influenced by a traditional Chippewa storytelling technique—a cycle of stories focused on a central subject. Like some of Faulkner's highly innovative works, such as *Go Down, Moses* and *As I Lay Dying, Love Medicine* makes a large demand upon its readers, who must assemble the fragments of the narrative to see the "large vision" that Dorris insists is there. This experimental novel challenges its readers to see connections and patterns in its intricate text where much is implied but rarely made explicit. Believing that "one of the attractive characteristics of *Love Medicine* is its subtle complexity," John Purdy sees this novel as an integral work revolving "around four of its characters: June, Marie, Nector, and Lulu." The latter three are involved in a "love triangle" over a half-century in duration. Though she does not appear much in the novel and does not narrate her own story, June is a haunting presence at the heart of the work because of her self-destruction (Silberman 101). The novel begins with her death and concludes with her son Lipsha symbolically bringing "her home" (*LM* 272, *LMN* 367). The reverberations of her life throughout the book serve as another unifying device.

But if *Love Medicine* is a novel and not a collection of stories, then the existence of two versions of the work becomes much more problematical and raises some perplexing questions. Which version reveals Erdrich's "real intentions"? Which version of *Love Medicine* is "definitive"? Which version is the better work of art? Why did Erdrich decide to substantially change a novel that was so highly regarded by both the critics and the public? What constitutes *Love Medicine,* a work with a complicated textural history that includes the publication of parts of the book, sometimes in different form, in periodicals before incorporation in the novel? Is a work that exists in multiple versions, such as *Love Medicine,* "a single version of the work or all the versions taken together?—and if it is all the versions taken together, is the work constituted by the *process* of its revisions, one after another, or by all the versions considered as existing simultaneously, as they might in a variorum edition giving a complete account of the successive readings?" (Stillinger v).

Love Medicine *and Textual Pluralism*

The usual assumption of scholars who have published criticism on *Love Medicine* is that while the two versions of the novel are not substantially different, the 1993 *Love Medicine* must be the more authoritative because it is the latest version of the text. This assumption of the textual stability of *Love Medicine* is a commonplace belief founded upon one of the basic premises of twentieth-century criticism and editing—the idea that there can be only one "definitive" or "correct" or "best" text, which is the latest one the author has approved. Since the 1960s this assumption has been challenged by James Thorpe, Hans Zeller, Jerome McGann, Donald Reiman, Peter Shillingsburg, James McLaverty, and most recently by Jack Stillinger. Stillinger has explored the problem of multiple versions with greater thoroughness and sophistication than any other contemporary theorist, especially in his *Coleridge and Textual Instability*, and I will summarize his ideas on multiple versions that are relevant to the problem of the two versions of *Love Medicine.*

Stillinger rejects the traditional notion that the latest text must be the best; he also refutes a more recent theory that the earliest text is the best because it reveals the author's first and therefore real intentions. Instead of textual stability and the notion of a single best text, he argues for "textual instability" or "textual pluralism"—the idea that there is no one version of the text that is "correct," "most authoritative," or "best."

> These theories are also related to ideas about authorial intention. The latest-text theory is based on the notion that the latest is best because it is the best representative of the author's intention; the earliest-text theory is based on the notion that the earliest text (rather than the latest) is where the author's "real" intention resides; and the

> newest theory, which I shall here call textual pluralism, is based on the idea that each version of a work embodies a separate authorial intention that is not necessarily the same as the authorial intention in any other version of the same work. (119)

Stillinger argues that for obsessive revisers like Wordsworth and Coleridge (and I would add Erdrich as another good example) the theory of textual pluralism, which allows for the uniqueness of aesthetic character and authorial intention of each version, is a much more sensible way to see their work than the other approaches that neglect the work's "extended textual history" (121). In addition to being true to a work's textual history, Stillinger's notion that "a work is constituted by all known versions of the work" and not one single most authoritative version, has the advantage of enhancing the "richness" and "complexity" of the author's writing (132, 140).

Stillinger also suggests that obsessive revisers like Wordsworth and Coleridge become readers and interpreters of their own writing and deliberately add "their intentions in the process of revision" (107), and thus their poems can be profitably examined by critics who are trying to ascertain the author's ideas (or "ideology") embodied in the work. Prompted by his realization that the two most difficult of the Coleridge's seven major poems have "relatively little revision" in them, Stillinger presents this tentative generalization: "the more revision in a Coleridge poem, the greater the likelihood of receiving determinate (authorial) meanings—and, conversely, the less revision, the greater the indeterminacy in situations where the lines come 'by chance or magic . . . as it were, something given'" (246). If Stillinger is correct, then an analysis of the revisions in *Love Medicine* reveals Erdrich's ideas that are embodied in the novel since it has been so extensively revised. In short, by regarding *Love Medicine* as constituting both versions of the novel, instead of merely selecting the early or late version, readers can comprehend the textual history of the book and have a better chance of understanding it in all its complexity and richness.

Although the paperback cover of the 1993 book proclaims that "this is a publishing event equivalent to the presentation of a new and definitive text," it is probably best to conclude that neither *Love Medicine* is "definitive," and that each should be regarded as unique. Sounding like a deconstructor of her own work, Erdrich rejects the idea of a single "best text" when she was asked if the expanded 1993 *Love Medicine* was intended to replace the original 1984 *Love Medicine:* "I have no great plan for the reader here—some may prefer the first version without the additions, others the next. I don't think of the books as definitive, finished, or correct, and leave them for the reader to experience" (Chavkin and Chavkin 247). In fact, Erdrich seems to share with some contemporary critics and theorists influenced by deconstructionism, such as Jack Stillinger, the belief in the legitimacy of multiple versions of the text and has remarked: "There is no reason to think of publication as a final process. I think of it as temporary storage" (Chavkin and Chavkin 232).

The Politics of the New Love Medicine

While the 1984 book attracted enormous attention, the 1993 edition did not. Reviewers and critics, with few exceptions, ignored the publication of the 1993 edition.[3] Critics have continued to select for their study either the original *Love Medicine* or more often the expanded version of the novel, with little or no explanation for their choice.[4] The assumption seems to be that the two versions are not substantially different and the additions to the novel do not change one's interpretation of the work.

In the few cases where critics provide any explanation for the purpose of the new and expanded version, they suggest that the main reason for it is to "help make clearer and more coherent connections to the planned tetralogy" (Wong, "Louise Erdrich's *Love Medicine*" 181). It is likely that the source for this explanation is the author herself. Marion Wood, Erdrich's editor at Henry Holt, reports: "New things were taking shape that she [Erdrich] felt needed a beginning [in the first novel]" (Devereaux 30). Perhaps because some interviewers were puzzled or even unsympathetic to the idea of revising such a successful and admired novel, Erdrich seems to downplay the difference between the two versions. While admitting to Elizabeth Devereaux that she would not be pleased if a novelist changed a book that was important to her, she claims that after the original publication of *Love Medicine* she discovered more stories that appeared to belong to it and therefore the additions to the expanded *Love Medicine* seemed the natural step (30). "I feel this is an ongoing work, not some discrete untouchable piece of writing," Erdrich informed David Streitfeld (15). But she also qualifies that statement: "When I went back to *Love Medicine,* I didn't tamper with what is there. If I did that, I'd feel funny" (15).

Actually Erdrich did revise parts of her novel, and in any case, the addition of four new chapters and the new section of "The Beads" influences one's reading of the entire book. And while she does include material that provides bridges and links to her other novels that comprise her vast Chippewa epic, the revisions and additions to the expanded *Love Medicine* are much more elaborate than her comments would suggest. In fact, she added so much new material that it is difficult to grasp exactly how the two versions of the novel differ and what the primary purpose of the changes and additions is.

Although one might be tempted to conclude after examining the numerous and varied changes and additions in the 1993 *Love Medicine* that the revision is extraordinarily complex and that no argument can explain the source of the new edition, actually a careful exploration of the changes reveals the premise behind the 1993 version—the need for a *Love Medicine* that is more effective than the 1984 book in conveying its political ideology. Erdrich has emphasized that "any human story is a political story" and that writers do not have to express political opinions openly in fiction to convey their politics; actually, she suggests, such overt expression is often counterproductive, for the subtler and more artistic work can change more minds than the preaching of didactic protest novels. With these assumptions in mind, Erdrich created the 1984 *Love Medicine.* Art must come first, and the politics would be implicit in the art. But for those whose first concern is more for political intent rather than art, Erdrich's subtle writing lacks force and commitment. In an essay-review of *The Beet Queen,* Leslie Silko harshly attacked Erdrich's fiction, which she believed lacked political commitment, and even suggested that Erdrich was ambivalent about her Native American origins.[5] According to Erdrich, as a result of careless reading Silko criticized her characters in *The Beet Queen* because she incorrectly assumed they were Chippewa when in fact they were whites and thus "they must have seemed shockingly assimilated" (Chavkin and Chavkin 237). Even more sympathetic reviewers than Silko, however, have grossly misinterpreted Erdrich's work, and they may have caused her to wonder if perhaps the 1984 *Love Medicine* might be too open to misreading, especially by those inclined to view the characters as the usual negative stereotypes of Indians.

James McKenzie relates how his students at the Turtle Mountain Reservation feared that the 1984 *Love Medicine* would confirm white stereotypical views of Indians as drunk, violent, and sexually deviant and encourage racism. McKenzie believed their fears unfounded until he consulted some of the reviews of the novel, especially those of Robert Towers and Marco Portales, which unsettled him because of their misreadings in which the characters are seen in the stereotypical ways his students feared. In the *New York Review of Books* Towers generalized:

> From the medley of individual faces and voices a few generic, or tribal, features gradually emerge. The men get drunk as often as possible, and when drunk they are likely to be violent or to do wildly irresponsible or self-destructive things. Even Grandpa Kashpaw (Nector), the most able and ambitious of the lot, achieved his political standing in the Chippewa community only because Marie repeatedly dragged him back from the bootlegger's and sometimes sat "all night by the door with an ax handle so he would not wander off in search of liquor." . . . Meanwhile the women, with the exception of the stalwart Marie, are likely to take up with any man who comes along. (36)

In the *New York Times Book Review,* Portales describes June Kashpaw as a "leggy Chippewa prostitute who has idled her days away on the main streets of oil boomtowns in North Dakota," certainly a gross simplification of June (6). Portales also simplified and misinterpreted another scene in which Nector and Marie have consensual intercourse; he concluded incorrectly that Nector raped Marie when in fact Marie deliberately "snares" Nector. When Erdrich revised *Love Medicine* for the 1993 version, she altered this scene in "Wild Geese" to make clear that sexual intercourse does not occur, probably because some people such as Portales misinterpreted the sex act for rape in the 1984 *Love Medicine.* Erdrich explains: "And the encounter between Marie and Nector was mistakenly ambiguous. I never meant it to be a rape and took a word or two out in the republished *Love Medicine* to make that clear. Reading it over, I too found it confusing and wanted to clarify his act (wrong, but not technically a rape)" (Chavkin and Chavkin 234). Erdrich makes clear the nature of their sexual encounter by having Nector state in the 1993 *Love Medicine:* "I touch her with one hand and in that one touch I lose myself" (*LMN* 65). Erdrich also alters another line to leave no doubt that the sexual encounter here does not culminate in coitus. When Marie says, "I've had better," Nector, the narrator of "Wild Geese," informs the reader: "I know that isn't true because we haven't done anything yet" (*LMN* 65). Originally the line suggested otherwise: "I know that isn't true, that I was just now the first . . . " (*LM* 61). In "Flesh and Blood" Marie remarks to her daughter Zelda that this place is "where I met your father" and then reflects to herself, "For all I knew, it was the place we made Gordon" (*LM* 114); but in the 1993 version of the novel, this reflection is omitted since the sexual encounter between Marie and Nector does not culminate in intercourse (*LMN* 149). Because Marie is so young, Nector's sexual behavior is improper in this scene (and more so in the 1984 version of it) in which she "snares" her husband, but intercourse does not occur. Now the revisions reduce the chance a reader can stereotype Nector as a rapist. In any case, Erdrich's dramatic revision of this scene suggests that after the publication of the 1984 *Love Medicine* she was concerned about misreadings, especially those where the Chippewa are simplified and reduced to whores, rapists, drunks, and other traditional stereotypes of Indians.

Although Erdrich has stressed that people should be politically committed in their personal life but not in their art, for to do so makes the art "polemic and boring" (Chavkin and Chavkin 241), apparently she decided at some point after the initial publication of *Love Medicine* that it did not adequately express her political ideology, and she needed to revise the novel to make it more political without becoming polemical. It is worth noting that in interviews Erdrich and Dorris stated that they deliberately set out to compose a novel that would not be as political in its subject matter as other Native American fiction. Instead, Dorris stressed, their focus would be on a reservation community, "not on the conflict between Indians and non-Indians," in order to remind readers "that in the daily lives of contemporary Indian people, the important thing is relationships, and family and history, as it is in everybody's life, and not these sort of larger political questions, although they do impinge" (Jones 7). In another interview, Dorris returns to this subject and remarks that while in some early drafts of the novel the work was more political they made a "conscious decision, in the way Louise wrote the book, to have it all centered in a community in which the outside world is not very present or very relevant in some respects. This is a world that is encompassed by that community, and it isn't so much the outside world of discrimination or wealth or anything like that" (Coltelli 23–24). When the Chavkins asked Erdrich about the reason for the few references to political and historical events in the novel, she responded: "In later books, there is more involvement with the political life of the country, and of course reservation people are gravely impacted. There wasn't room for a large political spectrum but I think the suggestion that great events influence the way people live day to day is implicit" (251). Erdrich and Dorris' intention to write a novel that attempted to universalize Indian lives and make them accessible to non-Indian readers while not ignoring the impact of white civilization was praised by Louis Owens, who suggested that readers could identify with Erdrich's characters "much more easily" than some others by major Native American writers (205). Apparently Erdrich decided after the publication of the 1984 *Love Medicine* that she had been too successful making her novel "accessible," and she needed to make it "more Indian."

Like the 1984 *Love Medicine,* the expanded version is not overtly political; it avoids didacticism and expresses its politics subtly. Nevertheless, the 1993 *Love Medicine* embodies a powerful political vision that is absent in the original novel. This new vision includes four interdependent objectives: (1) to argue for the importance of preserving American Indian culture and resisting complete assimilation into the dominant white culture; (2) to undermine the popular stereotypes of American Indians; (3) to promulgate a feminism that is in accord with traditional American Indian culture, underscoring the crucial role of motherhood and independent women who are activists for Indian rights; and (4) to present a more affirmative vision than the one in the 1984 *Love Medicine,* which for some readers reinforced the notion that the situation of American Indians today is hopeless, and to suggest that there are possible political solutions to the dire problems confronting American Indians.

In order to see how these interrelated objectives manifest themselves in the 1993 *Love Medicine,* I will focus on the five major new additions to the novel, where the new vision of the work is clearest. My intention is to reveal how the inclusion of "The Island," the second part of "The Beads," "Resurrection," "The Tomahawk Factory," and "Lyman's Luck" completely transforms the 1984 work by adding a political dimension to the novel absent in the 1984 book. My analysis is not intended to be exhaustive but to describe the major changes and reveal the ideology behind them.

"The Island"

In an article published in 1985 entitled "Where I Ought to Be: A Writer's Sense of Place," Erdrich stated: "Contemporary Native American writers have . . . a task quite different from that of other writers. . . . In the light of enormous loss, they must tell the stories of contemporary survivors while protecting and celebrating the cores of cultures left in the wake of the catastrophe." This is an eloquent expression of her purpose in *Love Medicine,* and it is likely that in the 1993 expanded version of the novel Erdrich, not happy how this task was accomplished in the original *Love Medicine,* intends to add to and to clarify the stories of her contemporary survivors so that readers will respond more sympathetically to them. The theme of preserving and celebrating the core of Chippewa culture that has survived historical and contemporary oppression gains prominence in the 1993 *Love Medicine,* where some of the key characters reveal much greater awareness than in the earlier version of the novel of the need to reject assimilationism and instead return to traditional Chippewa values.

This theme of the importance of repudiating assimilationism and returning to one's heritage is central to "The Island," which focuses on Lulu Nanapush as a young woman. "The Island," the only undated story in *Love Medicine,* is narrated by Lulu, who has just returned to the reservation after unhappy years at a government boarding school. Erdrich has placed the new story between "Wild Geese," narrated by Nector, and "The Beads," narrated by Marie. "The Island" provides the voice and perspective of Lulu, the third party in the love triangle that might be viewed as the main plot of the novel. "Wild Geese" and "The Beads" present the interpretations and perspectives of Nector and Marie on the crucial times of their youth. "The Island" adds balance to the novel by providing Lulu's perspective, and as a result the reader has a greater understanding of the roots of her unconventional behavior that scandalizes her community. The reader gains insight into Lulu's formative years, absent in the 1984 *Love Medicine,* and better understands the nexus of forces that helped shape her character and outlook.

Although in the 1984 *Love Medicine* Lulu is at times vital and exuberant, it is quite possible readers will view her as a sexually promiscuous woman whose primary goal is shamelessly seducing men. Erdrich regards Lulu as "heroically sensual" (Chavkin and Chavkin 224) and does not intend for the reader to see Lulu as a heartless man-chaser.[6] The problem occurs because the 1984 *Love Medicine* does not clarify the source of Lulu's wildness. In the 1984 edition of the novel, Lulu is a major character only in "Lulu's Boys," "The Plunge of the Brave," and "The Good Tears," all of which focus on her affairs. It is quite possible that many readers will share Marie's harsh view of Lulu as a slut who "went with anybody in the bushes" (*LM* 125, *LMN* 161). While Erdrich does include in the 1984 *Love Medicine* material that supports her view of Lulu as "heroically sensual," the cumulative impact of the numerous details of Lulu's sexual behavior undermines the positive interpretation of her character. "The Island," first published in *Ms.* in 1991 and revised and expanded for publication in the 1993 *Love Medicine,* corrects this problem by allowing the reader to understand the origin of Lulu's "wild and secret ways" (*LM* 216).

Although it is not clear in the original publication of *Love Medicine,* the loss of her mother Fleur Pillager profoundly influences Lulu's character; in fact, "The Island" implies that it is the single most important formative influence. Lulu's narration of her return to the reservation to live with her Uncle Nanapush and his wife Rushes Bear, after a disillusioning time at a government boarding school, continues the story where Nanapush's account ends in *Tracks.* "The Island" begins with this young woman's lyrical confession: "I never grew from the curve of my mother's arms. I still wanted to anchor myself against her. But she had tore herself away from the run of my life like a riverbank. She had vanished, a great surrounding shore, leaving me to spill out alone" (*LMN* 68). Water imagery helps unify the fragmented narrative of this novel, and the metaphoric evocation of Lulu alone in a boat and her mother Fleur as a shore or riverbank is suggestive. As the novel makes clear, the worst death for a Chippewa is drowning, for according to traditional Chippewa belief, the victim becomes a wretched ghost who can never find peace but is forced to wander forever. The water imagery of the novel implies that surviving in this world is a matter of not sinking but staying afloat despite all of life's trials and tribulations. Lulu's mother abandoned her and left the child adrift on the hostile seas of life. Lulu had wanted to "anchor" next to her mother, but Fleur "had tore" herself away, like a receding riverbank. Except in nightmares, a riverbank or shore remains stationary and secure; it is the boat that pulls up anchor and leaves. The metaphor that Lulu uses here evokes the perversion of the natural order by suggesting that the riverbank or shore has deliberately moved away and abandoned the boat, which is then left to drift about and find, if possible, a safe port in which to anchor.

Yet implicit in this feeling of being abandoned is the unconscious and irrational feeling of responsibility for the situation—and the origin of this peculiar feeling requires some explanation. Abandoned by her mother, Lulu is sent to a government boarding school, where the primary objective is to transform "uncivilized Indians" into "true Americans." At these schools Indians are punished for speaking their native languages and are encouraged to forget their heritage. A victim of the government's exploitation herself, Fleur is implacably opposed to assimilationism, and "The Island" implies that Lulu feels guilty for betraying her mother by attending a government boarding school. In the early version of this story in *Ms.,* her guilt is clearer than in the expanded but subtler version published in the 1993 novel: "I had come back from government school. While I was there, I had turned my back on my mother, and now I needed her forgiveness, but she didn't live in the old house in the woods anymore" (39). Although the 1993 *Love Medicine* is not so explicit about Lulu's feeling of guilt, Lulu does reveal that she continually ran away from the government school mainly because she missed "the old language in my mother's mouth" and was punished for doing so (*LMN* 68). Both in the *Ms.* and 1993 *Love Medicine* versions of the story, mother and ethnic heritage are inseparably linked. In both stories, the sought-for mother who has vanished is present in spirit and aids the daughter. Lulu imagines that she hears Fleur's consoling words in Chippewa, "mysteriously keeping me from inner harm" (*LMN* 69).

The insertion of Chippewa words into the 1993 *Love Medicine* underscores the importance of language as the foundation for culture and identity. Erdrich believes that there is a connection between self and language; "what you express and who you are" are related, she explains to Mickey Pearlman (154). Moreover, the government's suppression of Lulu's speaking Chippewa had to "have been an act that destroyed the self" (Pearlman 154–55). The association of speaking your native tongue, remaining true to your heritage, and empowering yourself is suggested in the 1993 *Love Medicine* by the inclusion of actual Chippewa words. Some might consider the inclusion of these foreign words, which almost all readers will not understand, as exotic; actually Erdrich is merely suggesting the inextricable connections between identity, heritage, empowerment, freedom, and language. In both texts of "The Island," the old language is associated with Chippewa heritage; in contrast, English is associated with assimilationism.

Lulu's search for her mother is, then, a search for her language, her heritage, and her identity. "I needed to find a person who would tell me where I was from," Lulu says in the *Ms.* text (39). On the literal level, she must travel to the island where her eccentric relative, the primitive Moses Pillager, lives alone with his numerous cats, in order to find out where her mother resides; but, in a symbolic sense, Lulu must go to the island to unite with the Pillager spirit (the embodiment of her heritage) and discover her roots; and then she must purify herself by burning out the corrupt assimilationism that still clings to her after her residence at the government boarding school. In fact, Lulu does "unite" with Moses not only spiritually but also sexually, and that results in the birth of Gerry Nanapush, who eventually grows up to become an activist and trickster hero, inspired by the legendary Chippewa trickster Nanabozho (Chavkin and Chavkin 252).

The source of Lulu's unconventional moral code which leads to many affairs and her unconventional behavior is evident in "The Island." The conventional moral code with its rigid definitions of right and wrong that she must have been taught at the government school is replaced by the relativistic code born out of her love affair with Moses. "Nothing would look the same after loving Moses Pillager. Right and wrong were shades of meaning, not sides of a coin" (*LMN* 76). Lulu's repudiation of her government-school values and her embracing the Pillager spirit also results in her rejection of a white goal-oriented lifestyle. "The richest plan is not to have one," Nanapush tells her, and she lives existentially in the moment, without regrets for the past or hopes for the future (*LMN* 76). Lyman succinctly explains his mother in "The Tomahawk Factory" of the expanded novel. "You know Lulu Lamartine if you know life is made up of three kinds of people—those who live it, those afraid to, those in between. My mother is the first" (*LMN* 302). The intrepid Lulu lives passionately for experience, refusing to curtail her desires to adhere to the codes of others. It is the primitive Moses Pillager who leads her to envision the Promised Land of her heritage and her freedom from the values and moral codes of the dominant culture.

Lulu's affair with Moses initiates a pattern of relationships with men in which she feels empowered by being in control of the affair. The two become lovers and at the same time mother to each other, for each of them has been profoundly hurt and desperately needs a parent and a protector, someone with whom to experience unconditional love. Lulu has been without love at a time when she was especially vulnerable to the slings and arrows of outrageous fortune, and therefore the union with Moses is a transforming one. Lulu indicates that she is permanently changed as a result of her being abandoned and then visiting the island where she is reconnected with her heritage; she is able to reconstruct her identity and create a new self forged out of the crucible of harsh experience.

> I was not immune, and I would not leave undamaged. To this day, I still hurt. I must have rolled in the beds of wild rose, for the tiny thorns—small, yellow—pierced my skin. Their poison is desire and it dissolved in my blood. The cats made me one of them—sleek and without mercy, avid, falling hungry upon the defenseless body. I want to grind men's bones to drink in my night tea. I want to enter them the way their hot shadows fold into their bodies in full sunlight. I want to be their food, their harmful drink, to taste men like stilled jam at the back of my tongue. (*LMN* 82)

It is useful to note that at the beginning of "The Good Tears," Lulu repudiates this cat metaphor: "They used to say Lulu Lamartine was like a cat, loving no one, only purring to get what she wanted. But that's not true" (*LM* 216, *LMN* 276). The implication is that Lulu's self-perception has changed, perhaps as a consequence of how she is viewed by the community.

With her pregnancy in the final stage, Lulu realizes that she must leave the island, even though Moses will not be able to go with her. The early version of the story published in *Ms.* is more explicit than the 1993 *Love Medicine:*

> For the first time since I went to the island, I couldn't sleep. I was watching the air, the heat go from the fire. I was hoping that I would bear the baby well, hoping that I wouldn't die. As I thought these things, I understood that I had followed the directions to my mother's house. By coming here, I had done what I needed to do. (42)

Lulu desires a mother in this crucial time of her life but realizes that she cannot reunite with her actual mother; instead she must be supported by her spirit. This idea is subtly suggested in the 1993 *Love Medicine,* where Lulu imagines that Fleur speaks in Chippewa and sings to her. The brief reference to the protective spirit keeping Lulu from harm is more explicit in the *Ms.* version, which concludes the story with boat and water imagery:

> "*You must get up now,*" she said. "*Daughter, it is morning and you must travel. You must start out on the road that leads into this life. As the day lengthens the road is steeper, harder to walk. You must keep going. On the black rocks, by the edge of the lake, I will wait for you. I will not go away as evening gathers. Don't be afraid. Cross the water, cross the rough waves. Where the owls drop the bones of mice and bent seed of pines, I will be sitting. I will be mending your boat.*" (42)

The water imagery in the 1993 *Love Medicine* version of the story is not extensive at the conclusion, but the penultimate sentence of this new chapter suggests a parallel between the need to leave the island for a safer pregnancy, with a guiding midwife or mother, or remain and sink to one's death in a permanent Chippewa hell: "I knew that this baby, still tied to my heart, could drag me under and drown me" (*LMN* 84). Even though Lulu realizes that she cannot literally reside with her mother again, her search for her is successful—she has found her through a return to her heritage and will be with her in spirit. Her mother will "speak" to her—her Chippewa belief and culture will provide the guidance and support that she needs as she crosses the water with its rough waves.

"The Beads"

While Lulu's search for her mother leads to her reconnection to her heritage, Marie's search in "Saint Marie" for a maternal figure results in an encounter with Sister Leopolda, who, as Jaskoski observes, turns out to be not a "true 'parent'" but "a wicked stepmother" whom one sees in fairy tales (55); in fact the search culminates in a grotesque and disastrous confrontation in which Marie is physically and psychologically brutalized by Sister Leopolda, a deranged mixed-blood nun, whose self-hatred and contempt for Indians have caused her to assimilate so totally that she is unable to acknowledge her Indian ancestry. The 1984 *Love Medicine* implies that the mixed-blood Marie is ashamed of her Indian ancestry; for example, she calls Nector a "damn Indian" (*LM* 59) in "Wild Geese" and in "Saint Marie" she also reveals her contempt for her Indian lineage: "the black robe women . . . were not any lighter than me. I was going up there to pray as good as they could. Because I don't have that much Indian blood" (*LM* 40); "I looked good. And I looked white" (*LM* 45). By the end of the 1984 *Love Medicine* she does not seem prejudiced, but there is no reason presented for this dramatic change. While the 1993 expanded *Love Medicine* also suggests that the young Marie is ashamed of her Indian ancestry with these same passages (*LMN* 43, 48), the added second part of "The Beads" makes clear why Marie changed. Here Marie reconnects with her heritage, primarily as a consequence of bonding with her mother-in-law, the old-time traditional Rushes Bear. In short, the second part of "The Beads" parallels "The Island" in its political ideology.

Both stories stress the importance of motherhood, a major theme in the 1993 *Love Medicine,* which is associated with the preservation and perpetuation of Native American heritage. In the novel mothers are not only responsible for giving birth to the new generations but also for acting as standard bearers of traditional Chippewa belief and customs. Marie and Lulu will carry on the tradition of Rushes Bear and Fleur. When daughters are separated from the mothers, as is the case with June, the danger is that they will lose contact with their heritage and suffer the consequences, such as loss of purpose, destruction of identity, and alienation from their culture.

In the second part of "The Beads," Marie tells the story of the unexpected arrival of her mother-in-law, Rushes Bear. She is a strong-willed, extremely difficult woman who seems to consider Marie her enemy. Although Marie had faced down the raging nun in "Saint Marie," she feels anxious in the presence of Rushes Bear. After a period of enduring her increasingly irascible behavior, Marie orders her to leave, only to be told that Rushes Bear has no place to go. Marie does not throw her out, as she had intended to do.

Marie's tolerance and generosity reap rewards. The second part of the new section of "The Beads" focuses on Marie's pregnancy in which her life is saved by Rushes Bear and Fleur, with her legendary knowledge of old-time Chippewa medicines. During the difficult delivery, Marie hallucinates and at one point sees herself "as from a distance, floating calm, driven by long swells of waves" (*LMN* 102). Perhaps influenced unconsciously by her association with these traditional women of the older generation, she also recalls a word "out of childhood, out of memory, an old word I had forgotten the use of, *Babaumawaebigowin*" (*LMN* 102). Marie knows that "it was a word that was spoken in a boat," but she cannot recall its precise meaning (*LMN* 102).

Later Marie dreams of eating with Rushes Bear and Fleur, who accept her as she is and do not make the kinds of critical comments about a woman's appearance that Nector and other men do: "Nobody said, 'Two years ago your waist was thin as a girl's' " (*LMN* 103). Marie moves in and out of consciousness, as Rushes Bear and Fleur sit by her bed, speaking "only the old language" (*LMN* 103). At one point Marie hears her word, "*Babaumawaebigowin,* and I understood that I was to let my body be driven by the waves, like a boat to shore" (*LMN* 103). Marie follows these directions and "that way, sometime the next afternoon, my child was born" (*LMN* 103).

Erdrich uses the boat metaphor to suggest a connection between Lulu and Marie. Both are in boats adrift on the perilous seas of life, where the possibility of drowning is never far away. Both women have been cut off from their heritage, and both are in search of a mother to protect and guide them. Erdrich also implies that Rushes Bear and her daughter-in-law Marie "are in the same boat" and that they recognize this reality at the end of this chapter. Both Fleur and Rushes Bear demonstrate their disgust with the wayward Nector by rejecting his offer of money for helping Marie during her life-threatening pregnancy. Rushes Bear tells Nector that he shames her and that she no longer has a son but only a "daughter," only Marie. Looking over the bleak edges of their lives, both Rushes Bear and Marie realize they can not depend upon Nector and that they need each other as they face their common enemy of existential loneliness. At the conclusion of "The Beads," the two women establish a bond of love that transcends their past differences. The story concludes with an explanation of their transformations:

> I never saw this woman the same way I had before that day. Before that birth of the child, a son after all, Rushes Bear was a hot fire that I wanted to crush. After that, things were different. I never saw her without knowing that she was my own mother, my own blood. What

> she did went beyond the frailer connections. More than saving my life, she put the shape of it back in place. . . . I took care of the old woman every day of her life because we shared the loneliness that was one shape, because I knew that she was in that boat, where I had labored. She crested and sank in dark waves. Those waves were taking her onward, through night, through day, the water beating and slashing across her unknown path. She struggled to continue. She was traveling hard, and death was her light. (*LMN* 104–5)

"Resurrection"

"Resurrection," the fourteenth chapter of the expanded *Love Medicine,* consists of two interrelated stories. The first story occurs in 1982 shortly after the death of Nector and reveals both the toughness and tolerance of Marie as she copes with her self-destructive son Gordie. Within this story is the second story that is a flashback to the honeymoon of Gordie and June, where the readers see a much more sympathetic and human Gordie than the monstrous substance abuser who would hurt his own mother. In the 1984 *Love Medicine,* Gordie is a major character only in "Crown of Thorns," where he appears as a one-dimensional character, a deranged alcoholic who at the end of the story is "crying like a drowned person, howling in the open fields" (*LM* 188). In the 1984 *Love Medicine,* the alcoholism of Gordie is not associated with the historic exploitation of Indians; in fact, Gordie's behavior in "Crown of Thorns" might well have reinforced for some readers the stereotype of the drunken Indian. This new story powerfully conveys the horrors of substance abuse on the reservation while viewing it primarily as a social problem that has its origin in the unfortunate consequences of the colonization of Indians. Similarly, June in the original *Love Medicine* appears in only a few brief scenes in the novel where she is usually seen as self-destructive—for example, as a child encouraging her peers to hang her, or as an adult, walking out into a snowstorm to her death. In this story, though, June, like Gordie, appears more complicated and sympathetic than the troubled child in "The Beads" or the promiscuous woman in "The World's Greatest Fishermen." The most sympathetic character of the novel, however, is Marie, and this story reveals aspects of her character not seen in the 1984 *Love Medicine.*

The first part of "Resurrection" presents the grieving widow coping with a son whose substance abuse has become suicidal. The omniscient narrator reveals that since residing with other old people at the Senior Citizens home, Marie has begun speaking the native language of her childhood and "holding to the old strengths Rushes Bear had taught her, having seen the new, the Catholic, the Bureau, fail her children, having known how comfortless words of English sounded in her ears" (*LMN* 263). Gordie is a perfect example of this failure, and confronted with the alien dominant culture that Marie considers largely responsible for the grim situation of Gordie and other Indians who have lost their connection to their heritage by trying to assimilate, she becomes even more committed to traditional Chippewa values. This commitment to Chippewa heritage is suggested subtly in the story when Marie discovers Nector's pipe as she is going through her husband's belongings in order to "shut her mind on loss by keeping busy" (*LMN* 259). The unassembled pipe and the bag in which the pieces are stored are described in some detail. The pipe is a symbol of Chippewa heritage and its values, and Marie reverently returns the pieces of the pipe to their bag, not fitting the pieces together for "Nector once said," to fit them together "was to connect earth and heaven" (*LMN* 260). Marie will save the pipe for Lipsha; and in *The Bingo Palace* the story of Lipsha and this pipe assumes great importance. "Resurrection" follows "Love Medicine," the story that reveals the resilience of Lipsha, and the juxtaposition of these two stories implicitly contrasts Gordie and Lipsha, both of whom have suffered because of June's neglect of them. While "[Lipsha's] personality seems to transform personal pain into wonder," Gordie can not cope with life's disappointments and disasters (Chavkin and Chavkin 223). It is appropriate that Marie intends to pass down the pipe to Lipsha, who as the son of June and Gerry Nanapush is connected to the Pillagers, the old-time Indians who remain loyal to their heritage.

While "Resurrection" does present the union between June and Gordie as doomed, it also humanizes them, making it less likely they will be interpreted as the sluttish squaw and the violent drunk. The chapter implies that Gordie's self-destructive substance abuse is caused partially by his desperate attempt to cope with June's death. For example, he refuses Marie's offer to wear a particular shirt since "it was June's," and thus would serve as a painful reminder of her (*LMN* 263). June is also humanized in this new chapter and presented more positively than in the 1984 *Love Medicine.* For example, unlike the young Marie she is not ashamed of her Indian blood. When she approaches the white resort owner, she does so as an equal—"she didn't act much like she knew she was an Indian" (*LMN* 268).

The tragic consequences of assimilation are implied in the flashback, which portrays the time when Gordie and June elope. They rent a dismal cabin in a rundown resort. Their honeymoon is strangely joyless and enervated, and the grim setting suggests that this relationship is doomed. When the two go skinny-dipping in the lake and try to make love in the water, the attempt is unsuccessful and they sink, linking this image with the pattern of imagery of actual and symbolic drowning in the novel. Later, in their cabin, they try to make love again, but "making love felt like work. It wasn't any fun, but they couldn't stop. . . . They went on and on until they gave up and fell asleep right in the middle of it, mouths open, hot, unhappy, bitten by insects, on a mattress with little buttons that left round sore marks all over them" (*LMN* 271). Later neither one of them desires to have sex again. The flashback concludes with a grim image that aptly symbolizes their union; they lie side by side, "like two people carved on stone caskets, staring up at the starless ceiling" (*LMN* 272). The isolation of the two young lovers is reminiscent of Moses Pillager and Lulu in "The Island," and the sexual descriptions of the two couples become representative of their spiritual and psychological states. Cut off from their heritage, June and Gordie are doomed, and their listless, passionless sex symbolizes the emptiness of their lives. Lacking a strong identification with their culture, out of contact with their souls, they self-destruct. In contrast, when Lulu reconnects with her heritage on the island, her identity and vitality are restored, as symbolized by the joyous lovemaking with Moses Pillager. The celebration of sexuality in "The Island" culminates in pregnancy and the continuation of the vital Pillager blood line.

The title of this new chapter refers to Marie's resurrection in which she transforms her grief over her husband's death and her sorrow over Gordie's self-destruction into life-affirming healing of the spirit. The preceding chapter, "Love Medicine," culminated in Marie's poignant bonding with Lipsha, forgiving him for his disastrous attempt to concoct a fraudulent love medicine and presenting him with her beads, whereupon Lipsha goes outside to dig dandelions. "The spiked leaves full of bitter mother's milk. A buried root. A nuisance people dig up and throw in the sun to wither. A globe of frail seeds that's indestructible" (*LMN* 258). It is Marie who can weather the dark forces and who embodies the maternal spirit that can bring new life into a land of decay and death. While "Resurrection" graphically portrays the devastating problems of substance abuse that put so many Indians at risk, it also suggests hope for the future in the figure of Marie. She can serve as the mother to the best of the new generation and teach them about their heritage. Unlike Gordie and so many others who are prisoners of the past, Marie has the capacity to subordinate painful memories to the immediacy of the present.

"The Tomahawk Factory" and "Lyman's Luck"

"The Tomahawk Factory" explores the ambivalent relationship between Lulu and Marie, clan rivalries and reservation politics, the theme of assimilationism vs. allegiance to one's heritage, and the economic realities on the reservation that contribute to familial conflict and cultural estrangement.[7] In "Lyman's Luck," which functions as a kind of epilogue for "The Tomahawk Factory," Lyman envisions a possible economic solution to some of the problems presented in the preceding story; Erdrich, in contrast to this businessman-hustler, is ambivalent about gambling as a solution, as the reader discovers in the next novel in the series, *The Bingo Palace,* which explores this solution, so full of contradictions, in much more depth. The placement of these two chapters immediately before the final chapter of the novel gives them special importance and heightens both the impact of the problems Erdrich explores here and Lyman's envisioned solution. These two chapters are substantially different from the other chapters in the book, for their focus is more on the social and economic problems of the community than was seen in the previous chapters. Moreover, the tragicomic tone of the preceding chapters created by the cumulative impact of stories of abused children, suicide, alienation, violent behavior, loveless sex, random deaths, and broken families, is alleviated here by the farcical satire and the lighthearted humor that are different from the dark comedy and survival humor in the other parts of the novel.

In the 1984 *Love Medicine* Lulu's threat of paternity suits blocked Nector's plan for a factory, but in the 1993 *Love Medicine* Lyman, son of Nector and Lulu, builds the factory. In the 1993 *Love Medicine* Lyman, the narrator of this chapter, becomes an important character. In the 1984 *Love Medicine* he is a minor character whose function is to tell the story in "The Red Convertible" of the psychological deterioration of his brother Henry Junior, a Vietnam vet who commits suicide by drowning; Lyman narrates the story, but he is primarily an observer—the real focus is on Henry Junior. In the 1993 *Love Medicine* Lyman embodies the problematical situation of the contemporary Native American, who is torn between his need to maintain his allegiance to the beliefs and values of his heritage and the desire to assimilate and become a "successful" modern American. Lyman's conflicting emotions are exacerbated by his grief and guilt over the death of his brother, his uneasiness about the opposition to his factory, and his ambivalent feelings over his illegitimate birth and his disappointment that his father never acknowledged him but became a substitute father of Lipsha. Somewhat cynical, he is not particularly concerned that he is exploiting Chippewa culture for money, even if the traditionalists, such as his mother Lulu, "now heavy into politics," are. The chapter not only explores the problem of assimilationism but also reveals aspects of the characters of Lulu, Marie, Lyman, and Lipsha not evident in the original version of the novel.

The reaction of Lyman to his brother's death and his subsequent career are substantially different in the two versions of *Love Medicine*. In the 1984 *Love Medicine* the carefree Lyman becomes morose after his brother's death. Lulu explains: "He could not snap out of it but slowly improved his outlook by working. He became a contractor, hired on his brothers, and in that way supported us all" (*LM* 228). In contrast, the

Lulu in the 1993 version of the novel explains: "He could not snap out of it but went down lower, lower, to where nobody could drag him up. He stayed alone in the oldest shack, where he could party all he liked. The rest of us stuck together on that strip of land that was once sun beat and bare of trees" (*LMN* 289). In the 1993 *Love Medicine* Lyman expands upon Lulu's succinct account of his life after Henry's drowning. "The Tomahawk Factory" begins where the "Red Convertible" ends, and Lyman presents a detailed account of his reaction to his brother's suicide.

In fact, the death of Henry Junior transforms Lyman from the carefree person with a talent for making money into a cynical man distraught over his brother's terrible death, which according to Chippewa belief results in Henry Junior becoming a ghost forced to wander forever without peace. Lyman has a difficult time coping with the reality that while some Native Americans succeeded, others suffered and were destroyed: "If I bobbed to the surface, others went down" (*LMN* 298).

After almost a year of depression and substance abuse, Lyman, as he comically relates it, resurrects himself when he realizes that he needs to contact the IRS; later he learns "the whole thing was a mistake." "Out of a typo, I was formed," he sardonically observes, appreciating the irony of the situation (*LMN* 301). Before too long, Lyman becomes part of the Bureau of Indian Affairs, and ignoring his mother's accusations that he has "sold out," he moves up the ranks of the bureaucracy. The "traditionals" are his opponents, and he disparagingly refers to them as "back-to-the-buffalo types" (*LMN* 303). In this new chapter the largely apolitical Lulu and Marie of the 1984 *Love Medicine* have become radicals allied to the American Indian Movement. Apparently, with Nector dead, the two women are "now free to concentrate their powers," and they become leaders of the "local agitating group of hard-eyes, a determined bunch who grew out their hair in braids or ponytails and dressed in ribbon shirts and calico to make their point" (*LMN* 303).

In this chapter Erdrich satirizes both the bureaucrats, such as Lyman, and the kind of radical activists who oppose for the sake of opposing, such as Lulu. In contrast to Marie, Lulu "led her gang of radicals in black spike heels and tight, low-cut dresses blooming with pink flowers" (*LMN* 303). But if Erdrich satirizes the pettiness and hypocrisy of reservation politics, she saves her harshest satire for Lyman because of his exploitation of Chippewa culture. This chapter subtly contrasts the cynicism of the assimilationist Lyman with the inveterate idealism of Lipsha. Both Lipsha and Lyman are descendants of the Pillagers, but Lipsha has remained true to his heritage while Lyman has not. "The Pillagers had been the holdouts, the ones who wouldn't sign the treaties, the keepers of the birch bark scroll and practitioners of medicines so dark and helpful that the more devout Catholic Indians crossed their breasts when a Pillager happened to look straight at them" (*LMN* 312). Unlike the situation in the original novel, in the 1993 *Love Medicine* Lipsha's stature in the community is enormous as a consequence of his allegiance to his Pillager ancestry.

Although Lipsha, Marie, Lulu, and other Chippewas work at Lyman's factory out of economic desperation, they are hostile to the idea of the mass production of the fraudulent Indian artifacts, which makes a mockery of Chippewa heritage. Tension at the factory reaches the explosion point as a consequence of the workers' instinctive dissatisfaction with their participation in the manufacture of these imitation artifacts. Lulu warns Lyman that the workers are unhappy and calls the fake artifacts "ka-ka" (*LMN* 314). This Chippewa word is said to children "to express that something is bad or dirty" (Baraga 179). Lyman refuses to admit that the manufacture of these fake artifacts exploits Chippewa culture but claims that he is proud of the products.

Some months later Lyman learns that he should have heeded Lulu's warning about the unhappy workers. Marie and Lulu become involved in a bitter argument, which culminates in Marie's outrage. Her response here is that of a self-assured leader so different from the apolitical Marie of the original *Love Medicine.* "From deep in her body she began to gather breath until she'd swelled, powerfully, all eyes on her, into the sound of her own private war cry, a *windigo* yell that at once paralyzed and mobilized every worker on the line" (*LMN* 318). This cry brings all work in the factory to a halt, as the rival clans ready themselves to take sides if fighting should occur. Everyone in the room, including Lyman, looks at Lipsha, as if to see what he will say to do about this situation. And Lipsha, after glancing at Lulu, smiles his "Pillager grin," "a grin that foresaw the end of Anishinabe Enterprises," and then with magisterial solemnity he brings down his toy tomahawk "with the crack of a sentencing gavel" (*LMN* 319). In the next moment, chaos erupts as the workers riot in an orgy of mayhem. In "a kind of organized joy," the workers completely destroy the factory, and Lyman is devastated (*LMN* 320).

The story concludes with an epiphany that reveals that Lyman achieves some kind of spiritual breakthrough when he is reconciled to Marie. When he apologizes to her for his past rudeness, he realizes in that moment that while he was always desperate for the love of his absent father, perhaps what he really needed was a mother. He asks Marie if Nector ever talked about him. Marie does not actually speak but communicates through look and touch, or at least Lyman imagines that she does. "She was going to tell me that the drowned could stop wandering, go home. . . . [that] I could come back, make my way down the narrow roads" (*LMN* 323). Marie alleviates Lyman's anxiety over his brother's drowning and his frustration over Nector's failure to acknowledge him. The narrow roads Lyman can return on are those of the Pillagers, his ancestors, who will show him the way to his true identity. When Lyman takes Marie's hand, he notices a "raised white scar," her stigmata from her confrontation with Sister Leopolda, and it prompts him to apologize and "feel forgiven" (*LMN* 324). In a heightened moment signifying the spiritual breakthrough Lyman has achieved, the two "danced to the center of the floor" (*LMN* 324).

In the next story Lyman appears to have decided to return down "the narrow roads" he had envisioned in "The Tomahawk Factory." Narrated by an omniscient narrator, the new penultimate chapter of the novel entitled "Lyman's Luck" is brief and focuses on the practical implications of Lyman's resurrection which was suggested at the end of "The Tomahawk Factory." Lyman's entrepreneurial spirit has not been destroyed with his factory; it is still alive, but this time instead of exploiting Indian culture he will develop an enterprise that is in accord with his heritage. Lyman anticipates the Indian gaming regulatory act and decides that he will make money for himself and other Indians by setting up Chippewa gambling casinos. "It was going to be an Indian thing, too" (*LMN* 326).

Lyman has a political conscience now and sees his gambling business as a way for Indians not only to find steady employment but to revenge themselves on the white culture that has oppressed them. Lyman's new political conscience is a remarkable change from his earlier contempt for the "back-to-the-buffalo types." In a passage that might aptly serve as the premise of the political ideology of the new version of *Love Medicine,* Lyman bitterly reflects on the injustice Native Americans have suffered over the years: "They gave you worthless land to start with and then they chopped it out from under your feet. They took your kids away and stuffed the English language in their mouth. They sent your brother to hell, they shipped him back fried. They sold you booze for furs and then told you not to drink" (*LMN* 326).

Lyman concludes that the answer to this injustice is for Indians to get smart and use federal law to their own advantage—that is, to use legal gambling to bring wealth to the reservation. "He'd . . . teach Chippewas the right ways, the proper ways, the polite ways, to take money from retired white people who had farmed Indian hunting grounds, worked Indian jobs, lived high while their neighbors lived low, looked down or never noticed who was starving, who was lost" (*LMN* 327). He envisions a future for the Chippewa in which they will be successful and control their destiny while remaining loyal to their culture. The waters that previously have drowned Indians will now allow them to bob to the surface. Lyman "saw the revenue trickling and then rolling and flooding into the tribal bank accounts. He saw the future, and it was based on greed and luck" (*LMN* 328).

Conclusion

It would be a mistake to conclude that the 1984 *Love Medicine* is completely apolitical. In the first version of the novel one does recognize Indian issues, including sovereignty, assimilationism, Indian activism, substance abuse, problems of the Indian Vietnam War veteran, clan rivalries, ambivalence over Indian identity, reservation politics, and cultural alienation. These issues are developed and presented more directly in the expanded 1993 version as a result of Erdrich's greater immersion in

Chippewa and Turtle Mountain culture and history. While one of her motivations in republishing *Love Medicine* is to connect it better to the other novels comprising her vast Chippewa epic, she also revised and expanded the book in order to express her new political commitment.

It is likely that Erdrich concluded after the publication of the 1984 *Love Medicine* that the novel was too pessimistic. It vividly presented the dire problems of the contemporary Indian—poverty, dysfunctional families, sexual promiscuity, abused and abandoned children, alcoholism, and cultural estrangement—but it did not present practical solutions to these problems, or indicate even in a more general way that solutions were possible. Nor did it clearly indicate the origin of these problems. The 1984 *Love Medicine* is largely ahistorical compared to the 1993 *Love Medicine.* History and current events do not much impinge upon the 1984 *Love Medicine* characters, who seemed isolated from mainstream America, and by and large, with the exception of Gerry Nanapush, they have little knowledge of or interest in politics. All of this changes in the more affirmative 1993 edition of the novel, where the "Indianness" of the book and especially of the need to return to one's heritage are underscored.[8] A number of the characters reconnect with their heritage, and even at times speak in "the old language," some of which Erdrich includes in the expanded edition. A number of the major characters now are politicized, including some women who become activists, and the characters who might have been seen as negative stereotypes of Indians in the 1984 *Love Medicine* are presented more sympathetically. Perhaps an apt symbol of how much the book is changed is the figure of Lyman. In the 1984 *Love Medicine* he is an insouciant, apolitical minor character, but in the 1993 version even this typical entrepreneur-hustler preoccupied with making money speaks like a radical Indian activist.

In short, then, it should be clear that the two versions of the novel present different visions because of different authorial intentions. Neither version can be considered "definitive," for each is unique, embodying Erdrich's "real intentions" at the time she composed that version of the novel. As for the question of which edition is the better work of art, the answer will not please those who desire to work according to "general" or "objective" principles; the fact of the matter is that the answer to the question of which is "better" will depend upon the individual's specific aesthetic and political values. Jack Stillinger sardonically observes, "In theory, everybody can be right in such matters, and the one who is rightest will be the one who musters the best rhetoric" (140). In any case, if future critics of *Love Medicine* are to understand this complex work properly, they must see the value of employing the theory of "textual pluralism" and recognize the need to focus upon the whole textual process and read the different versions of the novel in relation to one another and the author's developing intentions.

Notes

1. Rainwater suggests that Erdrich includes structural features that "frustrate narrativity" to create in her reader an "experience of marginality," a view of her work that Erdrich approves (Chavkin and Chavkin 230).

2. Ruoff observes: "Indian oral literatures are a vibrant force . . . that strongly influence the written works of Indian authors" (5). For an excellent overview of these oral literatures see Ruoff 5–52.

3. Notable exceptions to the failure to review the expanded *Love Medicine* are Rubinstein, Streitfeld, Bomberry, and Bennett. Bennett is the only reviewer to discuss insightfully some of the differences between the two versions. Only two critics analyze in detail some aspects of the expanded *Love Medicine.* Focusing upon "The Island," Mermann-Jozwiak explains Lulu's powers by arguing that her encounter with Moses Pillager transforms her into a kind of windigo, the cannibalistic demon of Chippewa myth. Smith focuses upon how some of the additions in the expanded version enhance the trickster aspects of the novel (100–103).

4. While Gish in this book states that he uses the 1984 *Love Medicine* because he considers it to be superior to the expanded edition, Purdy uses the 1993 book despite his belief that it is "a less engaging read" than the original version. Usually, though, scholars and critics do not provide any explanation for their choices of editions.

5. Louis Owens defends Erdrich, observing that Silko herself does not assume the role she would have Erdrich embrace.

6. In a 25 January 1998 letter to me Ruoff remarked that Lulu is an earth mother and trickster who repopulates the reservation with children from a variety of fathers from various backgrounds. "This is particularly relevant to a reservation such as Turtle Mountain or the one in *Love Medicine* because of its

mixture of peoples. Like the 'Yellow woman' figures in Southwest mythology, Lulu goes outside traditional boundaries to bring fresh bloodlines into the tribe. She is similar to the girl(s) in the 'Star Husband' tales so prevalent in the Plains and in the Algonquian mythology, who go outside the tribe, follow a strange Star Man or Bird Man to another world and eventually give birth to a baby (or twins). Thus her love adventure results in a child (or children) who becomes a culture hero important to the tribe."

7. Ruoff remarks in the Afterword to this book that "The Tomahawk Factory" originally was a section of the unpublished "Tracks," but Erdrich rewrote the story and included it in the 1993 *Love Medicine.*

8. But at least one critic found the new and expanded *Love Medicine* still politically wanting. Bomberry concludes that the novel portrays "Indians, especially the Indian woman, in a negative light," and "What *Love Medicine* gives us is a snapshot of hopelessness and despair" (77–78).

Works Cited

Baraga, Frederic. *A Dictionary of the Ojibway Language.* St. Paul, Minnesota Historical Society Press, 1992. Rpt. of *A Dictionary of the Otchipwe Language* (1878).

Bennett, Sarah. Rev. of *Love Medicine: New and Expanded Version,* by Louise Erdrich. *Studies in American Indian Literatures* 7.1 (Spring 1995): 112–18.

Bomberry, Victoria. Rev. of *Love Medicine: New and Expanded Version,* by Louise Erdrich. *Wicazo Sa Review* 101 (1994): 76–78.

Chavkin, Nancy Feyl, and Allan Chavkin. "An Interview with Louise Erdrich." *Conversations with Louise Erdrich and Michael Dorris.* Ed. Allan Chavkin and Nancy Feyl Chavkin. Jackson: UP of Mississippi, 1994. 220–53.

Coltelli, Laura. "Louise Erdrich and Michael Dorris." *Conversations with Louise Erdrich and Michael Dorris.* Ed. Allan Chavkin and Nancy Feyl Chavkin. Jackson: UP of Mississippi, 1994. 19–29.

Devereaux, Elizabeth. "*Love Medicine* Redux: New and Improved, but Why?" *Publishers Weekly* 23 November 1992: 30.

Erdrich, Louise. "The Island." *Ms.* January–February 1991: 39–42.

——. "Where I Ought to Be: A Writer's Sense of Place." *New York Times Book Review* 28 July 1985: 1, 23–24.

Jaskoski, Helen. "From the Time Immemorial: Native American Traditions in Contemporary Short Fiction." *Since Flannery O'Connor: Essays on the Contemporary American Short Story.* Ed. Loren Logsdon and Charles W. Mayer. Macomb: Western Illinois UP, 1987. 54–71.

Jones, Malcolm. "Life, Art Are One for Prize Novelist." *Conversations with Louise Erdrich and Michael Dorris.* Ed. Allan Chavkin and Nancy Feyl Chavkin. Jackson: UP of Mississippi, 1994. 3–9.

Lyons, Gene. "In Indian Territory." Rev. of *Love Medicine: A Novel,* by Louise Erdrich. *Newsweek* 11 February 1985: 70–71.

McKenzie, James. "Lipsha's Good Road Home: The Revival of Chippewa Culture in *Love Medicine.*" *American Indian Culture and Research Journal* 10.3 (1986): 53–63.

Mermann-Jozwiak, Elisabeth. "'His Grandfather Ate His Own Wife': Louise Erdrich's *Love Medicine* as a Contemporary Windigo Narrative." *North Dakota Quarterly* 64.4 (1997): 44–54.

Owens, Louis. "Erdrich and Dorris's Mixedbloods and Multiple Narratives." *Other Destinies: Understanding the American Indian Novel.* Norman: U of Oklahoma P, 1992. 192–224.

Pearlman, Mickey. "Louise Erdrich." *Conversations with Louise Erdrich and Michael Dorris.* Ed. Allan Chavkin and Nancy Feyl Chavkin. Jackson: UP of Mississippi, 1994. 151–56.

Portales, Marco. "People with Holes in Their Lives." Rev. of *Love Medicine: A Novel,* by Louise Erdrich. *New York Times Book Review* 23 December 1984: 6.

Purdy, John. "Crossing the Waters to a *Love Medicine* (Louise Erdrich)." *Teaching American Ethnic Literatures: Nineteen Essays.* Ed. John Maitino and David R. Peck. Albuquerque: U of New Mexico P, 1996. 83–100.

Rainwater, Catherine. "Reading Between Worlds: Narrativity in the Fiction of Louise Erdrich." *American Literature* 62.3 (1990): 405–22.

Rubinstein, Roberta. "Louise Erdrich Revisits the Complex World of the Chippewa." Rev. of *Love Medicine: New and Expanded Version,* by Louise Erdrich. *Chicago Tribune* 14 November 1993: sec. 14: 3, 11.

Ruoff, A. LaVonne Brown. *American Indian Literatures: An Introduction, Bibliographic Review, and Selected Bibliography.* New York: Modern Language Association, 1990.

Silberman, Robert. "Opening the Text: *Love Medicine* and the Return of the Native American Woman." *Narrative Chance: Postmodern Discourse on Native American Indian Literatures.* Ed. Gerald Vizenor. Albuquerque: U of New Mexico P, 1989. 101–20.

Silko, Leslie. "Here's an Odd Artifact for the Fairy-Tale Shelf." Rev. of *The Beet Queen,* by Louise Erdrich. *Impact/Albuquerque Journal* 8 October 1986: 10–11.

Smith, Jeanne Rosier. *Writing Tricksters: Mythic Gambols in American Ethnic Literature.* Berkeley: U of California P, 1997.

Stillinger, Jack. *Coleridge and Textual Instability: The Multiple Versions of the Major Poems.* New York: Oxford UP, 1994.

Streitfeld, David. "Love and Its Risks." Rev. of *Love Medicine: New and Expanded Version* by Louise Erdrich. *Washington Post* 13 February 1994: sec. WBK: 15.

Towers, Robert. "Uprooted." Rev. of *Love Medicine: A Novel*, by Louise Erdrich. *New York Review of Books* 11 April 1985: 36–37.

Wong, Hertha D. "An Interview with Louise Erdrich and Michael Dorris." *Conversations with Louise Erdrich and Michael Dorris*. Ed. Allan Chavkin and Nancy Feyl Chavkin. Jackson: UP of Mississippi, 1994. 30–53.

———. "Louise Erdrich's *Love Medicine:* Narrative Communities and the Short Story Sequence." *Modern American Short Story Sequences: Composite Fictions and Fictive Communities*. Ed. J. Gerald Kennedy. Cambridge: Cambridge UP, 1995. 170–93.

5

Narrative and Ethos in Erdrich's "A Wedge of Shade"

William J. Scheick

Louise Erdrich's four novels are collections of loosely connected stories associated more by the generational interaction of the people they concern than by any substantial development of plot. These works lack a conventional structure comprised of a beginning, middle, and end. And instead of decidedly central protagonists, these works present many characters whose memories and identities are as loosely connected as are the stories in which they appear. In this regard, Lipsha Morrissey's belief that "beginnings are lost in time" (*BP* 129) applies not only to his specific situation of being an orphan who is uncertain of the name of his father but also to the more general ongoing struggle among his known relations to sort out parentage and lineage from the "tangled bloodlines" reaching far into the past (*BP* 17).

The various narratives of these people are similarly tangled. If we apply Lipsha's description of his aunt's reminiscences, we may likewise say that these sundry accounts amount to "one story hinging into the next" (*BP* 48). However much these pieces apparently hinge together in one or another way, they never neatly integrate, never become a satisfying whole, never redeem what has been termed a "lost coherence" (Kiely 235) in the world depicted in Erdrich's fiction. In this regard, Erdrich's narrative manner is very much like Lyman's old dance shirt: "the light shines through the worn-out places where the weave has thinned and pulled," so much so that "all through it the threads look ready to part" (*BP* 163). The condition of Lyman's time-worn dance shirt represents the state of Native-American tradition and culture in the late twentieth century; and it also represents the narrative texture that Erdrich designs sympathetically to convey this condition.

If her readers mentally process their discontent with this absence of a satisfying integration of character identity and of overall narrative design, they will necessarily linger over the available bits and pieces at once related to and separate from each other in her work. Erdrich has confessed her own tendency to linger over segments more than the aggregates to which they belong; speaking of her first manuscript she has said:

> I have since divided up and re-used pieces of that manuscript elsewhere. It has become the old junked car in the yard front, continually raided for parts. It is the form of all else, still a tangle. (Chavkin 238)

Erdrich's personal engagement with, and her evidently deliberate abandonment of her readers to, vignettes or story-parts that are always more striking than the whole to which they loosely belong suggest the aptness of applying a device of art criticism to her work. Atomizing Erdrich's work by attending to the *detail,* the fine-arts technique of assessing the whole in terms of a crucial part, would encourage very close scrutiny of the building blocks of her artistry. At the micro-level of the *detail* we may see better what is reprised throughout Erdrich's work as a whole, and in turn we may perceive better the ethos informing her artistic manner.

"A Wedge of Shade," a short story which appeared in 1989, serves well as such a *detail.* Although this story has never been reprinted in any of Erdrich's books, its unidentified narrator is Dot, a fact that relates this story most immediately to *The Beet Queen.* "A Wedge of Shade" is, then, at once related to Erdrich's cycle of four books and also a separate undertaking with a narrative integrity of its own. It is, in other words, at once a well-crafted short story and an illuminating *detail* from Erdrich's larger project.

Divided Country

In "A Wedge of Shade" Dot recounts her return, after more than a six-month absence during the 1970s, to Argus, North Dakota, to tell her mother that she has married Gerry Nanapush. She arrives in the middle of a heat wave, which only worsens her discomfort over her strained relationship with her mother. That Gerry has a criminal record as a result of his political activism on behalf of Native American affairs is another complication in her mission. Her attempted communication with her mother fragments as they both await Gerry's arrival. When they do finally see him in the distance, he is detained by the police for questioning. After an equally disjointed encounter with her Aunt Mary in a meat locker, Dot and her mother return home to find Gerry waiting for them. Following some mutual staring between Gerry and Dot's mother, who makes a grudging concession that they are "probably related" (40), both of them work together and successfully repair two broken fans. Later, in the dark all three lie on the floor to sleep, with Gerry positioned between Dot and her mother.

The world depicted in "A Wedge of Shade" consists of numerous antitheses. The story, which occurs within a single day, begins with the blaze of noon and ends with the darkness of night. The antitheses of hot and cold likewise come into play, especially in the scenes when Dot enters her mother's sweltering home (where the fans are broken) and later when she enters her aunt's frigid meat locker. The fans repaired by Gerry and Dot's mother create a breeze, in contrast to the stillness of everything outside the house. Outside, too, "the water has been sucked from everything" (35), while inside Dot initially swallows glass after glass of water and later in her car drains two cans of soda. And if in this June terrain of Argus "nothing casts shadows," Gerry appears to be "a little wedge of moving shade" as he approaches the house (35, 37).

As the coalescence of the appearance of Gerry and the phenomenon of shadows suggests, not only natural and human environments evidence contrary features or forces. The people in these environments also seem to be reverse images of each other. For example, Dot thinks that

Gerry and her mother look "like two opponents," though they seem to her to be "more alike than [she is] like either one of them" (40). And as for her own relationship with Gerry, Dot speaks of herself as "the wrong woman for him" because she is "paler, shorter, un-magnificent" (37).

More insistent are the incongruities within Dot's family, such as the differences between Aunt Mary and her sister, Dot's mother. The division between them, developed earlier in *The Beet Queen,* is only suggested in the counterpoint between the meat freezer and the sweltering house in "The Wedge of Shade." In the short story, however, Dot and her mother are explicitly contrasted. Whereas Dot describes herself as "short, boxy, more like [her] Aunt Mary," she sees her mother—"I don't look like her," she insists—as "tall and broad-square" (35).

If nature and people alike evidence antithetical features, so too do human cultures. Gerry, whose activism allies him to Native American culture, wears a black T-shirt, which Dot notices is "the opposite of the construction workers" (37). The construction workers, as representatives of Anglo-American culture, are developing land for housing sites, thereby transforming it away from its former and opposite agricultural use. This contrast is virtually emblematized in the Dot's image of "the horizon . . . show[ing] through the gaps in the framing," through the spaces in the subdivision "spars and bones of the houses" (36), an observation we will consider again shortly. Cultural, not just physical, features contribute to the incongruency between Dot and her mother. Whereas Dot, who is more like her commercially savvy aunt, has become thoroughly acclimated to Anglo-American culture, her more traditional mother "doesn't know about convenience stores, has no credit cards for groceries or gas, pays only with small bills and change" (40).

In short, wherever Dot looks, even when she notices "the purple-black" and "the pale-whitish" sausages in her aunt's meat locker (38), she sees a "divided country." This image emerges in Dot's mind when her mother and Gerry seem to her to be "like two opponents from the same divided country, staring across the border" (40). But the image applies to more than this specific encounter between Gerry and her mother; and it applies to more than the ancestral history of family feuds and "tangled bloodlines" alluded to by Dot's mother and explored in the course of

Erdrich's novels. "Divided country" is an apt trope for all the antitheses in "A Wedge of Shade." This trope suggests that existence—including nature, people, families, and cultures—is for some inexplicable reason divided into antagonistic features and forces.

The Turn of the Day

Such dichotomies are inexplicable; they are mysterious. "A Wedge of Shade," like Erdrich's other works (Ruppert 233), suggests that in creation some sacred mystery exists far beyond human ken. Such a suggestion occurs at the very start of the story, when Dot indicates that the sky is like "a thin whitish-blue veil" or like "a flat gauze tarp" (35). These images imply a distinct limitation in Dot's, and humanity's, ability to perceive clearly some meaning in the flow of events and the nature of things. And on occasions (such as Dot's arrival in Argus) when "nothing casts shadows" (35), then even natural phenomena seem to be so insubstantial as to be useless in slaking one's desire for axiomatic signification and personal orientation.

This implied occlusion of vision is also expressed in the recurrent motif of the stage in "A Wedge of Shade." Dot may "have rehearsed" how she was going to tell her mother of her marriage to a criminal, but her "lines melt away" because "the staged drama" in which she finds herself "speaking like a bad actor" is a production where "everything is suddenly forced, unnatural," as if she and others are merely "reading lines" (36). In one sense, Dot's experience here refers to the drama set in motion years ago between her and her mother. In another and larger sense, Dot's experience is part of some macro-drama, some "choreography design," some "performance" marred by "terrible timing," in which she is hardly the only person struggling to "discover the right answer" (37, 38, 39). Even the construction workers seem to participate "in a practiced recital"; they move "back and forth," as if caught between some sweeping mysterious principle of antithesis akin to the many polarities we have already observed in the world of "A Wedge of Shade."

This motif of *theatrum mundi,* in conjunction with the imagery of veils and gauze, intimates a world unaccountably defined by a rhythm of antithesis where people are vaguely impelled to search for an apparently elusive role and theme. The ritualistic celebration of such a mystery in the scheme of things is an important feature of Chippewa culture (Johnston; Allen 59), as it is as well of many other Native American cultures.

A sense of mystery surfaces, for example, in Thomas King's *Green Grass, Running Water,* which features four timeless Native Americans, at once male and female, who represent mythic forces. These four escapees from a mental institution seem in their odd way driven by some sacred cosmic purpose in the midst of a Canadian Blackfeet family that appears to be adrift in time. This family and its acquaintances are characters in search of a theme, for a life-plot that truly includes them; for as Native Americans, they find themselves playing minor, barely observed roles in another culture's theatrical version of reality. Their own story, the life-narrative in which they once had major parts, has been lost, at least temporarily. In the mysterious scheme of things, King's novel indicates, this version still exists apparently submerged in the reservoir of mythic lore that comprises humanity's collective memory. And shards of this sunken heritage surface in the variation of reality presently "dreamed" into existence by Anglo-American culture.

Relatedly in *Love Medicine* Lulu says, "I know the grand scheme of the world is beyond our brains to fathom, so I don't try, just let it in" (221). Apt, too, in this regard is Lipsha's intuition in *The Bingo Palace* that no matter what he does or how much he changes, he "will never get away from here" and will "always be the subject of a plan greater than myself" (21). Like Lipsha, other Native Americans in *The Bingo Palace* "watch so hard" at the course of events, including the thinning of and the pulling at the weave of their culture, because they "don't know how it will work out, come to pass" (6). Like Lipsha, they too surmise both that "beginnings are lost in time" and that "the end of things are unpronounceable" (129). Dot, too, must struggle "to try and focus" (37) while performing in a *theatrum mundi* where purpose and design seem veiled. She, too, waits upon some revelation of, some conclusion to, the mysterious drama in which she appears to be "a bad actor."

What Dot, Lipsha, Lulu, and others in Erdrich's fiction anxiously experience is the working out of fate or destiny, the choreography of a scheme beyond the edge of their consciousness yet including their actions. In an important passage in "A Wedge of Shade" Dot vaguely intuits the correspondence of specific moments in time with some obscure larger pattern: "I have this intuition as we near the house, in the fateful quality of light, as in the turn of the day the heat continues to press and the blackness, into which the warmth usually lifts, lowers steadily: We must come to the end of something; there must be a close to this day" (40). Here small matters—the end of a particular day, the end of a daughter's particular encounter—are nuanced to intimate a larger context—the "fateful quality of light" and "the end of something" beyond what is measured in the course of a specific day.

A clue to this coalescence of the quotidian and the universal surfaces as well if we pause over the association of several antitheses embedded in this passage: day and night, light and dark, hot and cold, lifting and lowering. As we have already seen concerning the prevalence of antitheses in "A Wedge of Shade," nature, people, families, and cultures—existence, in short—seems for some inexplicable reason to be, as it were, a country divided into antagonistic forces. But it is important here to note that in Dot's unfocused insight, "the turn of the day" promises a cyclic passing of one opposite into the other, much like the back-and-forth rhythm of the "recital" of the construction workers. Accordingly, upon reaching home Dot and her mother find Gerry, whose detainment is redressed by his release; whereas they had tried to greet Gerry earlier, now he reverses the procedure: "it is [their] turn to be received" (40). It is equally important to notice that the perception of such an alternation of turns, of the recital-like back-and-forth pattern of things in "the turn[ing] of the day," encourages whatever hope Dot is able to muster.

The Horizon through the Gaps

Dot's hope lies in her unwitting appreciation of this larger scheme of the turning of things, a scheme that seems to underlie and possibly redeem her uncomfortable experience of fragmented moments, her entanglement in seemingly irresolute contraries, and her "speaking like a bad actor" in a production where "everything is suddenly forced, unnatural." Without knowing it, she finds hope in a ceremonial sense of time, which "is cyclic, rather than linear, accretive rather than incremental, and makes few distinctions between momentous events and daily, ordinary events" (Rainwater 416).

The hope likewise offered in King's *Green Grass, Running Water* resides in the perception of existence as "running water," as an incessant recycling flow of uncontainable possibilities. Even if Anglo-American culture seeks to obstruct this originative fluidity, to make adamantine its present version of reality through "power and control" (109), in fact (as the escapees, the reedited video western, the resistance to filming the Sun Dance, and the rupture of a dam in the novel mutually suggest) reality is as unconfinable and as mutable as gushing water. Everything has been and will always be "potential" or "imagination" (223). Since, accordingly, "there are no truths . . . only stories" (326)—or as Nanapush says in *Tracks,* "all substance [is] illusion" (223)—then narratives like King's novel may contribute to a cyclical revision of the present that better includes Native American experience and better fulfills their search for a theme, a purpose. Just wait and remember, King implies, and the present theatrical rendering of reality will eventually burst its imaginary bounds. Possibly the next life-narrative will recover Native American and Anglo-American cultures and better integrate them into a richer life-story for both cultures. This cyclic feature of Native American ceremonial time, frequently represented as a circle, is as structurally important in Erdrich's artistic use of Chippewa culture as it is in King's artistic use of Blackfeet culture.

For the Chippewa the circle (in whole or in part) is the sign of the Great Spirit evident nearly everywhere in natural phenomena, including organic cycles. As pertinently represented in the Plain tribes' medicine wheel, the circle is a common Native American sacred symbol for time itself (Tedlock 216; Allen 56–59). This regard for the circle includes variations on the image of the arc or curve. In *The Bingo Palace* Lipsha provides a clue to Erdrich's Chippewa regard for the curve: "the straight-edged shape is not a Chippewa preference" because everything "is round, everything in nature. There are no perfect boundaries, no natural borders except winding rivers" (80). Pauline, in contrast, possesses features—

all "angles and sharp edges" (71)—that suggest an intrinsic association with the Anglo-American culture and the Christian religion she unsuccessfully adopts.

The same distinction informs "A Wedge of Shade." If we return to Dot's image of "the horizon . . . show[ing] through the gaps in the framing," we see precisely this contrast between straight-edged lines in the foreground and the swell of the curved horizon in the background. Insofar as "A Wedge of Shade" narratively turns with the turn of the day, Erdrich's art aligns itself with the Chippewa regard for the circle. In fact, Dot's image of "the horizon . . . show[ing] through the gaps of the framing" is an apt objectification of Erdrich's narrative manner, an objectification related to the image (in *The Bingo Palace*) of Lyman's old dance shirt, with "the light shin[ing] through the worn-out places where the weave has thinned and pulled." Both passages suggest how Erdrich's piecemeal narrative rendering of the underlying antitheses of daily experience also insinuates "through the worn-out places" in the weave, "through the gaps of the framing," some distant mystery—a circular force—beyond the horizon of human consciousness.

In "A Wedge of Shade" this sacred force is intimated through the curve, a segment of this circular force; and appropriately the narrative round of Erdrich's fiction is comprised of segments never rounded off to completion. As a result, we as readers share in Dot's effort "to try and focus," an effort persisting beyond the end of any given episode in Erdrich's work. All Dot and we have is "the *turn* of the day" [italics added] with its back-and-forth cycles of light and darkness, hot and cold, lifting and lowering, receiving and being received, farming and real estate. This pattern is as cyclic as is ceremonial time, and even the day which lapses in the course of the story will necessarily pass into other days, other arches or curves along the larger segmented wheel of time.

Of Wedges, Hills, and Ethos

Gerry, too, strikes Dot, at an unconscious level, as an horizon, a curve along this mysterious sacred wheel. As we already saw, Gerry participates in the rhythm of balanced antitheses characterizing this wheel:

he wears a black shirt, the converse of the white shirts of the construction workers whose activity represents forces he opposes; he is tall and dark, in contrast to Dot's shortness and paleness; he receives Dot and her mother at their home, reversing their earlier attempt to receive him; he repairs the fans to create a breeze indoors, in counterpoint to the hot stillness outdoors; and he seems to Dot like a wedge of shade in a landscape (at once physical and psychological) bereft of shadows. At the end of the story, when Gerry positions himself between Dot and her mother on the floor to sleep, he appears to be a special link that in some way reconciles the many differences between a mother and her daughter.

This final image of Gerry reads: "I hold hands with Gerry as he settles down between my mother and me. He is huge as a hill between the two of us, solid in the beating wind" (40). Gerry unites mother and daughter by unknowingly participating in the circle-force of time which (as we saw Lipsha indicate) informs the Chippewa preference for the "natural" roundness of things. When Dot describes Gerry as "huge as a hill," she unconsciously figures him as an arc or curve along this universal circle-force. She unconsciously senses that he is bringing her *closer* to some rapprochement with both her mother and all the other antitheses in her life.

The hill image applied to Gerry not only suggests a segment of curve along this universal circle of unity; the hill image also can be configured as a wedge, the image Dot applied to Gerry earlier. The images of the hill and wedge coalesce in their paradoxical joining of antithetical possibilities. A wedge can be a device that separates two things, and in contrast, a wedge can be a device that tightens and secures two things. A hill likewise separates like a wedge; but seen as an arch, a hill also connects like a wedge. In the recesses of Dot's mind, Gerry appears to participate in this mystery of the wedge and hill; he encourages Native American resistance to Anglo-American development, and he furthers the reconciliation of Dot and her mother.

This emphasis on mutually constitutive antitheses, of curve-like segments that participate in a universal circuit, is fundamental to Erdrich's art. Her fragmented narratives are broken circles, piecemeal arcs, all apparently mysteriously inclined toward some distant completion or revelation. But as the comments about fate that we noted earlier indicate, usually this tendency toward fulfillment is not clear to Erdrich's characters. Fleur, who is believed to possess magical powers, may be a noteworthy exception. At the end of *Tracks,* for instance, with her hair "falling in a wide arc" Fleur ritualistically causes the trees on her lost land to "fall away . . . in a circle" (223). This peculiar event anticipates a subsequent turn of events, recorded elsewhere in Erdrich's fiction, when Fleur's land comes round to her again.

Dot and most other Erdrich characters, however, do not enjoy any mystical assurance concerning such fated circuiting. Dot continually finds herself with "lips half open" and "half smiles" only "half believing" and feeling "paralyzed halfway" (35, 36, 38). And Erdrich's readers, likewise narratively caught between chaos and unity, share in Dot's experience of halfness. They, too, encounter divisions that (like anything designated as halves) seem latently to imply deferred fulfilling complements.

In making these observations I mean that Erdrich's work appears to be designed to evoke a response from its readers. Erdrich's narrative device of deferred closure, of a faintly implied structure of incomplete circularity, encourages the implied reader to "draw . . . new boundaries" so that, as one theory of reader-response criticism holds, "the virtual background (the real 'me') will take on a different form" (Iser 285, 293). This effect, in other words, bares an ethical charge; for making ethical judgments in response to a text is not only a most natural act for readers, it is also an inevitable act whereby readers *in some manner* make spiritual, intellectual, or emotional use of what they encounter in a text (Booth). Moreover, a reader may be alerted to these personal implications most especially by narrative devices such as structure, devices which tend to convey ethos less ambiguously than does characterization (Scheick 18–40).

The effect, the narrative ethos, of Erdrich's structural deferral of closure that conversely faintly implies a possible fulfilling ontological circularity, may stimulate a feeling of discontent much like the one described by the narrator of *The Bingo Palace:* "The story comes around, pushing at our brain, and soon we are trying to ravel back to the beginning, trying to put families in order and make sense of things. But we start with one person, and soon another and another follows, and still another until we are lost in the connections" (*BP* 5). Here the narrator reflects on various characters' encounters with their "tangled bloodlines," and their experience aptly applies to the reader's encounter with these characters' "tangled" storylines. Similar to these characters, Erdrich's readers are likely to struggle to "make sense of things," and they are likely to get lost while trying to make connections among so many narrative fragments, so many oral remnants of memory and identity. In this way, however, the reader potentially becomes attentive—either vaguely or distinctly discontent with the apparent absence of a more satisfying unification of the temporal fragments of each character's experience and the segments of each narrative's design. Or, as a critic of Erdrich's works has astutely observed, the reader may enter "a state of marginality" that fosters revisionary "epistemological insight" into "the conventional expectations associated with ordinary narrativity" and ordinary life (Rainwater 422).

A distinct or indistinct sentiment of discontent over the apparent absence of a more aesthetic joining of episodic segments may—through a desire for what is absent—open the way to a compassionate intuition concerning human possibilities. In Erdrich's work, as we also saw in King's, such an intuition certainly may include a desire for a better integration of marginalized groups, such as Native Americans, or a keener insight into the textuality of our present lives, so open to revision (Rainwater 422). But in terms of its largest ethical implications, Erdrich's narrative structure of curve-like segments (apparently suggesting a distant sacred circle-like whole) directs the reader to sense the mysteriousness of being. Particularly emphasized is the mystery of the present historical diminishment (fragmentation) of a temporal world that may be veiled to human vision but is nonetheless inherently replete with spiritual nurture (unity). For Erdrich, we unfortunately see without mystically perceiving. So, as Nanapush says in *Tracks,* "There was so much we saw and never knew" (34).

Works Cited

Allen, Paula Gunn. *The Sacred Hoop: Recovering the Feminine in American Indian Traditions.* Boston: Beacon Press, 1986.

Booth, Wayne C. *The Company We Keep: An Ethics of Fiction.* Berkeley: U of California P, 1988.

Chavkin, Allan, and Nancy Feyl Chavkin, eds. *Conversations with Louise Erdrich and Michael Dorris.* Jackson: UP of Mississippi, 1994.

Erdrich, Louise. "A Wedge of Shade." *New Yorker* 6 March 1989: 35–40.

Iser, Wolfgang. *The Implied Reader: Patterns of Communication in Prose Fiction from Bunyan to Beckett.* Baltimore: Johns Hopkins UP, 1974.

Johnston, Basil. *Ojibway Ceremonies.* Lincoln: U of Nebraska P, 1982.

Kiely, Robert. *Reverse Tradition: Postmodern Fictions and the Nineteenth Century Novel.* Cambridge: Harvard UP, 1993.

King, Thomas. *Green Grass, Running Water.* Toronto: HarperCollins, 1993.

Rainwater, Catherine. "Reading Between Worlds: Narrativity in the Fiction of Louise Erdrich." *American Literature* 62.3 (1990): 405–22.

Ruppert, James. "Mediation and Multiple Narrative in *Love Medicine.*" *North Dakota Quarterly* 59.4 (1991): 229–41.

Scheick, William J. *Fictional Structure and Ethics: The Turn-of-the-Century English Novel.* Athens: U of Georgia P, 1990.

Tedlock, Dennis, and Barbara Tedlock, eds. *Teachings from the American Earth: Indian Religion and Philosophy.* New York: Liveright, 1975.

6

Of Vision Quests and Spirit Guardians

Female Power in the Novels of Louise Erdrich

ANNETTE VAN DYKE

When Native American women are thought of at all, and in the annals of American history that is seldom, two images come to mind: that of the exotic princess, guide and benefactor of white men—a good Indian—and that of squaw—a kind of savage beast of burden, subject to the whims of her mate, the befeathered Indian chief—a bad Indian. In both of these stereotypes Native American women are defined by their relationship to men and are not seen as powerful in their own right. However, as Paula Gunn Allen demonstrates in *Sacred Hoop,* and as early chronicles from American history show, Native American women were seen by their own people as "powerful, socially, physically, and metaphysically" (48), nothing like the common idea of the weaker sex applied to upper-class white women. Allen says of Native American women today: "Most Indian women I know are in the same bicultural bind: we vacillate between being dependent and strong, self-reliant and powerless, strongly motivated and hopelessly insecure," trying to deal "with two hopelessly opposed cultural definitions of women" (49).

As a Native American writer, Louise Erdrich is concerned with countering these stereotypical images and the cultural bifurcation of Native American women. By virtue of being female, her independent and feisty women characters exemplify a kind of power central to life on the reservation—what Erdrich calls "transformational power." In contrast, the males must seek to find their power and place. For example, in *Tracks,* Nanapush toys with the idea of representing his tribe to the United States government, but it is Fleur on whom the hopes of the tribe are pinned to transform or arrest the encroaching white civilization. In *Love Medicine* and in *Bingo Palace,* Marie and Lulu become the real power on the reservation, despite the outward show of control by the tribal government official, Lyman Lamartine. In *Bingo Palace,* Marie's daughter, Zelda, has also become a powerful force on the reservation. This essay explores the power of women as seen in two sets of mothers and daughters, Fleur/Lulu and Marie/Zelda—power which comes from the Chippewa vision quest and spirit guardian and which often takes on a peculiarly sexual form for Chippewa women.

In an interview, Erdrich makes clear that the bifurcation of Native American women's roles and status is of major importance to her. She says: "We are taught to present a demure face to the world and yet there is a kind of wild energy behind it in many women that *is* a transformational energy, and not only transforming to them but to other people" (Bruchac 82). Because of her three daughters and sisters, she has "an urgent reason for thinking about women attuned to their power and their honest nature, not the socialized nature and their embarrassed nature and the nature that says, 'I can't possibly accomplish this'" (Bruchac 82).

In the encounters between Erdrich's male and female characters, this transformational power is often sexual. In discussing her poem "Jacklight," Erdrich notes that "[j]acklighting and hunting are both strong metaphors for me of sexual and love relations between men and women. In the male tradition, men are the hunters and women are their prey"[1] (George 243). However, Erdrich believes that instead "[t]here must be an exchange, a transformation, a power shared between them. . . . [I]t is this transformation where we arrive at a different stage of power" (George 243). Further, some of Erdrich's characters use their "sexuality in the same way that the men in the poems are using the jacklight, to attract in an animal way, to paralyze and fascinate. The difference is that [they are] . . . defiant because . . . men are still in control" (George 244). This defiant use of sexuality is illustrated in the poem, "The Lady in the Pink

Mustang," in which the lady, "whose bare lap is floodlit from under the dash," lures truckers into her power: "She owns them, not one will admit what they cannot / come close to must own them. She takes them along . . . " (*Jacklight* 17).

Explaining the transformational power, Erdrich also says: "When, in some of the poems, it takes the form of becoming an animal, that I feel is a symbolic transformation, the moment a woman allows herself to act out of her own power" (Bruchac 82). An example of this appears in the poem, "The Strange People," in which an antelope woman defies the hunter who thinks he has killed her, and yet she still waits for one with whom she could share the transformational power:

> Safely shut in the garage,
> when he sharpens his knife
> and thinks to have me, like that,
> I come toward him,
> a lean gray witch,
> through the bullets that enter and dissolve.
>
> I sit in his house
> drinking coffee till dawn,
> and leave as frost reddens on hubcaps,
> crawling back into my shadowy body.
> All day, asleep in clean grasses,
> I dream of the one who could really wound me." (*Jacklight* 68–69)

In her novels, Erdrich has used the concept of the transformational power in developing the characters of Fleur, Lulu, Marie, and Zelda, among others. Traditionally, the Chippewa went on vision quests and had spirit guardians whose animal characteristics the recipient often took on.[2] Consequently, the transformational power also has a particularly Chippewa spiritual character which lessens as it is affected by Euro-American culture. Throughout the novels *Tracks, Love Medicine,* and *Bingo Palace,* the water spirit man, Misshepeshu, plays a prominent role lending his animal characteristics to Fleur, her daughter Lulu, Moses, and Lipsha—all in the Pillager line.[3] He is also featured on Nector's pipe bag handed down to Lipsha and Zelda.

In *Tracks* Fleur is described as having a good deal of transformational power illustrated in her animal characteristics which she takes on from her spirit guardian, Misshepeshu. She is described as having: "shoulders . . . broad and curved as a yoke, her hips fishlike, slippery, narrow. An old green dress clung to her waist, worn then where she sat. Her glossy braids were like the tails of animals, and swung against her when she moved, deliberately, slowly in her work, held in and half-tamed" (*T* 18). She also has "sly, brown eyes and . . . teeth, strong, sharp and very white" (*T* 18) which seem to be wolf-like Pillager characteristics.

Fleur exudes sexual power. She is always the hunter and never the prey, although some of the male characters attempt to be the aggressor. Eli follows the trail of a wounded deer he has shot to Fleur at her cabin near the lake and tries to claim the deer she is skinning. She denies his claim to it, and finally, he helps her skin it and gives the meat to her. After that he is obsessed with her and goes to the elder Nanapush for instruction. Nanapush tries to warn him away because Fleur is dangerous. She is "so impossible and yet available at the same time, that even the dried-out and bent ones around the store could see enough to light a slow fuse in their dreams" (*T* 55). She is "a woman gone wild, striking down whatever got into her path" (*T* 45). When Eli leaves to return to Fleur, Nanapush likens her to a bear: "It's like you're a log in a stream. Along comes this bear. She jumps on. Don't let her dig in her claws" (*T* 46).

Erdrich presents Fleur as firmly in control of the relationship between her and Eli. After Eli has a relationship with Sophie, Fleur uses her sexual power to punish him by ignoring him. According to Nanapush,

> After three days of Fleur's avoidance, he longed for her with the vigor of their first encounters, when . . . those two had coupled outdoors, against trees, down on pine-needle couches or out in the bare yard. After a week, he needed her with twice the force of their first meetings, and after two he was in desperate pain. His blood pounded at the rustle of her skirts. If she brushed him by accident his skin felt scorched. The fire spread. He even strained for her like a flame toward air. (*T* 106–7)

The descriptions of Fleur in *Tracks* are almost always animal-like; she is Erdrich's character who acts the most out of her own transformational power or who, we might say, is most herself. For instance, Eli believes that Fleur is mating with her spirit guardian Misshepeshu in the frozen lake at night. Eli describes her as moving, "[s]tealthly, smooth as an otter sliding from a log" (*T* 106). She stays under the frozen crust of the lake longer than a human could stand. When he wakes in the night, her hair is "a damp braid tossed against [him] . . . and once, from along her neck, [he] . . . picked a curl of black weed from the bottom of the lake" (*T* 107).

Fleur's powers are formidable and in *Bingo Palace,* the reader sees her win back her land once again using her gambling skills—this time from the Indian Agent. She returns to the reservation from the Twin Cities with a innocent-looking boy and a white Pierce-Arrow as her bait. Her hair hangs in long braids down her back, "bound together with a red strip of cloth" like the old-time warriors used to wear their hair "to meet an enemy" (*BP* 139). She is the woman acting out of her own power: "[S]he'd always acted as though she owned everything and nothing: sky, earth, those who crossed her path, road, and Pillager land. It was because she owned herself" (*BP* 140).

However, times change, and in *Love Medicine* the female characters are less themselves, having lost knowledge of the old ways and having been affected by Euro-American culture and Catholicism, forcing them to take on the bicultural split between strength and weakness. In spite of this, Lulu, Fleur's daughter, acts as a bridge character. Although she was sent to boarding school, which had the effect for most of erasing the Native culture, Lulu has a potent legacy from her mother. It is almost as if Lulu cannot help but be herself—be in her power. Erdrich's addition of the section "The Island" to the "new and expanded version" of *Love Medicine* illustrates this. This section shows Lulu's vision quest; before its addition, the reader did not see her seeking and coming into her transformatory power. Lulu has inherited her mother's sexual powers. She has become "a Pillager kind of woman with a sudden body, fierce outright wishes, a surprising heart" (*LMN* 71), but she has no guidance for her power since her mother is not around.

Like her mother, she sees herself in control of any relationships with men. Nector Kashpaw has indicated his interest in her, and she has returned that interest. However, when Nector is suddenly caught by Marie (to be discussed later), she says Nector would have been hers if she'd "jumped" for him, but since she doesn't "jump for men," he was apparently lost. She had thought of "maybe stepping high" for him when she discovered his attachment to Marie. She had wanted to meet Nector halfway, neither being the pursued nor pursuer—to share power.

However, in her anger at the situation and to irritate Nector's mother, Margaret Rushes Bear Kashpaw, she decides to seek out her very strange cousin, Moses Pillager, who survived the illness that killed the rest of her mother's relatives. Moses lives on an island in the middle of the lake with his cats, becoming cat-like himself and following his spirit guardian, Misshepeshu, who is alternately described as the big cat and as the horned lynx who lives in the lake.

Lulu is at puberty, the traditional age for a vision quest. She practices for Moses by kissing her arm. She notices "how the eyes of grown men stuck to" her at the store (*LMN* 75). Seeking she knows not what, Lulu goes to the island to charm Moses and to test her powers. The trip to the island is her vision quest, and Moses is no ordinary man:

> He was surprising, so beautiful to look at that I couldn't tell his age. His heavy hair coursed all the way down his back, looped around his belt. His face was closely fit, the angles measured and almost too perfect. My mother's face was like that too—too handsome to be real, constructed by the Manitous. (*LMN* 77)

Lulu uses her sexual powers to ensnare Moses, who is really old enough to be her father but who has remained animal-like and innocent. "I had dusted him, chilled him in the shape of my shadow when I stood against the sun. I had loosened the air, stolen the strings from his hands and legs, bent him like a stem of grass marking my trail" (*LMN* 80). He tries to leave, but she holds him and pulls him to her: "My black eyes opened wide, my *windigo* stare caught him, and I let him see the sharp flash of my teeth. He followed both of his hands as they flew forward and stroked me" (*LMN* 80). But something happens and Lulu loses control; she doesn't know if she is "acting from [her] . . . own intentions" or not.

He comes to her cat-like—licking her and exploring her curiously until they share transforming power: "Suddenly his breath went deep and ragged in my ear. There was no more light from the fire, and I couldn't feel where he ended or began. He was made of darkness—weightless, fragile, lifting and falling around me with each breath" (*LMN* 81).

Moses is brought back from the invisible state in which he hid from the spirits in the time of disease. He gains his voice; he says his name "which harbored his life" (*LMN* 82) and which had not been said in fear of death. He becomes more human.

Lulu's quest fills her with the desire for more of the transformational union. It is as if she can never get enough, and how often can one expect such mystical transport? She says:

> To this day, I still hurt. I must have rolled in the beds of wild rose, for the tiny thorns—small, yellow—pierced my skin. Their poison is desire and it dissolved in my blood. The cats made me one of them—sleek and without mercy, avid, falling hungry upon the defenseless body. I want to grind men's bones to drink in my night tea. I want to enter them the way their hot shadows fold into their bodies in full sunlight. I want to be their food, their harmful drink, to taste men like stilled jam at the back of my tongue. (*LMN* 82)

Lulu's vision quest has other results. She finds her mother in her understanding of the power she has been given, and she again hears her mother's voice keeping her from harm. As a result of her liaison with Moses, she gives birth to Gerry Nanapush, the magical trickster whom no jail can hold. Through her exuberant animal-like sexuality she has eight children, all by different fathers, some of them married to her and some not. She feels no remorse and says she is "in love with the whole world and all that lived in its rainy arms." She would "open . . . and let everything inside" (*LMN* 276) so that after a while she "would be full" (*LMN* 277). She continues to be known for her catlike characteristics: "loving no one, only purring to get what she wants" (*LMN* 276).

As a respected elder, Lulu causes plenty of trouble. In another new chapter in *Love Medicine,* she allies herself with her rival Marie, and together they change the plans for the tomahawk factory into making "'museum-quality' artifacts" (*LMN* 303). Later, they quarrel and the whole factory is destroyed. The factory manager, Lyman says of his aging mother, Lulu, that "[s]he has no fear, and that's what's wrong with her" (*LMN* 302)—Lulu is always herself.

Lulu also uses her Pillager power to delay the hunt for her escaped-convict son Gerry Nanapush. She dresses herself perfectly as if for a pow-wow and leads her questioners on for hours. Then when they take her off to jail, she "dances the old-lady traditional, a simple step, but complex in its quiet balance, striking. She dances with a tucked-in wildness, exactly like an old-time Pillager" and before they can take her away in the federal car, she gives "the old-lady trill, the victory yell that runs up our necks" (*BP* 265) before the news cameras. The reservation joins her, "[d]rawing deep breaths, hearts shaking" (*BP* 265), and she has created a unifying act.

Of course, if one wished, the character of Lulu could be used to reinforce the stereotype of Native American women being promiscuous. However, with the addition of "The Island" section that appears more difficult, for it puts her sexuality into the realm of the spiritual if the reader is paying attention at all. The new material may be, in fact, a reaction to the propensity that some reviewers have for seeing novels as anthropological documents and in reading the characters as racial stereotypes as happened in several reviews of *Love Medicine*.[4] One reviewer saw only stereotypes in Erdrich's female characters: "Meanwhile the women, with the exception of the stalwart Marie, are likely to take up with any man who comes along" (Towers 36).

Another reviewer also using sexual and racial stereotypes saw the scene in the "Wild Geese" section between Nector and Marie as a rape (Portales 6). However, perhaps to counter such interpretation, Erdrich has rewritten this scene so that even the most recalcitrant reader has to deal with Marie's sexual power. Marie is a mixed-blood girl of fourteen, the right age for a vision quest. She is from a marginal reservation family when she enters the convent. She wants to become a saint to rectify her position. There she meets Sister Leopolda, whom she does not know is her biological mother. Partly a result of Leopolda's physical mistreatment of her, she has a vision in which she takes on the characteristics of the water spirit man who "casts a shell necklace at your feet, weeps gleaming chips that harden into mica on your breasts. . . . He's made of gold" (*T* 11). Marie is "rippling gold." Her "nipples flashed and winked. Diamonds tipped them" (*LMN* 54).

When Marie descends from the convent, she has come into her power. She seizes her chance to improve herself by ensnaring Nector Kashpaw, who is from a well-thought-of family on the reservation. Nector thinks she is "a skinny white girl" (*LMN* 64) making off with the nuns' valuables, perhaps with a chalice hidden under her skirt. What he finds is the "chalice" of her sexual power:

> Her breasts graze my chest, soft and pointed. I cannot help but lower myself the slightest bit to feel them better. And then I am caught. I give way. I cannot help myself, because, to my everlasting wonder, Marie is all tight plush acceptance, graceful movements, little jabs that lead me underneath her skirt where she is slick, warm, silk. I touch her with one hand and in that one touch I lose myself. . . . [S]omehow I have been beaten at what I started on this hill. (*LMN* 65)

After their physical encounter, Marie says, "I've had better." However, Nector thinks, "I know that isn't true because we haven't done anything yet. She doesn't know what comes next" (*LMN* 65). This time Erdrich has not left to chance that the reader will misunderstand that Marie is exerting her transformational power. Erdrich reinforces her intention that Marie is in control of her sexual power by deleting a line in the chapter "Flesh and Blood" in which Marie and her daughter, Zelda, go up the hill to see the dying Sister Leopolda. In the original version, when she points out to Zelda as they walk the place where she met Nector, Marie thinks: "For all I knew it was the place we made Gordon as well, but I never exactly said that" (*LM* 114). This line is deleted in the revised version.

In the scene in which Marie encounters Nector, she is also described in both animal and nature terms, another clue that she is acting "out of her own power" (Bruchac 82). She has "brown eyes" that "glaze over like a wounded mink's, hurt but still fighting vicious" (*LMN*). She is "rail-tough and pale as birch . . . the kind of tree that doubles back and springs up, whips, singing" (*LMN* 63–64). She has eyes, "tense and wild, animal eyes" that send "chills" up his neck. She "makes an odd raspfile noise, cawing like a crow" (*LMN* 64).

Nector's response to Marie finally is as if she is a wounded animal, but still she does not release him from her power. Sometimes he

> find[s] a wounded animal that hasn't died well, or, worse it's still living, so that I have to put it out of its misery. . . . I touch the suffering bodies like they were killed saints I should handle with a gentle reverence. . . . This is how I hold her wounded hand in my hand. . . . Her hand grows thick and fevered, heavy in my own, and I don't want her, but I want her, and I cannot let go. (*LMN* 66–67)

Marie turns her considerable powers to making her husband Nector one of the most respected men on the reservation—the tribal chairman—and to keeping his drinking under control. She mothers her own children and those discarded by others such as June and Lipsha. As a respected elder on the reservation, she returns to "the old language, falling back through time to the words that Lazarres had used among themselves, shucking off the Kashpaw pride, yet holding to the old strengths Rushes Bear had taught her" (*LMN* 263). Her mother-in-law Margaret Rushes Bear Kashpaw had given Marie and subsequently, Zelda, the strength to be attuned to their own powers as women and to reject the Euro-American image of women as weak and helpless and herself as marginal—a dirty Lazarre.

She is not able to extend that transformational power to all, however. Despite her mothering of June, June's childhood is so horrendous—being raped by her mother's boyfriend—that she never comes fully into her own power and she eventually chooses death by walking into a blizzard. June's considerable sexual power traps Marie's son Gordie, but it is the power of the jacklight, used to hunt and kill in defiance for what has been done to her and not shared power. Gordie's life is devastated by his marriage to June, and Marie must deal with her son's decline. In another new chapter added to *Love Medicine,* Marie gathers her strength and refuses to allow Gordie to leave the cabin again in search of alcohol. She thinks: "There was no question in her mind that if she let him go he would get himself killed. She would almost rather have killed him herself" (*LMN* 275). Gordie dies after drinking Lysol with Marie sitting at the cabin door with her axe.

June's harm extends to her own son, Lipsha, who she tries to drown as an infant. Lipsha is saved by the water spirit man, and therefore given his gift of touch and connected firmly to the Pillagers, Fleur, and Moses, who also have the water man as a spirit guardian. Lipsha remembers it as:

> Darkened and drenched, coming toward me from the other side of drowning—it presses its mouth on mine and holds me with its fins and horns and rocks me with its long and shining plant arms. Its face is lion-jawed, a thing of beach foam, resembling the jack of clubs. Its face has the shock of the unburied goodness, the saving tones. . . . I am rocked and saved and cradled. (*BP* 218)

When Lipsha seeks out his great grandmother Fleur for some love medicine, their connection is reaffirmed. Later Fleur performs her last transforming act—she trades her life for Lipsha's: "Outdoors, into a deep cold brilliance that often succeeds a long disruptive blizzard, she went thinking of the boy out there. Annoyed, she took his place" (*BP* 272).

For Marie's daughter, Zelda, the vision quest, which sets an adolescent on her adult path, comes late. At sixteen she "did not know what she wanted yet" (*LMN* 148). Like her mother and her biological grandmother Pauline (Sister Leopolda), she thinks of going up the hill to join the nuns in the convent, but she has not chosen any particular path. It is after she and her mother visit the dying Sister Leopolda that the incident which shapes her life occurs. Zelda's vision takes the form of her father's infidelity with Lulu Lamartine. She finds his farewell letter to her mother and goes to bring him back. Her father, Nector, sees her as a vision of Marie and instead of animal characteristics, common to women coming into their own power, she has the characteristics of an avenging angel:

> I see Marie standing in the bush. She is fourteen and slim again. I can do nothing but stare, rooted to the ground. She stands tall,

> straight and stern as an angel. She watches me. Red flames from the burning house glare and flicker in her eyes. Her skin sheds light. We are face to face, and then she begins to lift on waves of heat. Her breast is a glowing shield. Her arm is a white-hot spear. When she raises it the bush behind her spreads, blazing open like wings. (*LMN* 145)

In acting for her mother, Zelda aborts her natural self. She decides that she wants a white man who "would take . . . [her] away from the reservation to the Twin Cities, where . . . [she'd] planned her life all out from catalogs and magazines" (*BP* 46). Unlike her father, Nector, she would never be subject to love; she would never share her transformational power with a man. Instead she uses her sexual power to thwart the love of Xavier Toose:

> She was capable of hovering in a blanket, in a room where her own breath rose and fell, a plume of longing, all night. She could exist in the dark cell of her body. She was capable of denying herself everything tender, unspoken, sweet, generous, and desperate. She could do it because she willed it. She could live in the shell of her quilt as the cold night lengthened, and she could let a man's fires flash and burn, flash and burn, until they disappeared. (*BP* 244)

Nevertheless, despite Zelda's refusal of Xavier, she uses her power to control events on the reservation. As Lipsha says of her,

> When women age into their power, no wind can upset them, no hand turn aside their knowledge; no fact can deflect their point of view. . . . My aunt knows all there is to know. She has a deep instinct for running things. She should have more children or at least a small nation to control. Instead, forced narrow, her talents run to getting people to do things they don't want to do for other people they don't like. Zelda is the author of grit-jawed charity on the reservation, the instigator of good works that always get chalked up to her credit. (*BP* 13–14)

Zelda has raven-like hair "which still sweeps its fierce wing down the middle of her back," and she wears the legacy from her paternal grandmother, Margaret Rushes Bear Kashpaw, a skinning knife in a beaded sheath "at her strong hip" (*BP* 15). Despite her marriage to her white man, the "morose" Swede (*BP* 23), she named her daughter "Albertine" after her first love, Xavier Albert Toose, her denial of his love affecting her all of her life. Zelda is visited with a vision which accompanies the return of her father's ceremonial pipe—the pipe which was "Earth and heaven, connecting, the fire between that burned in everything alive" (*BP* 245). The pipe also had a "horned man radiating wavering lines of power . . . beaded into the other end" (*LMN* 259). In a series of painful visions connected to heart attacks, she sees that she has denied her own nature, her love for Xavier Toose. When she thinks of him, her heart "yawned open like a greedy young bird, ready to be fed" (*BP* 246). Finally, she stands before him, "new as if naked, but she had no shame" (*BP* 247). So, even though Zelda has denied her own nature and only accepted it as a mature woman, still she is not weak; she is transformed. She meets Xavier half way: "Light dashed itself upon Zelda, but she wasn't shaken. Her hands floated off the steering wheel and gestured, but she wasn't helpless" (*BP* 247).

Fleur, Lulu, Marie, and Zelda all exemplify Erdrich's transformational sexual power when women are most themselves. Erdrich counters the stereotypes of Native American women as weak by using the traditional Chippewa concepts of the vision quest and the spirit guardian, most often the water spirit man. Her characters are shown as taking on the animal characteristics of their spirit guardians and acting out of their own power. With the revisions in *Love Medicine,* and through *The Bingo Palace,* Erdrich brings these concepts firmly onto the contemporary reservation—offering images of strong, self-reliant, powerful Chippewa women.

Notes

1. The *Random House Dictionary of the English Language,* 2nd edition, defines jacklight as: "a portable cresset, or oil-burning lantern, or electric light used as a lure in hunting or fishing at night."

2. See Vecsey 121–43 for discussions of puberty and the vision quest.

3. See Van Dyke for a discussion of the role of the water spirit man in Erdrich's work.

4. See McKenzie 53–55 for a discussion of stereotypes in reviews of *Love Medicine.*

Works Cited

Allen, Paula Gunn. *The Sacred Hoop: Recovering the Feminine in American Indian Traditions.* Boston: Beacon Press, 1986.

Bruchac, Joseph, ed. "Whatever Is Really Yours: An Interview with Louise Erdrich." *Survival This Way: Interviews with American Indian Poets.* Tucson: U of Arizona P, 1987. 73–86.

Erdrich, Louise. *Jacklight.* New York: Holt, 1984.

George, Jan. "Interview with Louise Erdrich." *North Dakota Quarterly* 53 (1985): 240–46.

McKenzie, James. "Lipsha's Good Road Home: The Revival of Chippewa Culture in *Love Medicine.*" *American Indian Culture and Research Journal* 10.3 (1986): 53–63.

Portales, Marco. "People with Holes in Their Lives." Rev. of *Love Medicine,* by Louise Erdrich. *New York Times Book Review* 23 December 1984: 6.

Towers, Robert. "Uprooted." Rev. of *Love Medicine,* by Louise Erdrich. *New York Review of Books* 11 April 1985: 36.

Van Dyke, Annette. "Questions of the Spirit: Bloodlines in Louise Erdrich's Chippewa Landscape." *Studies in American Indian Literatures* 4.1 (1992): 15–27.

Vecsey, Christopher. *Traditional Ojibwa Religion and Its Historical Changes.* Philadelphia: American Philosophical Society, 1983.

7

Ethnic Signs in Erdrich's *Tracks* and *The Bingo Palace*

CATHERINE RAINWATER

What makes a novel "Native American"? Is its content or the author's ethnic identity the stronger decisive factor? In the latter case, what percentage of Indian or any other type of blood confers ethnic status upon one's writings? Is one-quarter enough, one-sixteenth too little? According to ethnologists, a sizable portion of Americans have at least one American Indian ancestor, yet no equal proportion of American writers claim to be Indian writers. So, does the nature of the author's experience as an Indian count more than his or her genetic heritage? How does such experience somehow make the text "Native American" when, after all, the novel is basically a Western genre that powerfully resists many kinds of non-Western expression? If both authorial experience and ethnic status determine the "Indianness" of a work, what accounts for a remark once made to me that the controversial Heyemeyohsts Storm, a mixed-blood Cheyenne writer, is not a "real" Indian author whose books should be taken seriously? What about the fact that works by Tony Hillerman (non-Indian) are sometimes included in discussions of "Native American" literature? And finally, since all American writers have descended from one or another ethnic group, why is some American literature read as though it belonged to an apparently monolithic, "dominant" culture while other such literature is treated as though its marginal status were beyond question?[1]

Posed seriously, questions such as these can lead us to a deeper understanding of what constitutes an ethnic sign in American literature or, indeed, in the literature of any ethnically diverse group. Werner Sollors, for example, who sees all of American literature as complexly inscribed with ethnic issues, has argued in "Literature and Ethnicity" that "American literature as a whole can be read as the ancestral footstep or coded hieroglyph of ethnic group life of the past and ethnic tensions in the present" (649).[2] William Boelhower likewise sees "deeply embedded" ethnic signs in all of American literature. He detects an "ethnic deconstructive energy" in American works that is sometimes ignored by critics too hasty to assign particular authors to an alleged monocultural "mainstream." Remarking the "uncontrollable" and "ubiquitous" nature of the ethnic sign throughout American literature, Boelhower contends that it is "a constant source of disturbance" even in "so-called dominant cultural texts" (37–38).

The ethnic sign as a constant source of a particular kind of disturbance marks many contemporary works by Indian writers, including Louise Erdrich, as distinctively "Native American." Such "disturbance" registers subtly as an event in the reading process, and it may be overlooked or screened out altogether by a careless reader who believes, for example, that the "Native Americanness" of a work is exclusively a matter of content or authorial identity, or that ethnic signs can be catalogued, *before* reading, as a list of exotic references to the Other. On the contrary, the most ordinary sign may become "ethnic" in the social semiotic exchange called "reading."

In Erdrich's novels, ethnic signs deprive the potential reader of a comfortable interpretive position relative to the text, a feature of her work that I have discussed elsewhere. Her works thus become ethnosemiotic encounters—events or sites of what Boelhower calls "costructured interpretation"—where negotiating the ethnic sign may result in a reader's intense, self-critical awareness of his or her own role not only in text production, but also in the acts of worldmaking that texts imply (Boelhower 23, 22). *Tracks* (1988) draws on a variety of oral storytelling strategies, including the self-conscious accommodation of cultural "outsiders" in the audience, and thus converts "reader" to "listener." This "reader-as-listener," in turn, confronts a variety of tropes deployed as ethnic signs with potential for renegotiating some of the terms of contact between dominant and marginal cultures. For instance, just as on the literally depicted, historical frontier in *Tracks,* the Anishinabe lose their lands in "a storm of government papers" (*T* 1), on the semiotic frontier comprising the novel, the potential reader must give up some ground in an authorial assault on the conventional position that he or she occupies as a reader.[3] Likewise, *The Bingo Palace* (1994) achieves similar ends, but while the reader is constructed as listener in *Tracks,* in *The Bingo Palace* the reader is constructed as viewer. This "reader-as-viewer," together with several characters including a collective narrator, struggles to decode "pictures" in pursuit of an elusive "larger story" (*BP* 3). This "larger story" eludes our grasp of "the whole of it" (*BP* 5), and decoding the "pictures" forces the "reader-viewer" to reassess the act of "looking" in which he or she is engaged. Indeed, Erdrich's "pictures" in *The Bingo Palace* might be considered semiotic equivalents of iconic gestures that are an important part of oral storytelling.[4] We might say that in *Tracks,* Erdrich stages ethnosemiotic encounters through the "mind's ear" of the reader, while in *The Bingo Palace,* she works through the "mind's eye."

The Snare Hidden in the Words

Even a superficial reader of *Tracks* must notice Erdrich's apparent preoccupation with listening. The word "listen" and its grammatical variants, not to mention synonyms, appear frequently throughout the novel. Moreover, Erdrich creates a gallery of listen*ers,* ranging from characters such as the eavesdropping Pauline Puyat and Boy Lazarre, to the silent (in this novel) Lulu (Nanapush's stated audience), to the novel's reading audience. Erdrich frequently prods the reader to think about the implications of listening to other people's stories, even when "listening" means "hearing" their voices in our heads as we read the words. We understand that to read is to share Pauline's ambiguous "crow" identity—in Nanapush's words, to live on the "scraps" of other people's lives. Indeed, a reader-listener is a kind of eavesdropper, perched like Crow inconspicuously outside the frame of action and savoring tidbits of other people's business.

Such a reader, like Pauline-as-Crow, must consider the unflattering implications of consuming the stories of others. Why *do* we read? Do our motives even slightly resemble Pauline's unsavory ones? What do we do with the stories we gather? Like Crow, readers are snoopers and potentially petty thieves.

Crow and Pauline also have the uncanny ability to be in two places at the same time: Pauline in one scene psychically appropriates Sophie's body to enjoy the effects of a love potion on Eli Kashpaw. This ability extends to the reader, who is simultaneously outside the text and "inside," imaginatively appropriating the lives and experiences of various characters. Erdrich even implies that like Pauline and Crow, the reader is responsible for the use of such voyeuristically acquired knowledge. Pauline (and potentially any listener) can "create damage" by repeating what she hears without regard to story's power to cure or kill (*T* 39).

The reader-as-listener shares with Pauline and Crow another important trait—"invisibility." Pauline is "invisible" primarily because none of the other characters pay her serious attention. Like Crow, she learns to take advantage of her inconspicuousness. The reader, on the other hand, is literally "invisible" through absence to the storyteller. Unlike oral storytelling, written storytelling is directed to an absent audience. In a series of paradigmatic equivalents of the reader, Erdrich implies that such absent, "invisible" listeners can be dangerous. Characters in the text repeatedly worry about who might be listening, including spirits and people who might act maliciously or irresponsibly (as Crow might, and Pauline does). To be overheard by spirits is dangerous because a person can become the object of their unwanted attention. Listening to some spirits can drive a person "windigo," infect him or her with the "invisible sickness" (maladies which, a reader should note, are connected in *Tracks* with listening to disembodied voices).

Clearly, the reader is urged to add him- or herself to the long list of potentially threatening and threatened listeners named in the narrative. Erdrich's implied agenda is to make such an invisible reader-listener aware of both responsibilities and liabilities incurred in hearing stories. While oral storytellers develop specific, dramatic methods for instructing the listening audience and for directing the responses of cultural outsiders, the novel's absent or invisible audience is more difficult to manage and, indeed, more likely to contain "outsiders." Nevertheless, Erdrich finds ways to direct her "absent" audience; Nanapush is Erdrich's responsible storyteller and authorial ventriloquist who subtly instructs the reader in an ethics of "listening." His stories remind the reader of the power of words over a hostile or irresponsible listener.

Rife with tropes or ethnic signs fostering an ethnosemiotic encounter, Nanapush's narration frequently challenges the reader-listener to reassess his or her involvement in storytelling. Nanapush uses story figuratively to "drown" the well-intentioned but meddlesome, ethnocentric Father Damien and, by implication, the reader, another outsider-listener. (Drowning is the worst means of death imaginable to a Chippewa.)[5] In a thinly disguised warning to the reader, an eavesdropper on his story addressed to Lulu, Nanapush threatens: "I talked both languages in streams that ran alongside each other. . . . I kept Father Damien listening all night. . . . Occasionally, he took in air . . . but I pushed him under with my words" (*T* 7). To emphasize his point, Nanapush equates words with water many times throughout his narrated passages. (Silence was a "frozen state" [*T* 8, 31], speech a "thawing" [*T* 205]; conversational "waters were . . . muddy" with rumors and lies [*T* 61], etc.). This trope of watery submergence, or "drowning," appears throughout each of Erdrich's novels, but in *Tracks* it is especially conspicuous as an ethnic sign serving to apprise the wary reader of the dangers of irresponsible consumption of other peoples' stories.

Nanapush also lets us know that story can be used to fend off Death, as well as to summon it. Nanapush defeats Death by "starting a story" and not letting Death "get a word in edgewise" (*T* 46). His words in this case imply that Death is yet another type of invisible listener—another unflattering, paradigmatic equivalent to the reader. Fortunately, Nanapush (and Erdrich) ultimately have the best interests of the reader in mind. Though they suggest that a powerful storyteller poses a threat to a careless reader-as-listener, they simultaneously offer the reader a variety of opportunities to revise ethnocentric, appropriative, and other destructive types of readerly habits such as those of Pauline, who "creates damage" (*T* 39) or of Father Damien, who would use against the Chippewa the knowledge that he had acquired in his "well-intentioned" but misguided efforts to help.

In overdetermining the equation between listening and reading, Erdrich defines at least one role of the reader in this text as that of an outsider to be either fended off altogether or, preferably, instructed in the art of listening to the Other. The "disturbing" (cf. Boelhower) trope of "drowning" is complexly encoded by Erdrich with its Chippewa, contextual meaning (drowning prevents the victim's entry into the spirit world) and with further meaning generated by the immediate narrative (verbal "drowning" perhaps, prevents the reader's entry into a Native American reality sustained by the text). "Drowning" thus becomes one of several highly charged ethnic signs in *Tracks*—part of a semiotic network of references instructing the reader to confront his or her own identity as a heedless consumer of the "scraps" of other people's lives, or as a responsible participant in storytelling. Erving Goffman, Andrew Wiget, and other scholars of oral performance remind us that audience "engrossment" includes listener accountability for yielding collaboratively to the power of the storyteller, whose many roles include being a transformer of the audience. In this novel that fashions semiotic equivalents to oral performance, the trope of "drowning" thus becomes a site of "co-structured interpretation," a site at which authorial demands on the reader call for various types of renegotiation—renegotiation of meaning as well as of the "listener's" place in the storytelling process. Consequently, *Tracks* may be seen as a subtly reappropriative gesture: whereas history has seen repeated incursions by non-Indians upon Indian "territory," contemporary "word warriors" such as Erdrich and other current Indian writers stand fast against ill-informed, misguided cultural appropriation of Indian "stories" (including histories, art, etc.).

Erdrich deploys another major trope as ethnic sign in *Tracks* and, as we shall see, in *The Bingo Palace.* This trope of the snare likewise causes the reader to ponder his or her own role as defined by the Native American storyteller. A most memorable scene in *Tracks* finds Clarence Morrissey about to fall into a snare set by Nanapush and Eli. Moving means possible death, and not moving means straddling the pit until fatigue brings the inevitable fall. The snare "had been invisible," says Nanapush, "and yet in one foot-pedaling instant as he fell, the certain knowledge of its construction sprang into Clarence's brain" (*T* 122–23). Clarence's position is the figurative equivalent of the reader's, potentially caught in the "snare" of words set by Erdrich through her ventriloquist character Nanapush, who is thoroughly knowledgeable of the "traps" set by storytellers like himself. For instance, he remarks of Father Damien, "I had taught him well [how to set verbal traps, so] . . . I saw the snare [in his argument] . . . the invisible loop hidden in the priest's well-meaning words" (*T* 185). Also paradigmatically replicated in Clarence's "spread-eagled" stance is his own bicultural identity. The halfblood straddles the space between two cultures, always a potential victim of snares set within the double-coded semiotic system that defines a cross-cultural reality. Only a small step is required to appreciate how this dilemma is, in turn, replicated in the position of the reader who must avoid a one-sided reading of a cross-coded, bicultural text such as *Tracks*. Erdrich has set a semiotic trap for her reader, for whom "the certain knowledge of its construction" should, ideally, spring clear.

In light of this implied equation between the snared Morrissey and the reader, the pattern of Clarence's and Boy Lazarre's scars—the legacy of Nanapush's trap—is itself a subtly encoded reference to storytelling. These scars lie on the mouth, neck, arm, and fingers (sources of the voice, on the one hand, and of signing and writing, on the other). Says Nanapush, "perhaps my snare did damage, taught a temporary lesson. The drag of Clarence's mouth was permanent." Lazarre's "fingers grew weak and numb" (*T* 123). Nanapush's "lesson" is ultimately a warning to the reader about the proper positions to assume when telling and listening to stories. Pauline's position is especially to be avoided; a counterexample of the ideal reader and straddling the bicultural gap in undesirable ways, she constructs a frightening, damaging, albeit cross-cultural reality from bizarrely interpreted "scraps" of Western and Native American "stories" that she has collected.

Erdrich's implied reader is informed and instructed; her ideal reader is not drowned by the words of the text, but perhaps she is instead like Fleur Pillager, a creature at home in the water, or like Nanapush himself, who can see "invisible snares" and who sees "the deadfall beneath [his] feet before [he] step[s]" (*T* 185). Fleur repeatedly escapes "drowning," and Nanapush perfects the art of ethical listening and storytelling. He wields the power of words with great finesse, able to inflict measured amounts of damage, able deliberately to "cure or kill." His keen senses extend even to the "reading" of messages in the "leaves" of his beloved trees.

Nanapush's perfected art contains a further lesson for the attentive reader. At the conclusion of *Tracks*, Erdrich introduces another ethnic sign requiring sophisticated response on the reader's part. On a note of ostensible defeat, Nanapush declares that the Chippewa are no longer anything more than a "tribe of file cabinets and triplicates, a tribe of single-space documents, directives, policy. A tribe of pressed trees. A tribe of chicken-scratch that can be scattered by a wind" (*T* 225). Though these metaphors at first appear merely self-deprecating, Nanapush the trickster must certainly be aware of their double-coded message for the alert reader, who knows that "pressed trees," or paper, are what books are made of, and that there is more than one way to "translate the language of . . . leaves" (*T* 210). Though the tribe may be reduced to papers made of cherished trees stripped from lost lands, Erdrich is living proof that Indians also write countercolonial stories on paper, stories aimed at the "invisible" listener-reader in an effort to recolonize the colonizer, if we understand colonization as involving the appropriation of mental space and the revision of interpretive frames of reference.[6] If Nanapush's literal strength ebbs with the disappearance of the actual trees, his storyteller's trickster power as Erdrich's ventriloquist increases with the use of the "pressed trees" as "leaves" of books. Erdrich's trope of the "tribe of pressed trees" refers subtly to a steadily increasing "tribe" of books such as those by Erdrich and other Native American writers that aim to revise not simply the record of the past, but the shape of the future. Their readers are, ideally, displaced from a position of careless-consumer-of-exotica to that of an active agent in a social semiotic revision of contemporary reality.

I See and I Am Caught

Like the other novels in Erdrich's "paper tribe," *The Bingo Palace* works for audience "engrossment" with an instructive, potentially world-altering purpose. Through a narrative equation between reading and looking at pictures, Erdrich shows how photographs and various other types of visual representations may be "traps," capable of ensnaring the viewer within fixed frames of reference. She shows us the power that lies in recognizing such "invisible snares," in seeing "the deadfall beneath [our] feet before [we] step" (*T* 185). Like her preoccupation with listening in *Tracks,* Erdrich's preoccupation with looking in *The Bingo Palace* appears designed to "disturb" the reader's conventionally stable interpretive position in relation to the narrative and, furthermore, to increase reader self-consciousness about interpretive acts. Enhancing reader awareness of visual decoding processes is a narrative equivalent of the instructive and affective "iconic gestures" of oral performance. Indeed, Erdrich's "gestures" expand the projected reader's awareness of the epistemic nature of representation and broaden the base of American Indian semiotic power through textualized, countercolonial moves, as we shall see.

The kinesic dimension of oral storytelling involves body language that communicates to the audience a wealth of information about possible responses to the narration.[7] Through a variety of gestures, oral narrators both express and delimit their own authority to suggest that the story itself is greater than the storyteller, that storytellers are not the final arbiters of meaning, and that, in fact, the story as told is a variant, not a "definitive text" belonging to a particular "author."[8] In *The Bingo Palace,* Erdrich fashions a collective narrative voice composed of tribal elders who, like a traditional oral storyteller, combine authority and humility. For example, they admit that, like the audience, they cannot always "grasp the whole" (*BP* 5) of the story being told. Through such proclaimed doubt, hesitancy, and overt interpretive struggles, Erdrich's collective narrator aligns itself with the audience and elicits creative audience participation in storytelling. As in oral literature, narrator and audience alike face interpretive problems and share responsibility for the story's effects.

The collective narrator in *The Bingo Palace* openly dialogues with the audience on the subject of looking at pictures; furthermore, both collectively narrated sections and those narrated by Lipsha Morrissey are rife with pictorial tropes that overdetermine the equation between seeing and reading. Overall, the narrative insists that looking at pictures is predicated on habits of perception that determine not only how we interpret, but also how we actively respond to such pictures. Fully aware of this fact, Lulu Lamartine and Zelda Kashpaw draw suspicious and unsuspecting "viewers" alike into the "snare" that their artful "designs" comprise, in Erdrich's view. Lulu's and Zelda's spider-like relationship to their prey resembles that between authors and readers, or between graphic artists and viewers. Both women manage others by subtly shaping a worldview before the eyes of their unsuspecting "victims." Lipsha, in particular, seems destined to fall prey to both women's "traps."

The novel opens with Lulu Lamartine's theft from the U.S. Post Office of a Wanted Poster depicting her son, Gerry Nanapush. She photocopies it, mails the copy to Lipsha Morrissey (Gerry's son), frames the original, and places it "where you couldn't help noticing it upon first entering her apartment" (*BP* 5). The collective narrator informs us that a deliberate design lies behind Lulu's visual arrangement. Determined to free her son from prison and to enlist the (witting or unwitting) aid of other people in her effort, Lulu sets up a mysterious pattern of events that begins with the photograph. Not even the "elders" understand exactly how she works her ultimately successful spell: "Lulu Lamartine was sending the picture of the father to the son. . . . Surely, it meant something. There was always a reason behind the things Lulu did, although it took a while to find them, to work her ciphers out for meaning. . . . [I]n her small act there was a complicated motive and a larger story" (*BP* 3). By the end of the novel, her plan has worked. When federal marshals come to arrest her for assisting a fugitive (a charge that will not stick), Lulu, dressed beautifully in ceremonial garb, cries out a "victory yell" (*BP* 265). On the scene to snap pictures of her in her "planned" victory are the media: "All of the North Dakota newspapers" will unwittingly publish photos of Lulu's victory and perhaps contribute to the further advancement of her scheme (*BP* 264).

Lulu's "snare" begins with a carefully placed picture in her apartment, along with a copy of it deliberately placed in Lipsha's possession. Despite themselves, those drawn into her design begin to fall under Lulu's control. The collective narrator's response to Lulu's plot corresponds to the model reader's response to "designs" of the sort set in motion by authors such as Erdrich herself: "Some of us tried to resist [looking at the picture of Gerry], yet were pulled in just the same. We were curious to know more, even though we'd never grasp the whole of it. The story comes around, pushing at our brains, and soon we are trying to ravel back to the beginning, trying to put families into order and make sense of things. But we start with one person, and soon another and another follows, and still another, until we are lost in the connections" (*BP* 5). This passage is a metacritical statement upon the act of looking at the "designs" that artists set up, whether verbal or visual. Once a reader begins to "see" the "picture," to detect the hint of a pattern, he or she is "pulled in . . . curious to know more." The careless reader is virtually ensnared in the view or vision of the world implied in the pattern, while the careful reader sees "the snare . . . the invisible loop hidden in the . . . words" (*T* 185) and begins to develop a more epistemologically sophisticated, larger vision of "reality" as a socially constructed, malleable phenomenon.

Like Lulu, Zelda Kashpaw and Fleur "Mindemoya" Pillager are powerful old women who have learned how to entangle others in their snares. Zelda "scans" Lipsha's mind with the "sudden zero-gaze" of a "medical machine," and she "reads" the "map of [his] feelings" before she weaves her own design around him (*BP* 18). Zelda means to use Lipsha to cement the relationship between Shawnee Ray and Lyman Lamartine. Knowing he has already succumbed to Lulu's power conveyed through the Wanted Poster, Lipsha now suspects he has fallen "into Zelda's range," as well: "I am drawn back specifically *to watch* [emphasis mine] the circle where that pretty [Shawnee Ray] Toose now appears[.] And Shawnee Ray herself . . . has she rolled me into each one of her snuff-can-top jingles [on her dress]? Sewed me into her dress with a fine needle?" (*BP* 19).

Schemers such as Lulu and Zelda are not the only arrangers of powerful designs. Erdrich shows that the individual mind itself is "authorial" in its arrangement of mental pictures, including those we call memories. As Lipsha says, "I see [the pictures in my memory], and I am caught" (*BP* 152). A victim of his own habits of mind as well as of other people's designs, Lipsha admits to "airbrushing" the past (*BP* 188). When he dislikes an experience, he revises it: "I try to recast the whole scene in my thoughts" (*BP* 190). This tendency to avoid "reading" the pictures before him and, instead, to see what he wants to see is largely responsible for Lipsha's fate. Though he claims a Pillager heritage, he seems to lack definitive Pillager traits, especially the ability to alter his apparent fate first by straightforwardly recognizing the "traps" such as Lulu's and Zelda's that lie in his path. Whereas Fleur has eluded the Lake Man of Matchimanito for years, even sending others to drown in her place, Lipsha seems unable to extricate himself from the simplest of "webs" (*BP* 21).

In fact, ill-fated Lipsha in *The Bingo Palace* takes the brunt of the collective narrator's criticism: "We weren't very pleased with the picture" of Lipsha's life (*BP* 8). He becomes the textual equivalent of the naive reader. Lipsha does not hear (he misconstrues Gerry's telephone message because he does not understand Chippewa), nor does he see (he "airbrushes"). He is an easy victim of other peoples' and his own artful semiosis. Indeed, the collective narrator contemptuously reduces him to a semiotic phenomenon—the "son of a poster" (*BP* 7)—a trope to be manipulated by someone more clever, such as Lulu. When he visits Fleur Pillager in her cabin, he cannot read or speak her "language" (literally, Chippewa, but also Fleur's "language" of power, not to mention fate, the "writing on the wall," so to speak). The visit leaves him dazed, as if under a heavy spell. "Weakening and dizzy," Lipsha says, "I look at the strange lines on her walls, between the neat stacks of letters, and pick out familiar patterns. . . . I am reading a set of words, a sentence, something that loops toward the window, which makes no sense to me and which I can't understand. . . . I [am] afraid that I have fallen under some sort of spell" (*BP* 135–36).

Indeed, Lipsha is a trope (a "son of a poster") in somebody else's "sentence" (Lulu's, Fleur's, and, of course, Erdrich's); he is under someone else's "spell" (as a character he is in their power, and as a trope he is a "sign" in their system, a "spelled" phenomenon). Because he is so naive,

Lipsha has little hope of seeing the "design" of the verbal and visual traps "spring clear" (*T* 34). For Lipsha, the consequence of such naiveté is death, for (as Nanapush tells us in *Tracks*) stories, including the stories contained in pictures, can "cure or kill." Saved from drowning as a baby abandoned in a slough, Lipsha nevertheless meets his apparently fated death by water, literally by freezing to death at the end of his trek with Gerry, who has successfully escaped from prison with Lulu's deliberate and Lipsha's unwitting aid. Frozen within the "designs" of others, Lipsha in death reminds us of Nanapush's remarks in *Tracks* concerning Father Damien, whom Nanapush "drowns" by "push[ing] him under with . . . words" (*T* 7).

Whereas Lipsha remains naive and dies as an example of a poor "reader," the collective narrator's "gestures" to the actual audience, as we have seen, include metacritical cues that make the careful reader aware of the power of "pictures" like those of Erdrich and other authors. Moreover, Erdrich further manages her audience through skilled deployment of the countercolonial trope, a type of "hook" that snags an attentive reader not only while reading *The Bingo Palace,* but possibly forever after. Adept readers, unlike Lipsha in Fleur's cabin, learn with the help of narrative cues to decode the "sentence" in which they are immersed; moreover, under Erdrich's "spell," such readers are also profoundly affected by her unique management of the ethnic sign.

Simply Extract the Hook

Implied throughout *The Bingo Palace* in the multiple overdetermined trope of ensnarement (photographs, webs, nets, and sewn and beaded garments) is the notion that stories contained in verbal and visual designs can change the world, beginning with the perceptual and interpretive habits of readers. Like Lipsha, readers and viewers may become implicated or "trapped" within the "design" of an authoritative consciousness, and this design may, in turn, affect their actions, especially their subsequent habits of interpretation. For some contemporary American Indian writers such as Erdrich, to change a reader's habits of interpretation amounts to a subtle, countercolonial, and reappropriative act. Like her character Fleur Pillager, who gambles to repossess lost Chippewa lands, Erdrich plays a textual game with the aim of appropriating the semiotic space of the novel, previously dominated by Eurocentric storytellers with Eurocentric frames of reference.

As we have seen, a significant portion of the narrative energy of her novels is devoted to bringing all preconceived frames of reference into question, especially through the example of Lipsha, the naive "airbrusher" who does not even know his own native language. Erdrich is not satisfied with raising questions, however. Her writings marshal the "deconstructive energy" of the ethnic sign in an ultimate countercolonial move designed to change her audience's ways of seeing, hearing, and knowing. After all, the ultimate colonial act is to appropriate the intellectual, psychological, and emotional space of the Other—to alter his or her sense of reality. Fleur Pillager, Lulu Lamartine, and Zelda Kashpaw each present to the attentive reader alternative schemes for the construction of "reality" that resist Eurocentric explanation, not the least of which schemes assume that well-managed stories can "cure or kill," and that storytellers and listeners alike are directly responsible for the beliefs, attitudes, and actions that stories engender. As originators of stories or as willing participants in the designs that others' stories comprise, we conspire in the ongoing creation, or destruction, of realities.

In *The Bingo Palace,* Erdrich's various tropes of ensnarement, especially the trope of the picture and the accompanying act of looking, serve as ethnic signs to "dispel" the Eurocentric "spell" that dictates a way of seeing and interpreting the world, as well as to introduce an alternative epistemology. The ethnic sign, with its disruptive, deconstructive energy, is a "hook." Generating hesitation and doubt, it helps to clear a space in the reader's mind for expanded interpretive possibilities; it redefines the position of the reader with regard to the text, now conceived as an opportunity to participate in, or to resist, the designs of the storyteller.

One passage from *The Bingo Palace* especially emphasizes how the ethnic sign serves as a "hook" for the author-as-fisherman who casts for the minds and hearts of the audience. A consummate gambler (and fisherman—recall how Fleur "reels in" her prey in the fateful card game in *Tracks* [23]), Fleur Pillager appears on the reservation dressed as a warrior with a white Pierce-Arrow and a strange, otherworldly white boy. This white boy, doubtless Erdrich's version of the Chippewa "evil gambler," plays cards with Fleur and Tatro, the Indian Agent. Tatro, like a hooked, "gasping fish" (*BP* 145), is easy prey in Fleur's design to repossess her lands. He wants to win the Pierce-Arrow so badly that he fails to see how Fleur has set him up: "Even the boy did not deflect his attention, though if Tatro had not been preoccupied, he would have asked questions enough to form an explanation. The automobile, the clarity of his own greed, concentrated him. He looked at the car, he looked at Fleur, and that is when we realized that the decoy was not the boy, as we previously believed, but the car. Large parcels and belongings would soon change owners" (*BP* 143). In the end, Fleur wins back everything, including the car. "As for the Agent, the car, you do not feed bait to a gasping fish. . . . You simply extract the hook" (*BP* 145).

This humorous scene is also a metacritical "picture" from which the alert reader may learn much. It is rife with cues alerting the reader to Erdrich's reappropriative aim, which, ironically, succeeds best in the case of the adept reader who has played the textual game fully enough to be thoroughly, but not naively, "hooked" into Erdrich's design. In this game, Erdrich as author corresponds to Fleur, the designer of the game. The reader corresponds to the sidelined collective narrator, who struggles to perceive Fleur's design, and to Tatro, who must ultimately cede some of his territory. Like Tatro, distracted by the whiteness of Fleur's dress, the whiteness of the Pierce-Arrow, and finally, the eerie whiteness of the strange boy, the reader is distracted by the whiteness of the page into thinking that he or she is engaged in the simple ("white," Eurocentric) "game" of *merely* reading a story. Such a reader does not at first, or perhaps ever, consciously realize that some of his or her mental space has been appropriated by a member of a "tribe of pressed trees." Though neither this metaphor of the reader-as-gasping-fish, nor the earlier metaphors of the reader as snared prey, is especially flattering, the fact is that, like Lipsha, Tatro, and Clarence Morrissey, we "are caught"—in a new frame of reference, the "trap" of the countercolonial design of Erdrich's story.

Erdrich's texts potentially revise the interpretive frames of reference through which readers will encounter other Indian writers' works, including Erdrich's. The members of her "tribe of pressed trees" are intertextually related not only to one another, but also to works by Indian authors such as Leslie Marmon Silko, N. Scott Momaday, Thomas King, Gerald Vizenor, and others who seem to share some of her cross-cultural aims. Such works open up a different kind of semiotic space within the overall "terrain" of North American literature, where until recently few Indian voices and worldviews have been present. An ethical and responsible storyteller, Erdrich leads her readers (Indian and non-Indian alike) to see that there are no innocent participants in storytelling, given its dramatic potential for transforming the world.[9]

Notes

1. Henry Louis Gates, Jr., makes some fascinating observations on this subject of authenticity. His discussion underscores the perils of simplistic assumptions about what makes a text "Indian" or "African American," etc.

2. See also Sollors' Introduction to *The Invention of Ethnicity*.

3. On the ethnic writer's management of the reader's interpretive position vis-à-vis the text, see Vévé Clark's excellent essay.

4. On the subject of audience accommodation through iconic gestures in Pueblo oral performance, see, for example, Andrew Wiget.

5. Several of Erdrich's characters remark that drowning is a death no Chippewa can survive. Their belief is that the drowned victim cannot begin the afterlife journey to the Land of Souls. On Chippewa beliefs about death, see Basil Johnston.

6. Gloria Bird discusses Erdrich's dialogue on colonialism in *Tracks*.

7. Wiget's essay explains this kinesic dimension of oral performance. See also Boelhower on the kinesic role of signs in literature, both oral and written.

8. See Elaine Jahner's remarks on narrator authority and responsibility in oral literature and in written texts by Native American writers (especially N. Scott Momaday) that derive from oral literature: "Metalanguages," 163; and "Indian Literature and Critical Responsibility," 7–12. See also James Flavin; and see James Ruppert's remarks on Erdrich's attempts to reproduce oral narrative in writing.

9. The *Tracks* portion of this essay was presented on 1 October 1993 at a meeting of the American Literature Association in San Antonio, Texas, as "'A Tribe of Pressed Trees': Louise Erdrich and the Reappropriation of America in *Tracks*."

Works Cited

Bird, Gloria. "Searching for Evidence of Colonialism at Work: A Reading of Louise Erdrich's *Tracks*." *Wicazo Sa Review* 8.2 (1992): 40–47.

Boelhower, William. *Through a Glass Darkly: Ethnic Semiosis in American Literature.* New York: Oxford UP, 1987.

Clark, Vévé. "Developing Diaspora Literacy and *Marasa* Consciousness." *Comparative American Identities: Race, Sex, and Nationality in the Modern Text.* Ed. Hortense Spillers. New York: Routledge, 1991. 40–61.

Flavin, James. "The Novel as Performance: Communication in Louise Erdrich's *Tracks*." *Studies in American Indian Literatures* 3 (1994): 1–12.

Gates, Henry Louis, Jr. "'Authenticity,' or the Lesson Little Tree." *New York Times Book Review* 24 November 1991: 1, 26–30.

Jahner, Elaine. "Metalanguages." *Narrative Chance: Postmodern Discourse on Native American Indian Literatures.* Ed. Gerald Vizenor. Albuquerque: U of New Mexico P, 1989.

———. "Indian Literature and Critical Responsibility." *Studies in American Indian Literatures* 5 (1993): 7–12.

Johnston, Basil. *Ojibway Ceremonies.* Lincoln: U of Nebraska P, 1982.

Rainwater, Catherine. "Reading Between Worlds: Narrativity in the Fiction of Louise Erdrich." *American Literature* 62.3 (1990): 405–22.

———. "'A Tribe of Pressed Trees': Louise Erdrich and the Reappropriation of America in *Tracks*." American Literature Association. San Antonio, Texas, 1 October 1993.

Ruppert, James. "Mediation and Multiple Narrative in *Love Medicine*." *North Dakota Quarterly* 59.4 (1991): 229–41.

Sollors, Werner. "Introduction." *The Invention of Ethnicity.* Ed. Werner Sollors. New York: Oxford UP, 1989. ix–xx.

———. "Literature and Ethnicity." *Harvard Encyclopedia of American Ethnic Groups.* Ed. Stephan Thernstrom. Cambridge, Mass.: Belknap-Harvard UP, 1981. 649.

Wiget, Andrew. "Telling the Tale: A Performance Analysis of a Hopi Coyote Story." *Recovering the Word: Essays on Native American Literature.* Ed. Brian Swann and Arnold Krupat. Berkeley: U of California P, 1987. 297–387.

8

Indi'n Humor and Trickster Justice in *The Bingo Palace*

Nancy J. Peterson

If it is fair to describe Louise Erdrich's *Tracks* as a novel entirely haunted by historical dispossession and tribal splintering, with only small hope for effective resistance, Erdrich's subsequent novel, *The Bingo Palace,* seems remarkably different in tone and plot. *The Bingo Palace* returns to the often startling moments of levity and absurdity that were apparent in Erdrich's first two novels, *Love Medicine* and *The Beet Queen,* moments that typically cannot be articulated within the lines of the tragic-historical narrative that haunts *Tracks.* In sharp contrast, *The Bingo Palace* foregrounds a classical comic plot—the romance plot—as it follows Lipsha Morrissey's uncontrollable passion for Shawnee Ray Toose, who has had a baby and an affair with his uncle Lyman Lamartine, a successful entrepreneur and respected tribal member.

Lipsha's desire for Shawnee Ray and his contest with Lyman to win her affection furnish the novel with some hilarious scenes. On his first date with Shawnee Ray, Lipsha's adrenaline rush turns to embarrassment at the U.S.-Canadian border, when he is arrested for drug possession—which might turn into material for serious consideration had the border patrol not mistaken an old-time pemmican fruitcake (that Zelda had given Lipsha and that he didn't want in the first place) for hash! Later in the novel, a verbal joust between Lipsha and Lyman over Shawnee Ray breaks out into a physical confrontation at a Dairy Queen and produces an impromptu food fight. "Doing a flying drop kick," Lipsha explains, "I knock into an entire large-size family who are carefully turning from the ice cream counter and balancing five-topping sundaes with whipped cream and cherries. The cherries explode into the air, the walnut bits zing sideways, the ice cream blobs collide at super speed," and the Dairy Queen erupts with "one big explosion" (*BP* 167). Driving away from the scene of the food fight, though, Lipsha and Lyman do not continue their battle but instead forge lines of connection, and Lipsha discovers that "mixing it up with Lyman doesn't unwedge either my friendship feelings for him or my love for Shawnee Ray" (*BP* 169). Because of this friendship, it is perhaps not so surprising that Lipsha and Lyman subsequently go together to Xavier Toose's to participate in a sweat lodge ceremony and fast for a spiritual vision. Even this very serious ceremonial endeavor, however, produces comic results: while Lyman has a vision that reconciles him to his brother Henry's suicide, Lipsha is visited by a skunk—literally.

By providing such moments of slapstick and humor, Erdrich insists that readers recognize Indians not as tragic victims but as comic actors and agents. This point is particularly important given that early reviewers of Erdrich's novels missed the humorous elements in them. In a 1986 interview conducted by Hertha Wong, Erdrich observes that literary critics tended to characterize *Love Medicine* as "devastating," but tribal people saw it as "funny" (Erdrich and Dorris 49).[1] We might wonder what lies behind such a dramatic contrast in interpretations, how it is possible for comedy in a novel like *Love Medicine* to be (mis)read as tragedy.

Part of the answer surely involves the tragically romantic narrative of native peoples as vanishing victims that became such a predominant trope in the late nineteenth century and that continues to reappear even today. This narrative gained legitimacy as it was communicated in and reinforced by the kinds of photographs taken of Indians at the time, particularly photos made by the famous Edward S. Curtis, who is perhaps best known for an image titled "The Vanishing Indian—Navajo,"[2] and by various photographers in the service of the federal government, employed to capture on film delegations of Indians when they came to Washington to conduct or protest treaty negotiations. In these photographs, the subjects sit stoically and solemnly facing the camera: almost never does one come across a person who is smiling. Given these photographs, a viewer might be tempted to interpret Native Americans as "naturally" serious, as "essentially" humorless, but Gerald Vizenor has suggested that such images are not accurate representations but the effects of photographic practices of the late-nineteenth and early-twentieth centuries, when camera technology (especially the length of time needed for proper exposure) required Indian subjects to remain unsmiling so that they could sit as still as possible while the shutter was held open (*Crossbloods* 48, 84–86). Elsewhere Vizenor contends that "tragic modes are inventions and impositions that attend the 'discoverers' and translators of tribal narratives" and that are related to white culture's desire to construct Indians as "vanishing" people (*Narrative Chance* 9–10). In opposition to what he calls this "*hypotragic* intrusion," Vizenor argues that native cultures have a profound (but typically unrecognized) connection to comic modes, as can be witnessed in trickster stories, oral traditions, and the communal emphasis of tribal narratives.

Clearly cross-cultural misinterpretation might lead to a reading of *Love Medicine* as devastating rather than funny, but the complex nature of tribal humor is another significant factor. The examples from *The Bingo Palace* mentioned above not only suggest Erdrich's interest in comic effects, but also point to the intermixture of comic laughter and serious matters that has made her vision of Native America so compelling. In various interviews, Erdrich has articulated a complicated approach to the issue of native humor, suggesting that laughter and a sense of humor are pan-Indian ceremonies, enabling tribal peoples to deal with the terrible hands they have been dealt. "Ironic survival humor," Erdrich calls it in a 1989 interview conducted by Bill Moyers, "enables you to live with what you have to live with." One of the things native peoples have had to learn to live with is injustice; after her comments about humor, Erdrich informs Moyers that "when you grow up and see your people living on a tiny pittance of land or living on the edge, surrounded by enormous wealth, you don't see the world as just" (Erdrich and Dorris 144).

Erdrich's comments anticipate one of the most significant observations in Kenneth Lincoln's *Indi'n Humor: Bicultural Play in Native America,* in which Lincoln argues that Indi'n humor is fundamentally connected to the wounds of history: "After five hundred years of dispossession—germ and conventional warfare, bounty hunting, guns, plows, telegraph poles, trains, barbed wire enclosures, land swindles, and outright stealing—native peoples still persist on some 53 million acres of reservation land left over from the great dirt grab. . . . [C]learly, humor both targets and takes some fatal sting out of history" (54–55). Indi'n humor thus acts as a survival strategy and as a healing ceremony. Lincoln's approach to Indi'n humor provides a means of understanding the complex comic dynamics of Erdrich's most recent novel as well as the ways in which *The Bingo Palace* moves toward an unprecedented development—the emergence of a new kind of Indi'n humor rising out of triumphant laughter and (postmodern) trickster justice.

Indi'n Humor

Early on in *The Bingo Palace,* Lipsha notes with amusement that the competition between Lyman and himself over Shawnee Ray is serious but not vicious. He relates this good-natured rivalry to their Indianness, in fact: "Reading is my number-one hobby," Lipsha confesses, "and I have browsed a few of the plays of the old-time Greeks. If you read about a thing like Lyman and me happening in those days, one or both of us would surely have to die. But us Indians, we're so used to inner plot twists that we just laugh" (*BP* 17). As individual men in love with the same woman, Lipsha and Lyman are adversaries, but as Indians, used to dealing with ironies and the twisted plots and words of the federal government, Lipsha and Lyman know how to recognize an absurd situation and laugh about it rather than come to blows. Lincoln's treatment of Indi'n humor pays particular attention to the bicultural dynamics evident in Lipsha's remark. As "a form of public teasing to raise Indian-white issues," Indi'n humor mediates conflicts between the dominant culture and Native America (Lincoln 25). Drawing on Freud's analysis of jokes as making sense out of nonsense, combining bewilderment and amazement, Lincoln demonstrates that Native American jokes are both playful and deliberate: jokes about Indian-white relations have to be taken "not too seriously, so as not to wreck the playful construct on the rocks of reality, and yet seriously enough to engage the mind in unpuzzling the real" (35). In other words, Indi'n humor enables the participants to laugh and lift their spirits, but it also prepares them to face a sobering reality—the reality of living in a society that privileges whiteness at every turn. The episode in *The Bingo Palace* when Lipsha encounters the bigoted Anglo gas station convenience store clerk illustrates what is at stake in this kind of joking. Lipsha has entered the store to buy condoms so he and Shawnee Ray can have their first intimate moment, but he is so nervous about the purchase and dazzled by the numerous choices that he quickly picks up two boxes of economy size, setting in motion the verbal combat that follows. When the clerk asks him if he is on a "'heavy date,'" Lipsha—having already noticed that the clerk is wearing a T-shirt with Big Sky Country written on it—sees the clerk's ugly grin and responds: "'Not really. Fixing up a bunch of my white buddies from Montana. Trying to keep down the sheep population'" (*BP* 70). The humorous jousting gets more intense, with Lipsha following up on the sheep innuendoes and the clerk resorting to racist innuendo, at one point asking Lipsha which species he belongs to. As Lipsha turns to leave the store he hears the clerk mutter "prairie nigger"—a phrase so wounding Lipsha can hardly believe he hears it right. "'What?'" Lipsha turns and asks, "'What'd you say?'" (*BP* 71). There is a standoff at this point, until Lipsha gets to the door of the store and cries out "'Baah . . . '" (*BP* 71). He gets the last line and the last laugh, at least for the moment, and triumphs to the extent that he gets the upper hand in a potentially devastating and dehumanizing situation.

Joking under these conditions becomes a way to turn pain into pleasure, as Lincoln suggests. But what are the limits of such joking? Can jokes be effective in renegotiating Indian-white power relations? *The Bingo Palace* takes on this issue in the subsequent meeting between Lipsha and the Big Sky Country clerk. After Lipsha has the amazing fortune to win the grand prize at bingo—a fully equipped van—he can't help but want to show it off. With Shawnee Ray unavailable, Lipsha heads for a party in Hoopdance and unfortunately encounters the same clerk with some of his friends. To put Lipsha in his place, they decide to force him to get the state of Montana tattooed on his buttocks. Although Lipsha tries to inject humor into the situation, even pleading for a different form of retribution ("'Just beat me up, you guys. Let's get this over with'" [*BP* 80]), the white guys are the only ones who laugh at this moment in this encounter. Luckily, for Lipsha, the tattooist is a fellow Chippewa, Russell Kashpaw, who listens attentively while the Anglos describe what kind of map they want Lipsha to have ("'Like [one] of those maps we did in grade school showing products from each region. Cows' heads, oil wells, missile bases, those little sheaves of wheat and so on'") and then gravely instructs the Anglos to tie Lipsha up and "'leave this place'" (*BP* 81). They follow Russell's directions precisely, and after the Anglos leave, Lipsha is surprised to have a vision of Russell as his "twin"—someone who has "the same thoughts in another brain" (81). As they exchange glances, Russell "suddenly grins" and says, "'I don't have a pattern for Montana'" (*BP* 82)—as if this were the only reason he doesn't follow through on the tattoo. And so Lipsha's butt is saved, literally. Bonding together, Russell and Lipsha create a comic conclusion to what has threatened to become a vicious joke. But violence is not entirely averted in Lipsha's encounter with the Anglos: his prized bingo van is totaled by the group. This final outcome serves as an important reminder that although joking can be a useful way to assuage the painful history of white oppression and racism, it isn't enough for Lipsha just to crack jokes. In order to enjoy laughter without the threat of violence erupting, the unequal relationship between the parties has to be addressed.

The title of Erdrich's novel points to one way of leveling the playing field: bingo. Bingo and other forms of gaming have become increasingly significant—and controversial—sources of revenue for Indian nations across America today. Proponents argue that bingo and casino games are making it possible to end the terrible impoverishment that has afflicted most reservations; critics argue that this economic boon comes with hidden price tags, and they contend that native involvement with gambling is detrimental to tribal traditions and values. There is no clear consensus among native peoples, although the establishment of bingo palaces and casinos on reservations across America has increased exponentially since the late 1980s. In recent essays, Gerald Vizenor has been vocal in his criticisms of bingo and gambling, arguing that these contemporary games are not in any way connected to Indian traditions like the moccasin game, that the legal circumstances permitting casinos on reservations could impinge on tribal sovereignty in the future, that the debates about bingo and gambling casinos have led to disturbing intratribal rifts.[3] Vizenor's criticism of contemporary Indian gaming is also ethical in nature: "Casino avarice with no moral traditions is a mean measure of tribal wisdom" ("Casino" 148).

In contrast to Vizenor's openly critical stance on this issue, Erdrich's novel exhibits ambivalence about bingo as an economic tool. The novel presents a critical side by following Lipsha's attachment to bingo. He wants to win money and the bingo van, not to end impoverishment on the reservation, but to impress Shawnee Ray. With the help of his mother's spirit (June, who died at the beginning of *Love Medicine*) and her notebook of winning bingo numbers, Lipsha begins to win money at bingo regularly. But by winning this money, he loses his touch—the mysterious power concentrated in his hands, which he had formerly used to heal people—all together. As in *Tracks, The Bingo Palace* questions whether economic gains for Indians ought to be arrived at by any means necessary. Except for Lulu, who is one of the few players who actually makes money playing bingo and who seems untainted by its excesses, the other players have a difficult time reconciling bingo and gambling with their traditions. Lyman, for one, is so interested in profits and in his plans to build an even grander bingo hall that he cons Lipsha into allowing him to be a co-signer of the savings account into which Lipsha is depositing his bingo earnings. When Lipsha goes to withdraw money from this account, he discovers the balance is zero—Lyman has taken all of his money, he has stolen from his own nephew. The link between gambling and corruption is developed further in the novel when Lyman, in a wagering fever, puts up Nector's peace pipe as collateral to get more money to spend gambling at a Las Vegas casino: he loses the money and the pipe.

Because of these events, Lipsha and Shawnee Ray (and Erdrich's readers) become increasingly concerned about the location of the bingo palace Lyman plans to build, for his bingo palace is destined for the shores of Matchimanito, to be located on Pillager land. Once more Fleur will be displaced: not by white lumber interests this time, as happens in

Tracks, but by her own grandson. The desire for bingo dollars allows Lyman to contemplate an unthinkable act of injustice, directed at someone of his own people, of his own family.

Fleur's reaction to her impending dispossession is curious, though. When Lipsha asks to visit with her, she "smiles . . . showing her sharp old teeth" (*BP* 132), registering on her face what Lipsha calls "fierce pleasure" (*BP* 132). When Lipsha reveals that the purpose of his visit is to ask for a potion that will make Shawnee Ray love him, Fleur instead transforms herself into a bear and with her "hot rasp[ing]" voice (*BP* 137) tells Lipsha "her bear thoughts, laughing in tongues" (*BP* 151). What does Fleur, who knows she is on the verge of being dispossessed, once again, have to laugh about? Why does she acquiesce in the taking of her land for a bingo palace?

To understand her laughter, we have to be able to conceive of the almost inconceivable: the possibility of Indian victory. Because of the dismal outcome of the Indian wars of the nineteenth century, any image of Indian victory has come to be charged with irony. Irony also lies at the heart of Lincoln's exploration of bicultural Indi'n humor: laughter as a survival strategy is created precisely out of defeat, out of something painful. But what about the possibility of conceiving a laughter that emerges from triumph and justice? Because of the tragedies of Indian history in America, we initially have to look elsewhere, outside of native culture, for such a prospect. "The Laugh of the Medusa," Hélène Cixous's often-cited French feminist essay, proposes such a kind of laughter, a laughter that occurs at a time of rupture, when "the new breaks away from the old" (875). In this essay, Cixous calls for a radical reconceptualization of woman's position in Western culture modeled on the black-power slogan of the sixties ("we are black and we are beautiful" [878]), so that what has been repressed or defined as a negative for woman can be reevaluated and seen as having extraordinary value. The essay takes its title from Cixous's feminist revision of the myth of Medusa: "You only have to look at the Medusa straight on to see her. And she's not deadly. She's beautiful and she's laughing" (885).

While not going so far as to claim that Erdrich's novel is "feminist," I do want to suggest a connection between Cixous's Medusa, whose laughter marks her empowerment and vision, and Fleur's "laughing in tongues."[4] Concerns of triumph and justice are linked to Fleur throughout the novel. In a flashback, the novel relates the incident when Fleur craftily seduced the agent who took possession of the Pillager land around Matchimanito into playing cards and losing badly. Erdrich's narrator tellingly comments about Fleur's strategy and success: "Fleur was never one to take an uncalculated piece of revenge. She was never one to answer injustice with a fair exchange. She gave back twofold" (*BP* 145). Fleur's bear laughter, then, voices not just survival but triumph; in the encounter with the agent, she got her land back. The implication is that she can laugh at the loss of her land to the bingo palace because she is able to envision a kind of bingo justice—a justice that will enable the Chippewa to get their land back two-or-more-fold. Appearing to Lyman in a dream—a dream that first arises while he is "staring into the lighted face of [a] video slot machine" (*BP* 147), gambling away all his money and Nector's sacred pipe—Fleur speaks in her rasping bear voice, repeating Nanapush's important words from *Tracks*: *"Land is the only thing that lasts life to life. Money burns like tinder, flows off like water, and as for the government's promises, the wind is steadier"* (*BP* 148). She then adds her own words of advice: *"This time, don't sell out for a barrel of weevil-shot flour and a mossy pork. . . . Put your winnings and earnings in a land-acquiring account. Take the quick new money. Use it to purchase the fast old ground"* (*BP* 148–49). Fleur shapes Lyman's vision of the importance of bingo money: it ought not to be used to create red versions of white capitalists but should buy back the land—acres and acres of it. In effect, she becomes a trickster figure, showing Lyman how to craftily take a new technology and use it to restore the tribe's grounding in tradition.[5]

As Erdrich describes it later in the novel, "temporary loopholes in the law" (*BP* 221) have made it possible for bingo palaces and casinos to spring up on reservations around the country. The legal background that the novel refers to shows that trickster maneuvers can be very effective even in contemporary America. In a 1987 decision, the U.S. Supreme Court ruled in *California v. Cabazon Band of Mission Indians* in favor of the Indians. The Cabazon Band had been running bingo games with prizes up to two hundred times higher than what was allowed by California state law, and they also had conducted poker and other card games; when California attempted to enforce state laws on Indian reservations, which typically fall under the jurisdiction of the federal government and tribal self-rule, the Cabazon Band fought back in court. In its ruling, the U.S. Supreme Court decided that a state has no right to *regulate* gaming on Indian lands, although it could *prohibit* gaming on Indian lands if similar kinds of gaming were prohibited in the state. If, however, the state permits a form of gaming (in the case of California, the state allowed bingo and other kinds of gaming to be used to raise money for charitable purposes), then tribes could operate such games and do so without state interference. Bingo parlors run by tribes had already been allowed before the Cabazon decision was handed down (federal agencies in fact had promoted bingo as a means of economic development for tribes), but the decision changed the playing field by giving tribes access to other, more lucrative forms of gaming. More important to many tribal members, however, was the way in which the Cabazon decision reaffirmed the principle of tribal sovereignty by treating the tribes as independent nations within the United States.

Because the Cabazon ruling made it possible for high-stakes bingo and other forms of gaming to be located on reservations throughout the country, the U.S. Congress almost immediately sought to codify the decision in what is called the Indian Gaming Regulatory Act (IGRA) of 1988. This act divided kinds of games into three tiers, each tier involving a different level of regulation. The IGRA declared that all "class I gaming"—traditional Indian games played for social or ceremonial purposes—was to fall under "the exclusive jurisdiction of the Indian tribes" and thus was not subject to any of the provisions of the act. "Class II gaming"—including bingo, poker, and other "non-banking" card games—was to fall under the jurisdiction of Indian tribes but would be subject to IGRA regulations. "Class III gaming"—slot machines, roulette, blackjack, baccarat, video poker, and other kinds of casino gaming—would be permitted only if "located in a State that permits such gaming for any purpose by any person, organization, or entity."[6] To establish class III gaming on a reservation, tribes were required to negotiate "compacts" with the state, but to even the playing field, the IGRA set a strict time period for conducting negotiations, and if an agreement was not reached within the time limit or if the state did not negotiate in good faith, the tribe could ask for federal intervention.[7] In any court action arising from failed negotiations, the IGRA declared that "the burden of proof shall be upon the State to prove that the State has negotiated with the Indian tribe in good faith."[8]

Although the IGRA was meant to establish clear guidelines for the appropriate regulation of gaming on Indian reservations and lands, it created some interesting loopholes. Because the language for "class III gaming" includes the phrase "for any purpose," a tribal attorney in Wisconsin—surely a trickster in his own right—was able to convince a federal judge that "since Wisconsin has a state lottery and since the lottery consisted of prize, chance, and consideration, and since all casinos had games consisting of prize, chance, and consideration, therefore, Wisconsin had to negotiate a compact with the tribes which would allow Indian casinos" (Kelly 1672). In other words, the wording of the IGRA and the outcome of the *Lac du Flambeau Indians v. State of Wisconsin* case of 1991 created a situation in which Indians could establish casinos in states that did not have casinos per se, but allowed only occasional "Las Vegas nights" to be staged by charities and churches. This has meant, in effect, that as of February 1994 reservation casinos existed in nineteen of the forty-eight continental United States.

Another kind of loophole concerns the definition of "Indian lands." The IGRA defines them as "all lands within the limits of any Indian reservation; and any lands title to which is either held in trust by the United States for the benefit of any Indian tribe or individual or held by any Indian tribe or individual subject to restriction by the United States against alienation."[9] What happens, though, if tribes—through their bingo and casino earnings—buy land? Can casinos or bingo parlors be set up on these newly purchased lands which are often not contiguous to their reservations? Although one court case has suggested the answer is no (*Siletz Tribe v. the State of Oregon*), other tribes continue to raise this very issue in court.[10] Because of the revolution in Indian gaming over the past decade, tribes are now poised to demand or buy back some of the land forcibly taken from them in the nineteenth century. No wonder Fleur laughs at the loss of her land to Lyman's bingo palace. When she laughs as a bear manitou, Fleur is surely thinking several moves ahead in the game; she is foreseeing conditions beyond the story told in this novel, conditions under which contemporary legal tricksters have been able to effect a kind of bingo justice.

Virtual Visions and Trickster Justice

Erdrich's tricksters in *The Bingo Palace* are most successful when, like Fleur in *The Bingo Palace* and Nanapush in *Tracks,* they figure out how to set in motion traditional strategies and goals adapted to contemporary conditions. Erdrich's characters in *Tracks* are in the process of being redefined as Chippewa, and not as Anishinabe; that is, they must confront the various ways in which the dominant culture is defining their land, their identity, their political status. To assert any measure of agency under these conditions, Nanapush learns to create false documents, learns to participate in alien and alienating discursive systems to achieve tribal goals. In *The Bingo Palace,* Erdrich's contemporary Chippewa learn to manipulate mass media and various postmodern technologies for their own purposes. In other words, Erdrich's novel suggests that postmodernism and native traditionalism are not incompatible and may in fact work together to create significant oppositional strategies.[11]

Erdrich's Chippewa live in a society driven by mass media, technology, and global commodification—a society and culture so saturated with images and representations that any connection with the Real—let alone Native American traditions—is tenuous at best.[12] But out of what some might call a dismal situation Erdrich creates new possibilities; her strong characters learn to put the new technologies to good use. Lipsha is one of those who learns to straddle the worlds of Native American traditions and postmodern technology. Waiting for spiritual insight on his vision quest, Lipsha finds that his head has become a tape deck: he "plays" audiotapes and videotapes in his mind, sometimes stopping to rewind and listen to or watch a particular moment again. Here is a contemporary version of oral memory.[13] Similarly, when the skunk from his vision quest later reappears to him, Lipsha invokes the language of both tradition and postmodernism: "'Excuse me,'" Lipsha addresses the skunk, "'I got the wrong vision. Could you change the channel?'" (*BP* 220). But the vision turns out to be the right one, for the skunk is a manitou who keeps repeating in slang "*This ain't real estate*" (*BP* 200, 218) to enable Lipsha to evaluate critically Lyman's plans for the bingo palace. Lipsha is able to see that "the money life has got no substance, there's nothing left when the day is done but a pack of receipts" (*BP* 221). And yet, he also glimpses Fleur's vision of bingo as a kind of trickster justice, in which "a clever operator . . . can use the luck that temporary loopholes in the law bring to Indians for higher causes, steady advances" (*BP* 221). Seeing this situation from two opposing vantage points, Lipsha significantly comments, "It's not completely one way or another, traditional against the bingo. You have to stay alive to keep your tradition alive and working" (*BP* 221).

Lipsha's both-and vision here might be seen from a conventional standpoint as a wobbly ethical stance, but it closely resembles the version of postmodern ethics Jean-François Lyotard articulates in *Just Gaming.* Like Lipsha, Lyotard works against universal concepts of justice, asserting that "One must judge case by case" (Lyotard and Thébaud 73–74). Similarly, the language associated with bingo in Erdrich's novel—gaming, chance, play—is also the language of Lyotard's postmodernism. Moreover, Erdrich's concept of trickster justice is analogous to the double-entendre of Lyotard's title: *Just Gaming* meaning merely playing, but also meaning a playful kind of justice. For Lyotard, "Justice . . . does not consist merely in the observance of the rules; as in all . . . games, it consists in working at the limits of what the rules permit, in order to invent new moves, perhaps new rules and therefore new games" (Lyotard and Thébaud 100).

The invention of a new game happens literally in Erdrich's novel. Lipsha wins his van by playing a form of bingo that does not exist in practice: he chooses his own numbers (actually the numbers June's spirit has given him) and writes them down on a blank bingo card. If bingo players were allowed to do so in real games, certain players could—by studying the distribution of numbers called in games over time and by analyzing the most favorable array of numbers—create cards that would be much more likely to win; hence, the evenhanded luck that characterizes bingo would be undermined. (In fact, this sense of impartial fairness is so important to the game that most bingo parlors will not even allow players to look through a stack of preprinted cards to select their own.) Moreover, as the efforts to amend the IGRA and to restrict gaming on Indian reservations suggest, bingo and casino income has enabled contemporary tribes to play if not a new game at least according to new rules in their negotiations with state and federal governments.[14]

Playing an old game by new rules through the combination of postmodern conditions and native traditions becomes extremely important in Erdrich's novel at the end when Lulu toys with the federal agents who are searching for her son, Gerry Nanapush, who has escaped from prison officials once again, this time via a "lucky" plane crash.[15] As they question her for information about Gerry, Lulu gives them the impression she is playing their game: she acts the part of a senile old Indian lady who doesn't quite have her wits about her and must circle around and around a subject before getting to the point. It takes forever for the agents to realize that Lulu might be leading them on a wild goose chase; meanwhile the communal "we" that narrates this episode is laughing and smiling behind the agents' backs, understanding Lulu's machinations clearly. Eventually, the duped agents decide to arrest Lulu—presumably for harboring stolen government property since she has taken and framed a Post Office wanted poster of Gerry and has it on display in her apartment, but readers suspect they arrest her simply to save face and assert their authority. Again, however, Lulu gets the upper hand: as she walks handcuffed out of the old people's home, surrounded by muscle-bound agents, she wears full ceremonial dress and clutches her eagle-feather fan—and *TV cameras* record the moment to broadcast on "the six o'clock news . . . all through the country" (*BP* 265). Lulu as a postmodern trickster in this final scene manipulates the situation so that these television cameras reproduce an image of police brutalizing a frail, old Indian lady—a representation that is both true, in the sense of the abusive treatment tribal people have experienced and continue to experience in the hands of legal officials and courts, as well as false, because readers know that Lulu has incredible strength and cleverness.

While the cameras continue to roll, Lulu "dances the old-lady traditional, a simple step, but complex in its quiet balance, striking. She dances with a tucked-in wildness, exactly like an old-time Pillager" (*BP* 265). Her image functions as a striking reminder to the American audience watching the six o'clock news across the country that Indians and their traditions continue to live and survive in the twentieth century, that these people are not docile victims who vanished at the end of the nineteenth century. And as the cameras continue to roll, Lulu begins "the old-lady trill, the victory yell that runs up our necks" (*BP* 265), prompting her tribal kin to join her. Lulu is clearly using the news media for her own purposes to circulate an electrifying image of triumphant native peoples. This image is efficacious not only for the audience of these newscasts but also for her own people: it is her trickster tactics, as well as her willingness to begin the trill by herself, that moves the people, that lifts their hearts, to join her.

This moment of triumph, unprecedented in Erdrich's other novels, points to the possibility of a future for native peoples in which traditions and tribes are revitalized and strong, where the wheel of history—like the sacred hoop Black Elk speaks of—has revolved and is putting Native Americans on top. But Erdrich's novel does not end with Lulu's victory; her moment of triumph is only one of five separate final chapters that bring the novel to a close. In these last chapters, Zelda finally recognizes her love for Xavier Toose; Lipsha is left in the middle of a blizzard in a stolen car with a kidnapped baby; Shawnee Ray has left Lyman and dreams of Lipsha returning to her; Fleur leaves Matchimanito and begins the journey toward the land of the spirits. In this way, Erdrich's novel resists a clear or firm resolution and strikes a kind of balance between rebirth and death that is analogous to the situation of contemporary Native Americans. In fact, in contrast to the end of *Tracks* when Fleur leaves Matchimanito without leaving tracks, at the end of *The Bingo Palace,* Fleur's journey to the land of the spirits is marked, and her tracks remain uncannily: "her tracks should have filled with snow," the collective narrator marvels. "They should have blown away with those rough songs from the wild dead we cannot hush. . . . And yet on clear and brilliant days and nights of black stars they are sometimes again left among us, Fleur's tracks, once more, so it is said that she still walks" (*BP* 273).

But as the collective narrator continues to reflect on Fleur's haunting presence, the possibility that the people are falling away from the traditional vision Fleur is associated with arises. The last reference to bingo and gaming for tribal peoples in the novel, "as we drown our past in love of chance" (*BP* 274), is ominous: this phrase raises the critical question of how far traditions can be adapted to postmodern conditions and still be thought of as traditions. Paul Pasquaretta's recent essay on casinos in Native American communities raises similar questions. By narrating the stories of gaming at two different reservations, the tragic controversy at Akwesasne in New York state and the great success story of the Mashantucket Pequots in Connecticut, Pasquaretta suggests that one reason the issue of gaming on reservations is so heated is because it directly involves slippery definitions of "Indianness." Because of this problematic, his essay ends with a question rather than a firm conclusion: "Will gambling provide a means to support the independent life of an indigenous community or contribute to the erasure of its boundaries and the complete assimilation of its people?" (714).

Erdrich's novel asks this question too, but goes one step further as it winds to a conclusion. Fleur's bear laugh returns and unnerves the collective narrator: "You have heard the bear laugh—that is the chuffing noise we hear and it is unmistakable. Yet no matter how we strain to decipher the sound it never quite makes sense, never relieves our certainty or our suspicion that there is more to be told, more than we know, more than can be caught in the sieve of our thinking" (*BP* 274). Here is a kind of laughter that is not recognizably humorous; it is "unmistakable" but indecipherable; its elusiveness chafes the listeners and thus animates the people to work, to strain, toward some kind of understanding. In this regard, Fleur's uncanny laugh resembles the sacred laughter that Black Elk describes as part of the *Lakota heyoka* ceremony, a healing ceremony that uses humorous antics and sacred clowns (*heyokas*) to lift the people's hearts and so prepares them to face a visionary, perhaps even terrifying truth.[16]

Given what is at stake in such serious laughter, it is no wonder that the Indi'n humor of Erdrich's novels has been so difficult for some readers to grasp. Like the *heyoka* ceremony, Fleur's laugh prepares the people to face potentially terrifying questions: What does it mean to be "Indian" at the end of the twentieth century? What does it mean to be "traditional" in a postmodern consumer culture? Without suggesting there is any one right answer to these questions, Erdrich's novel does take a firm stance on one thing: collective discussion of these issues is vitally necessary. By evoking the language of "we" and "our" at the end, *The Bingo Palace* affirms the ability of Native American communities to sustain and strengthen themselves, no matter how potentially divisive the issues they must face, through such collective analysis. This constitutes in the end perhaps the most significant comic characteristic of Erdrich's fictional world—the ability to hold on to the idea of community for Native Americans from within postmodern exigencies, postmodern conditions.

Notes

I am grateful to Catherine Rainwater for encouraging me to work on this topic, as well as to Aparajita Sagar and Marcia Stephenson for their many helpful comments and suggestions for further reading.

1. In addition to Kenneth Lincoln, whose work on Indi'n humor is discussed below, the only other scholar to analyze humor extensively in *Love Medicine* is William Gleason.

2. See Christopher Lyman's *The Vanishing Race and Other Illusions* for a marvelous analysis of the ways in which Curtis manipulated his images in the darkroom to reflect his own predetermined, romanticized views of Indians.

3. For Vizenor's views, see in particular "Casino Coups" and *Crossbloods* (x–xiii, 18–24). The violent confrontation over gaming at the Mohawk reserve Akwesasne is detailed in Rick Hornung's book. Whether or not contemporary gaming on Indian lands has any connection to traditional games and traditional stories is a tangled question. The earliest games of bingo in America used a large bowl to hold the markers with letters on them; perhaps this equipment is not so distant from the bowls that the Chippewa traditionally used to carry out various "dice" games: see Stewart Culin, especially 44–49, 61–68. But seriousness and ceremonialism distinguished these dice games and the moccasin game Vizenor mentions from "mere" gaming, as is apparent in many of the ethnographic accounts in Culin. Even if this sense of ceremony is missing from contemporary Indian casinos, it is present to some degree in Erdrich's handling of bingo in the novel since Lipsha receives his bingo guidance from his mother's spirit. The combination of chance and skill, of fate and choice, of life and death apparent in traditional Indian games is also rep-

resented in traditional Chippewa stories of the Great Gambler: see Vizenor's *Summer in the Spring* 124–31 for the myth and his novel *The Heirs of Columbus* for another retelling. Erdrich never directly invokes the story of the Great Gambler in *The Bingo Palace* or elsewhere, but it is clear from the acknowledgments to the novel that a love of card games is part of her Chippewa inheritance since it is associated with her Turtle Mountain grandfather, Pat Gourneau; see also the poem "Turtle Mountain Reservation" in *Jacklight* (82–85), which is dedicated to Gourneau and which has a grandfather figure within the poem who still uses words from the old language ("a word / that belongs to a world / no one else can remember" [82]) and yet enjoys playing bingo.

4. Hertha Wong's essay on Erdrich offers a compelling investigation of the (non)applicability of feminist criticism in relation to Native American women. Lincoln argues that the humor of Erdrich's novels is Indi'n and feminist.

5. In his well-known study *The Trickster,* Paul Radin writes, "Laughter, humour and irony permeate everything Trickster does" (x)—a description that pertains to Fleur's role in the novel at this particular moment. But unlike the traditional trickster, which Radin describes as being noted for tricks and exploits that oftentimes get beyond his control, Fleur is not laughed at: she is always the laugher in *The Bingo Palace.*

6. See 25 USC 2710.

7. Some native peoples who are critical of bingo and casinos point out that the requirement to negotiate compacts with the state in effect limits tribal sovereignty. They therefore argue that the IGRA does as much to harm tribal sovereignty as to support it, and they are opposed to casinos established on reservations because of this dilemma.

8. See 25 USC 2710, (d)(7)(B)(ii).

9. See 25 USC 2703, (4).

10. This is, in fact, what happened when the city of Duluth, Minnesota, worked together with the Fond du Lac Chippewa to create a gaming casino in downtown Duluth. The Fond du Luth Casino is clearly not located within the traditional reservation boundaries but on newly defined land. The affirmation of tribal sovereignty in the Cabazon ruling has been manifested in a number of other interesting trickster legal challenges: the assertion of the right to spearfish and to hunt and gather on ceded lands, as well as the filing of lawsuits to regain long-lost territory.

11. Erdrich is not alone in making this kind of conjunction. In an essay tellingly and playfully titled "Latin American Identity and Mixed Temporalities; or, How to Be Postmodern and Indian at the Same Time," Fernando Calderón cites "the Aymara group WARA, which plays ancestral Indian flutes to

the accompaniment of electric guitars" (64). Vizenor, who is White Earth Chippewa, is one of the few contemporary Native American writers who adamantly espouses Native American postmodernism. See his introduction and epilogue to *Narrative Chance:* "A Postmodern Introduction" and "Trickster Discourse" (3–16, 187–211). I would argue, however, that Erdrich's postmodernism is not as theoretical or linguistic as Vizenor's. Whereas Vizenor's fiction employs the kind of wild pastiche associated with "classic" postmodernists such as Thomas Pynchon or Donald Barthelme, Erdrich remains interested in using native storytelling modes in postmodern, postindustrial contexts. Another way to underscore this distinction is to observe that, while Vizenor cites Roland Barthes, Jacques Derrida, Michel Foucault, and other French poststructuralists, Erdrich's sense of postmodernism seems closer to the crisis in historicity that Fredric Jameson discusses as the most significant attribute of postmodernism.

12. Besides Vizenor, the contemporary Native American writer who comes closest to Erdrich's postmodern sensibility, in my view, is Sherman Alexie. In his most recent novel, *Reservation Blues,* a guitar given from Robert Johnson, a legendary blues artist, to Thomas Builds-the-Fire becomes a contemporary manitou.

13. Cf. Walter Ong's concept of secondary orality, which is a contemporary version of traditional oral structures and worldview created by the mass media.

14. The triumphant struggle of the Mashantucket Pequots of Connecticut to offer casino gaming on their reserve provides a fine example of the change I describe here: the state of Connecticut vehemently opposed the establishment of a casino on the reservation, but the Pequots sued them in court and won. The Foxwoods casino opened in February 1992, and even though the casino could offer only class II gaming, it brought in approximately $300 million in revenue for the tribe. When the state of Connecticut faced severe and ongoing financial crisis, however, Governor Lowell P. Weicker decided to enter into negotiations with the Pequots, giving them the right to run slot machines at the casino in return for a 25 percent cut of the slot revenues, with a guaranteed payment of at least $100 million. In 1994, the Pequots passed along $136 million to the state.

15. I should point out that the combination of native traditions and postmodern technologies is not always successful in *The Bingo Palace.* After Gerry's escape, Gerry calls Lipsha for help in fleeing to Canada, but speaks in "the old-time language," Anishinabe, to tell Lipsha where he is in case the phone line is being tapped. Despite Lipsha's intense concentration on these words, he cannot recall enough of the language to decipher his father's message with

any certainty. Humor moderates what might be a moment of despair, though, as Lipsha confesses: "I become confused. My father is either playing Star Wars games at Art's Arcade, or he is holed up at the Fargo library, or he is hiding curled up in the lodge dumpster of the Sons of Norway"—these are "three strange possibilities," Lipsha thinks to himself, as he continues to ponder the message (*BP* 233).

16. See *Black Elk Speaks,* 188–93.

Works Cited

Alexie, Sherman. *Reservation Blues.* New York: Atlantic Monthly P, 1995.

Black Elk, and John G. Neihardt. *Black Elk Speaks.* 1932. Rpt., Lincoln: U of Nebraska P, 1979.

Calderón, Fernando. "Latin American Identity and Mixed Temporalities; or, How to Be Postmodern and Indian at the Same Time." *boundary 2* 20.3 (1993): 55–64.

Chavkin, Allan, and Nancy Feyl Chavkin, eds. *Conversations with Louise Erdrich and Michael Dorris.* Jackson: UP of Mississippi, 1994.

Cixous, Hélène. "The Laugh of the Medusa." Trans. Keith Cohen and Paula Cohen. *Signs* 1 (1976): 875–93.

Culin, Stewart. *Games of the North American Indians. Volume 1: Games of Chance.* 1907. Rpt., Lincoln: U of Nebraska P, 1992. 2 vols.

Erdrich, Louise. *Jacklight.* New York: Holt, 1984.

Erdrich, Louise, and Michael Dorris. "An Interview with Louise Erdrich and Michael Dorris." With Hertha Wong. Chavkin and Chavkin 30–53.

——. "Louise Erdrich and Michael Dorris." With Bill Moyers. Chavkin and Chavkin 138–50.

Gleason, William. "'Her Laugh an Ace': The Function of Humor in Louise Erdrich's *Love Medicine.*" *American Indian Culture and Research Journal* 11.3 (1987): 51–73.

Hornung, Rick. *One Nation Under the Gun.* New York: Pantheon, 1991.

Indian Gaming Regulatory Act. 25 U.S. Code 2701-2721. 1988.

Jameson, Fredric. *Postmodernism, or, the Cultural Logic of Late Capitalism.* Durham: Duke UP, 1991.

Kelly, Joseph M. "American Indian Gaming Law." *The New Law Journal* 26 November 1993: 1672.

Lincoln, Kenneth. *Indi'n Humor: Bicultural Play in Native America.* New York: Oxford UP, 1993.

Lyman, Christopher. *The Vanishing Race and Other Illusions: Photographs of Indians by Edward S. Curtis.* Washington, DC: Smithsonian, 1982.

Lyotard, Jean-François, and Jean-Loup Thébaud. *Just Gaming.* Trans. Wlad Godzich. Minneapolis: U of Minnesota P, 1985.

Ong, Walter. *Orality and Literacy: The Technologizing of the Word.* London: Methuen, 1982.

Pasquaretta, Paul. "On the 'Indianness' of Bingo: Gambling and the Native American Community." *Critical Inquiry* 20 (1993–94): 694–714.

Radin, Paul. *The Trickster: A Study in American Indian Mythology.* London: Routledge and Kegan Paul, 1956.

Vizenor, Gerald. "Casino Coups." *Manifest Manners: Postindian Warriors of Survivance.* Hanover, NH: Wesleyan UP–UP of New England, 1994. 138–48.

———. *Crossbloods: Bone Courts, Bingo, and Other Reports.* Minneapolis: U of Minnesota P, 1990.

———. *The Heirs of Columbus.* Hanover, NH: Wesleyan UP–UP of New England, 1991.

———, ed. *Narrative Chance: Postmodern Discourse on Native American Indian Literatures.* Albuquerque: U of New Mexico P, 1989.

———, ed. and interpreter. *Summer in the Spring: Anishinaabe Lyric Poems and Stories.* 1981. Rev. ed., Norman: U of Oklahoma P, 1993.

Wong, Hertha. "Adoptive Mothers and Thrown-Away Children in the Novels of Louise Erdrich." *Narrating Mothers: Theorizing Maternal Subjectivities.* Ed. Brenda O. Daly and Maureen T. Reddy. Knoxville: U of Tennessee P, 1991. 174–92.

9

Afterword

A. LaVonne Brown Ruoff

Louise Erdrich has achieved phenomenal literary success since the publication in 1984 of *Love Medicine,* her first novel, and *Jacklight,* her first book of poetry. Publishing a book of fiction, poetry, or autobiography almost every other year since then, Erdrich has become a prolific writer, best-selling author, and critical success. Currently more scholarly articles are published each year about her work than about that of any other contemporary Native American author. Clearly her books have struck a cord.

Because I knew her before she became an acclaimed writer, I have been delighted by the literary stature she has gained. Michael Dorris first introduced us in 1979, when she was visiting Dartmouth and I was doing research there while on a fellowship in Native American Studies. In 1981, she asked me to comment on early versions of "Tracks" and some short stories. We got to know each other better in October of that year, when I attended her and Michael's wedding. Through the years, I have treasured her friendship.

The 1981 manuscript called "Tracks" was a wonderfully creative and imaginative book that was not quite ready for publication. One of my suggestions to her, which makes me laugh now, was to abandon linear plot and use a more disjointed narrative. The original "Tracks," which has never been published in its entirety, is not the same novel as *Tracks.* Erdrich has incorporated into the published version some episodes which originally appeared in the 1981 "Tracks," particularly versions of the card games among the meat-plant workers, the gang rape of a central female character, and what happened to the perpetrators. There were also allusions to water and Misshepeshu, developed much more fully in the published version. Nevertheless, the plots, characters, and narrative structures of the two books are very different. One of my favorite sections from the unpublished "Tracks" was the hilarious battle royal in the tomahawk factory, which opened this manuscript. Erdrich subsequently rewrote and inserted this incident into the revised *Love Medicine.*

At the time I was particularly impressed by her short stories "Gooseheart" and "Scales." When she and Michael Dorris visited Gene and me in 1982, she showed me her splendid collection of stories. Revised and expanded, these became her first novel, *Love Medicine.* Since its publication, I have often asked Erdrich if she was revising the original "Tracks." Her growth as an artist, however, has taken her far beyond the promise of this beginning effort. As she said in her 1993 interview with Allan Chavkin and Nancy Feyl Chavkin, "*Tracks* is very tangled, problematic for me, difficult. It was the first manuscript I finished, but I have since divided up and re-used pieces of that manuscript elsewhere. It has become the old junked car in the yard front, continually raided for parts. It is the form of all else, still a tangle" (238).

Why has Erdrich's fiction achieved such popularity? Critics and scholars have highly praised her skillful weaving of Ojibwe ethnohistory into her narratives, masterful use of oral tradition and multi-layered stories, powerful portrayals of characters (particularly women), hilarious humor that ranges from mock heroic battles to survival jokes, unerring depictions of popular culture, and lyrical descriptions of nature. Perhaps what most distinguishes Erdrich's fiction is its emphasis on community. Other Native American fiction writers have described their protagonists' quests for understanding their tribal and family heritages and have stressed the importance of achieving wholeness through integration within Indian traditions, family, and community.

Erdrich, however, charts a new path by describing in a series of novels the complex and shifting relationships of her characters within their families and communities. These novels form a chronicle of how these families of North Dakota Ojibwes survived, despite their loss of land and cultural sovereignty. Erdrich sharply depicts the marriages, love affairs, interfamily feuds, and blood relationships between Indian families and between natives and non-natives. She vividly portrays the infinite varieties of Indianness that exist from generation to generation on her fictional mixed-blood reservation, in the imaginary town of Argus, and in eastern North Dakota. Among the many forms of Indianness she describes are Nanapush and Fleur Pillager's staunch traditionalism in *Tracks;* Gerry Nanapush's mythic trickster adventures in *Love Medicine, Tracks,* and *Bingo Palace;* Pauline Puyat's (Sister Leopolda) bigoted religious assimilationism in *Love Medicine* and *Tracks;* Lipsha Kashpaw's tentative struggles to connect with the traditions of his tribal heritage in *Love Medicine* and *Bingo Palace;* Celestine James's diminished links to her Ojibwe roots in *Beet Queen;* and Jack Mauser's dim recollection of his Ojibwe ancestry in *Tales of Burning Love.*

Her focus on community has had an impact on the work of other Native American writers. Linda Hogan says she was influenced by the way Erdrich portrays characters within a community (personal communication). David Treuer's (Ojibwe) emphasis on an Ojibwe community in his *Little* (1995) also reflects Erdrich's influence.

Erdrich's most popular and most frequently taught novels are *Love Medicine* and *Tracks,* in which her interweaving of Ojibwe traditions and history is most evident. The fondness of readers, teachers, and critics for these books has tended to pigeonhole her as a writer about Ojibwe history, culture, and life, a categorization she has worked hard to escape. In a 1986 interview with John Blades in the *Chicago Tribune,* she expresses her hope that *The Beet Queen* will "establish her as an American writer—not just a writer about American Indians." Though she says that "I really don't mind being a Native American writer as long as people read my books," she also states that "my fondest hope is that people will be reading me 10 or 20 years from now as someone who has written about American experience in all its diversity." She expanded on this topic in her 1993 interview with the Chavkins. Asked if she was concerned about being labeled a "Native American writer" or "woman writer," Erdrich responded that she thought that such labels "originate in course descriptions. If the work survives, perhaps they will fall away. . . . The point we're striving for is one at which the criteria for the work is its worth to readers, its excellence, the qualities that shine out and endure" (230).

Certainly *The Beet Queen, The Crown of Columbus* (1992, co-authored with Dorris), and *Tales of Burning Love* are attempts to locate her novels outside a reservation or Indian community. *The Beet Queen,* which is less concerned with Native American characters than *Love Medicine* and *Tracks,* exemplifies her desire to explore the non-Indian side of her heritage and experience. In a *Chicago Sun-Times* interview with John Barron in 1996, Erdrich notes that *Love Medicine* and *Tracks* are her books most frequently taught in colleges. She laments that *The Beet Queen* is "a victim of reverse discrimination on campuses. But she is heartened by its huge acceptance in book groups."

The Crown of Columbus has been largely ignored by scholars. Thomas Matchie gives a perceptive reading of the novel in his "Exploring the Meaning of Discovery in *The Crown of Columbus,*" in which he examines its use of the detective story as well as its themes of pursuit and discovery and of being lost and found. Native American critic M. Annette Jaimes attacks the authors for opting for "the pop reading trends of the general American public to satisfy the contemporary taste for literary kitsch" (58). Much of the controversy about this novel has focused on what some have felt was a failure to treat with appropriate seriousness the devastating impact of Columbus's arrival on the futures of native peoples. In addition to being a romance, detective story, adventure tale, and postcolonial response to the consequences of Columbus's invasion, *The Crown of Columbus* is also a sharp academic satire. It contains one of the first portrayals of an Indian academic, the no-nonsense Vivian Two Star, who struggles to complete a study of Columbus that will secure her tenure while she copes with a dithering lover, a rebellious teenage son, and a howling newborn.

Tales of Burning Love, like all Erdrich's novels except *The Crown of Columbus,* is set in North Dakota. It is populated with a mixed-blood, assimilated protagonist (Jack Mauser) and strong women characters, Indian and non-Indian, who have had affairs with or married him. In "De Sade's Daughters," Lee Siegel examines the relationship of this novel to the new erotic writing by women, arguing that "for the first time in our literature since the 1930s, a social and political ideology is providing the touchstone for literary art" (98). Siegel concludes that in *Tales of Burning Love,* "masculine self knowledge is elaborately and imaginatively equated with a man's learning to enjoy sexual intercourse on his back" (98). Though Siegel has phrased her comment cleverly, she reveals that the critic ignores the revelations of character and compelling tales Erdrich has woven into the novel. Siegel also misses the Indian trickster influence on Erdrich's portrayal of Jack Mauser's sexual desires and adventures. Nevertheless, Siegel correctly sees the novel as a journey, in which Mauser must learn a series of lessons before achieving redemption. Siegel notes that unlike other contemporary women authors of erotic novels, Erdrich seeks to "re-educate" her male protagonist "rather than indict him" (100).

Erdrich is a gifted poet as well as a fine novelist. Her *Jacklight* and *Baptism of Desire* (1989) have been highly acclaimed for their lyric power, moving dramatic monologues, and delightful "Old Man Potchikoo" trickster narratives. Among her most moving poems in *Jacklight* are "Family Reunion" and "Indian Boarding School Runaways," which have been frequently anthologized. Both depict the survival of emotional ties to tribe and family. *Jacklight* also includes a series of poignant dramatic monologues called "The Butcher's Wife." One of the group of poems in *Baptism of Desire* focuses on visionary and religious ecstasy and humankind's relations with the divine, some of which recall images similar to those in the Book of Revelation and in Blake's prophetic poetry. Another group depicts lust, disillusionment, and longing, while a third examines the author's reactions to pregnancy, childbirth, motherhood, and relations between family members. Her poetry has been justly praised by critics for its powerful character portraits, vivid descriptive-reflective verse, and soaring lyricism.

Erdrich's narrative and poetic skill are combined in *The Blue Jay's Dance: A Birth Year* (1995), her first major work of nonfiction. This memoir of twelve months encompasses a pregnancy in winter, new motherhood in spring and summer, and a return to writing in the fall. *The Blue Jay's Dance* is a poignant and beautifully crafted book that combines deft insights into the interrelationship between mother and child, humankind's links with the natural universe, and the act of writing. The recipes that punctuate the narrative emphasize the sensuality of experience. After reading *The Blue Jay's Dance,* mothers are likely to exclaim, "Take that, Thoreau." Erdrich's insights into the physical demands of pregnancy, childbirth, and early infancy; the obsession new mothers and their babies have for each other; and the nonstop demands made by young children will remind all mothers of their experiences with their own youngsters. Her joy at her babies' births and growth is tempered by her sense of loss at the illnesses and deaths of her beloved maternal grandfather, Patrick Gorneau, and paternal grandmother, Mary Erdrich Korll. In lyrical prose, Erdrich describes life cycles of the plants, birds, and animals on her New England farm.

Most recently, Erdrich has published her first children's book, *Grandmother's Pigeon* (1996), a story about a tough-minded grandmother who abandons her family in the middle of their Pacific Coast vacation and rides a porpoise to Greenland. A year after her departure, the family finds in her room a nest with three eggs, which immediately begin to hatch. An ornithologist declares the baby pigeons part of an extinct species, news which brings the press to the family's home and disrupts their lives. The book has received considerable acclaim. In her review in the *New York Times Book Review,* Nancy Caldwell Sorel praised *Grandmother's Pigeon* as excelling "both in style and story. In fact, it soars" (49).

Erdrich's career since 1984 has been truly remarkable: she has written or co-authored ten major, creative books, edited *Best American Stories of 1993,* attracted enthusiastic audiences, won numerous literary prizes, and gained ever-increasing scholarly attention. She achieved all this while helping to raise three adopted children with varying degrees of learning disabilities, bearing three daughters, and mourning the deaths of her oldest, adopted son and two grandparents. The years 1996 and 1997 were especially hard because of her separation from Dorris and his tragic suicide on 10 April 1997. Despite their grief, Erdrich and the children are doing well. May the breath of *gitchi-manidoo* heal them and bring them peace.

Miigwech, Louise Erdrich, for all the word magic.

Works Cited

Barron, John. "Louise Erdrich Adds 'Burning Love' to Other Related Tales." Mixed Media. *Chicago Sun Times* 26 May 1996: B3.

Blades, John. "Louise Erdrich Taps a Slightly Lighter Vein in Quest to Shed Labeling." *Chicago Tribune* book section 31 August 1986: 14, 30.

Chavkin, Allan, and Nancy Feyl Chavkin. "An Interview with Louise Erdrich." *Conversations with Louise Erdrich and Michael Dorris.* Jackson: UP of Mississippi, 1994. 220–53.

Jaimes, M. Annette. "The Art of Pandering: Michael Dorris' and Louise Erdrich's 'The Crown of Columbus.'" *Wicazo Sa Review* 8.2 (1992): 58–59.

Matchie, Thomas. "Exploring the Meaning of Discovery in *The Crown of Columbus." North Dakota Quarterly* 59.4 (1991): 243–50.

Siegel, Lee. "De Sade's Daughters." *Atlantic Monthly* February 1997: 97–100, 102.

Sorel, Nancy Caldwell. "Wisdom of the Ancestor." Rev. of *Grandmother's Pigeon,* by Louise Erdrich. *New York Times Book Review* 10 November 1996: 49.

Selected Bibliography

Compiled by Allan Chavkin and Nancy Feyl Chavkin

Works by Louise Erdrich

Books

Imagination. Westerville, OH: Merrill, 1981.

Jacklight. New York: Holt, 1984.

Love Medicine: A Novel. New York: Holt, 1984.

The Beet Queen. New York: Holt, 1986.

Tracks. New York: Holt, 1988.

Baptism of Desire. New York: Harper & Row, 1989.

[With Michael Dorris] *The Crown of Columbus.* New York: HarperCollins, 1991.

[With Michael Dorris] *Route Two.* Northridge, CA: Lord John Press, 1991.

Love Medicine: New and Expanded Version. New York: Holt, 1993.

The Bingo Palace. New York: HarperCollins, 1994.

The Blue Jay's Dance: A Birth Year. New York: HarperCollins, 1995.

Grandmother's Pigeon. New York: Hyperion, 1996.

Tales of Burning Love. New York: HarperCollins, 1996.

The Antelope Wife. New York: HarperCollins, 1998.

Selected Fiction in Books and Periodicals

[With Michael Dorris] "Change of Light." *Redbook* October 1980: 78–79.

"Scales." *North American Review* 267 (March 1982): 22–27.

"The World's Greatest Fishermen." *Chicago* (October 1982): 159–68.

"American Horse." *Earth Power Coming: Short Fiction in Native*

American Literature. Ed. Simon J. Ortiz. Tsaile, AZ: Navajo Community College P, 1983. 59–72.

"Saint Marie." *Atlantic Monthly* March 1984: 78–84.

"Crown of Thorns." *Chicago* September 1984: 207+.

"Wild Geese." *Mother Jones* October 1984: 21+.

"The Beads." *North Dakota Quarterly* 52.2 (1984): 54–61.

"Lulu's Boys." *Kenyon Review* 6.2 (1984): 1–10.

"The True Story of Mustache Maude." *Frontiers* 7.3 (1984): 62–67.

"Destiny." *Atlantic Monthly* January 1985: 64–68.

"The Little Book." *Formations* Summer 1985: 1–6.

"The Beet Queen." *Paris Review* 27 (1985): 10–26.

"Mister Argus." *Georgia Review* 39 (1985): 379–90.

"Pounding the Dog." *Kenyon Review* ns 7.4 (1985): 18–28.

"Sita Kozka." *Ms.* 15 August 1986: 52+.

"Scars." *Boston Globe Magazine* 31 August 1986: 17+.

"Fleur." *Esquire* August 1986: 52–55.

"Chez Sita." *Minneapolis/Saint Paul Magazine* September 1986: 14.

"Knives." *Granta* 19 (1986): 135–49.

"Mary Adare." *New England Review and Bread Loaf Quarterly* 5.1 (1986): 30–49.

"Snares." *Harper's* May 1987: 60–64.

"Matchimanito." *Atlantic Monthly* July 1988: 66–74.

"A Wedge of Shade." *New Yorker* 6 March 1989: 35–40.

"The Bingo Van." *New Yorker* 19 February 1990: 39–47.

"The Leap." *Harper's* March 1990: 65–68.

"The Dress." *Mother Jones* (July–August 1990): 50+.

"Best Western." *Vogue* May 1990: 288+.

"I'm a Mad Dog Biting Myself for Sympathy." *Granta* 34 (1990): 137–43.

"Potchikoo." *Granta* (1990): 245–55.

"The Island." *Ms.* January–February 1991: 38–42.

"Mauser." *New Yorker* 8 April 1991: 38–42.

[With Michael Dorris] "A Baby Between Us." *Redbook* May 1991: 50+.

"The Crown of Columbus." *Mother Jones* May–June 1991: 24+.

"The Immaculate Conception of Carson DuPre." *The Sound of Writing.* Ed. Alan Cheuse and Caroline Marshall. New York: Doubleday, 1991. 91–95.

"Line of Credit." *Harper's* April 1992: 55–60.

"Flight." *American Short Fiction* 2.5 (1992): 28–38.

"Fleur's Luck." *Georgia Review* 47 (1993): 659–63.

"The Plunge of the Brave." *New England Review* 15.1 (1993): 57–70.

"Resurrection." *Glimmer Train Stories* 9 (1994): 7–22.

"Satan: Hijacker of a Planet." *Atlantic Monthly* August 1997: 64–68.

Selected Nonfiction in Books and Periodicals

"Where I Ought to Be: A Writer's Sense of Place." *New York Times Book Review* 28 July 1985: 1, 23–24.

[With Michael Dorris] "Sea to Sea on Route 2." *New York Times Magazine* 15 March 1987: 30+.

"Bangs and Whimpers: Novelists at Armageddon." *New York Times Book Review* 13 March 1988: 1+.

[With Michael Dorris] "Who Owns the Land?" *New York Times Magazine* 4 September 1988: 32+.

Foreword. *The Broken Cord: A Family's Ongoing Struggle with Fetal Alcohol Syndrome* by Michael Dorris. New York: Harper & Row, 1989.

Preface. *A Link with the River* by Desmond Hogan. New York: Farrar, Straus & Giroux, 1989.

"The Eighties and Me: Writers Reflect on How Their Books Helped Shape a Decade—and Vice-Versa." *Publisher's Weekly* 5 January 1990: 21–23.

"Full Circle: Sins of the Mother." *Family Circle* 3 April 1990: 134+.

"Manitoulin Island." *Antaeus* 64–65 (1990): 381–89.

"Kay Boyle: Power vs. Love." *Lear's* April 1991: 76–79.

"What Writers Are Reading." *Ms.* July 1991: 82–83.

"Foxglove." *Georgia Review* 46 (1992): 473–78.

"The Names of Women." *Granta* 41 (1992): 131–38.

"Beneath My House." *Harper's* March 1993: 30+.

"What My Mother Taught Me." *Ladies Home Journal* May 1993: 83–87.

"A Woman's Work: Too Many Demands, and Not Enough Selves." *Harper's* May 1993: 35–46.

Introduction. *The Best American Short Stories 1993.* Ed. Louise Erdrich. Boston: Houghton Mifflin, 1993.

"Skunk Dreams." *Georgia Review* 47 (1993): 85–94.

[With Michael Dorris] "The Power of Love." *New Choices for Retirement Living* December 1993: 26–30.

"Self-definition: Spirit." *Self* July 1994: 134.

"Snow Houses." *Architectural Digest* 51 (December 1994): 40–48.

"Enter Laughing." *Parents* April 1995: 93–95.

"When Your Baby Says Good-Bye." *Redbook* April 1995: 120+.

"Not Your Grandmother's Head Cheese." *New York Times Magazine* 10 March 1996: 98.

"The Garden Path." *New York Times Magazine* 21 July 1996: 37.

Works about Louise Erdrich

SELECTED CRITICISM

Aldridge, John W. *Talents and Technicians: Literary Chic and the New Assembly-Line Fiction.* New York: Charles Scribner's Sons, 1992. 92–100.

Bak, Hans. "Toward a Native American 'Realism': The Amphibious Fiction of Louise Erdrich." *Neo-Realism in Contemporary American Fiction.* Ed. Kristiaan Versluys. Amsterdam: Rodopi, 1992. 145–70.

Barak, Julie. "Blurs, Blends, Berdaches: Gender Mixing in the Novels of Louise Erdrich." *Studies in American Indian Literatures* 8.3 (1996): 49–62.

Barnett, Marianne. "Dreamstuff: Erdrich's *Love Medicine.*" *North Dakota Quarterly* 56.1 (1988): 82–93.

Barry, Nora, and Mary Prescott. "The Triumph of the Brave: *Love Medicine*'s Holistic Vision." *Critique* 30.2 (1989): 123–38.

Bataille, Gretchen. "Louise Erdrich's *The Beet Queen:* Images of the Grotesque on the Northern Plains." *Critical Perspectives on Native American Fiction.* Ed. Richard F. Fleck. Washington, DC: Three Continents Press, 1993. 277–85.

Beidler, Peter G. "Three Student Guides to Louise Erdrich's *Love Medicine.*" *American Indian Culture and Research Journal* 16.4 (1992): 167–73.

Bird, Gloria. "Searching for Evidence of Colonialism at Work: A Reading of Louise Erdrich's *Tracks.*" *Wicazo Sa Review* 8.2 (1992): 40–47.

Bowers, Sharon Manybeads. "Louise Erdrich as Nanapush." *New Perspectives on Women and Comedy.* Ed. Regina Barreca. Philadelphia: Gordon & Breach, 1992. 135–41.

Brady, Laura A. "Collaboration as Conversation: Literary Cases." *Essays in Literature* 19.2 (1992): 298–311.

Brehm, Victoria. "The Metamorphoses of an Ojibwa *Manido.*" *American Literature* 68.4 (1996): 667–706.

Breinig, Helmbrecht. "(Hi)Storytelling as Deconstruction and Seduction: The Columbus Novels of Stephen Marlowe and Michael

Dorris/Louise Erdrich." *Historiographic Metafiction in Modern American and Canadian Literature.* Ed. Bernd Engler and Kurt Muller. Paderborn: Ferdinand, 1994. 325–46.

Brogan, Kathleen. "Haunted by History: Louise Erdrich's *Tracks.*" *Prospects* 21 (1996): 169–93.

Carr, Susan. "The Turtle Mountain/Yoknapatawpha Connection." *Bulletin of the West Virginia Association of College English Teachers* 16 (1994): 18–25.

Castillo, Susan Perez. "The Construction of Gender and Ethnicity in the Poetry of Leslie Silko and Louise Erdrich." *Visions of History: Visions of the Other.* Ed. Earl Miner, Toru Haga, Gerald Gillespie, Margaret Higonnet, and Sumie Jones. Tokyo: International Comparative Literature Association, 1995. 637–45.

———. "The Construction of Gender and Ethnicity in the Texts of Leslie Silko and Louise Erdrich." *Yearbook of English Studies* 24 (1994): 228–36.

———. "Postmodernism, Native American Literature, and the Real: The Silko-Erdrich Controversy." *Massachusetts Review* 32.2 (1991): 285–94.

———. "Women Aging into Power: Fictional Representations of Power and Authority in Louise Erdrich's Female Characters." *Studies in American Indian Literatures* 8.4 (1996): 13–20.

Catt, Catherine M. "Ancient Myth in Modern America: The Trickster in the Fiction of Louise Erdrich." *Platte Valley Review* 19.1 (1991): 71–81.

Cid, Teresa. "Wanting America Back: *The Crown of Columbus* as a Tentative Epic in an Age of Multiculturalism." *The Insular Dream: Obsession and Resistance.* Ed. Kristiaan Versluys. Amsterdam: VU UP, 1995. 342–49.

Clarke, Joni Adamson. "Why Bears Are Good to Think and Theory Doesn't Have To Be Murder: Transformation and Oral Tradition in Louise Erdrich's *Tracks.*" *Studies in American Indian Literatures* 4.1 (1992): 28–48.

Cornell, Daniel. "Turning the Story Over: The Narrative Perspectives in Louise Erdrich's *Tracks.*" *Associacao Portuguesa de Estudos Anglo Americanos.* Aveiro: U de Aveiro, 1989. 43–55.

———. "Woman Looking: Revis(ion)ing Pauline's Subject Position in Louise Erdrich's *Tracks.*" *Studies in American Indian Literatures* 4.1 (1992): 49–64.

Crabtree, Claire. "Salvific Oneness and the Fragmented Self in Louise Erdrich's *Love Medicine.*" *Contemporary Native American*

Cultural Issues: Proceedings from the Native American Studies Conference at Lake Superior State University. Ed. Thomas E. Schirer. Sault Ste. Marie: Lake Superior State UP, 1988. 49–56.

Daniele, Daniela. "Transactions in a Native Land: Mixed-Blood Identity and Indian Legacy in Louise Erdrich's Writing." *RSA Journal: Rivista di Studi Nord Americani* 3 (1992): 43–58.

Desmond, John F. "Catholicism in Contemporary American Fiction." *America* 14 May 1994: 7–11.

Devereaux, Elizabeth. "*Love Medicine* Redux: New and Improved, but Why?" *Publishers Weekly* 23 November 1992: 30.

Downes, Margaret J. "Narrativity, Myth, and Metaphor: Louise Erdrich and Raymond Carver Talk about Love." *MELUS: The Journal of the Society for the Study of the Multi Ethnic Literature* 21.2 (1996): 49–61.

Flavin, James. "The Novel as Performance: Communication in Louise Erdrich's *Tracks*." *Studies in American Indian Literatures* 3.4 (1991): 1–12.

Flavin, Louise. "Gender Construction amid Family Dissolution in Louise Erdrich's *The Beet Queen*." *Studies in American Indian Literatures* 7.2 (1995): 17–24.

———. "Louise Erdrich's *Love Medicine:* Loving Over Time and Distance." *Critique* 31.1 (1989): 55–64.

Friedman, Susan Stanford. "Identity Politics, Syncretism, Catholicism, and Anishinabe Religion in Louise Erdrich's *Tracks. Religion and Literature* 26.1 (1994): 107–33.

Gaughan, Sara K. "Old Age, Folk Belief, and Love in Stories by Ernest Gaines and Louise Erdrich." *Louisiana Folklore Miscellany* 10 (1995): 37–45.

Gleason, William. "'Her Laugh an Ace': The Function of Humor in Louise Erdrich's *Love Medicine*." *American Indian Culture and Research Journal* 11.3 (1987): 51–73.

Grodal, Hanne Tang. "Words, Words, Words." *Dolphin* 18 (1990): 21–26.

Hafen, Jane P. "Sacramental Language: Ritual in the Poetry of Louise Erdrich." *Great Plains Quarterly* 16 (1996): 147–55.

Hessler, Michelle R. "Catholic Nuns and Ojibwa Shamans: Pauline and Fleur in Louise Erdrich's *Tracks*." *Wicazo Sa Review* 11.1 (1995): 40–45.

Holt, Debra C. "Transformation and Continuance: Native American Tradition in the Novels of Louise Erdrich." *Entering the Nineties: The North American Experience.* Ed. Thomas E. Schirer. Sault Ste. Marie: Lake Superior State UP, 1991. 149–61.

Jaskoski, Helen. "From the Time Immemorial: Native American Traditions in Contemporary Short Fiction." *Since Flannery O'Connor: Essays on the Contemporary American Short Story.* Ed. Loren Logsdon and Charles W. Mayer. Macomb: Western Illinois UP, 1987. 54–71.

Khader, Jamil. "Postcolonial Nativeness: Nomadism, Cultural Memory, and the Politics of Identity in Louise Erdrich's and Michael Dorris's *The Crown of Columbus.*" *ARIEL* 28.2 (1997): 81–107.

Kolmar, Wendy K. "'Dialectics of Connectedness': Supernatural Elements in Novels by Bambara, Cisneros, Grahn, and Erdrich." *Haunting the House of Fiction: Feminist Perspectives on Ghost Stories by American Women.* Ed. Lynette Carpenter and Wendy K. Kolmar. Knoxville: U of Tennessee P, 1991. 236–49.

Kroeber, Karl, et al. "Louise Erdrich: *Love Medicine.*" *Studies in American Indian Literatures* 9.1 (1985): 1–29.

Lansky, Ellen. "Spirits and Salvation in Louise Erdrich's *Love Medicine.*" *Dionysos* 5.3 (1994): 39–44.

Larson, Sidner. "The Fragmentation of a Tribal People in Louise Erdrich's *Tracks.*" *American Indian Culture and Research Journal* 17.2 (1993): 1–13.

Lee, Robert A. "Ethnic Renaissance: Rudolfo Anaya, Louise Erdrich, and Maxine Hong Kingston." *The New American Writing: Essays on American Literature since 1970.* Ed. Graham Clarke. New York: St. Martin's, 1990. 139–64.

Lincoln, Kenneth. "'Bring Her Home': Louise Erdrich." *Indi'n Humor: Bicultural Play in Native America.* New York: Oxford UP, 1993. 205–53.

Ludlow, Jeannie. "Working (In) the In-Between: Poetry, Criticism, Interrogation, and Interruption." *Studies in American Indian Literatures* 6.1 (1994): 24–42.

Magalaner, Marvin. "Louise Erdrich: Of Cars, Time, and the River." *American Women Writing Fiction: Memory, Identity, Family, Space.* Ed. Mickey Pearlman. Lexington: UP of Kentucky, 1989. 95–112.

Manley, Kathleen E. B. "Decreasing the Distance: Contemporary Native American Texts, Hypertext, and the Concept of Audience." *Southern Folklore* 51.2 (1994): 121–35.

Maristuen-Rodakowski, Julie. "The Turtle Mountain Reservation in North Dakota: Its History as Depicted in Louise Erdrich's *Love Medicine* and *Beet Queen.*" *American Indian Culture and Research Journal* 12.3 (1988): 33–48.

Maszewska, Jadwiga. "Functions of the Narrative Method in William Faulkner's *Absalom, Absalom!* and Louise Erdrich's *Tracks.*" *Faulkner, His Contemporaries, and His Posterity.* Ed. Waldemar Zacharasiewicz. Tubingen: Francke, 1993. 317–21.

Matchie, Thomas. "Exploring the Meaning of Discovery in *The Crown of Columbus.*" *North Dakota Quarterly* 59.4 (1991): 243–50.

———. "*Love Medicine:* A Female *Moby-Dick.*" *Midwest Quarterly* 30.4 (1989): 478–91.

———. "Louise Erdrich's *Scarlet Letter:* Literary Continuity in *Tales of Burning Love.*" *North Dakota Quarterly* 63.4 (1996): 113–23.

McCay, Mary A. "Cooper's Indians, Erdrich's Native Americans." *Global Perspectives on Teaching Literature: Shared Visions and Distinctive Visions.* Ed. Sandra Ward Lott, Maureen S. G. Hawkins, and Norman McMillan. Urbana: National Council of Teachers of English, 1993. 152–67.

McKenzie, James. "Lipsha's Good Road Home: The Revival of Chippewa Culture in *Love Medicine.*" *American Indian Culture and Research Journal* 10.3 (1986): 53–63.

Medeiros, Paulo. "Cannibalism and Starvation: The Parameters of Eating Disorders in Literature." *Disorderly Eaters: Texts in Self-Empowerment.* Ed. Lillian R. Furst and Peter W. Graham. University Park: Pennsylvania State UP, 1992. 11–27.

Meisenhelder, Susan. "Race and Gender in Louise Erdrich's *The Beet Queen.*" ARIEL 25.1 (1994): 44–57.

Mermann-Jozwiak, Elisabeth. "'His Grandfather Ate His Own Wife': Louise Erdrich's *Love Medicine* as a Contemporary Windigo Narrative." *North Dakota Quarterly* 64.4 (1997): 44–54.

Mitchell, David. "A Bridge to the Past: Cultural Hegemony and the Native American Past in Louise Erdrich's *Love Medicine.*" *Entering the Nineties: The North American Experience.* Ed. Thomas E. Schirer. Sault Ste. Marie: Lake Superior State UP, 1991. 162–70.

Nelson-Born, Katherine A. "Trace of a Woman: Narrative Voice and Decentered Power in the Fiction of Toni Morrison, Margaret Atwood, and Louise Erdrich." *LIT: Literature Interpretation Theory* 7.1 (1996): 1–12.

Owens, Louis. "Erdrich and Dorris's Mixedbloods and Multiple Narratives." *Other Destinies: Understanding the American Indian Novel.* Norman: U of Oklahoma P, 1992. 192–224.

———. "Acts of Recovery: The American Indian Novel in the 80's." *Western American Literature* 22.1 (1987): 53–57.

Pasquaretta, Paul. "Sacred Chance: Gambling and the Contemporary Native American Indian Novel." *MELUS: The Journal of the Society for the Study of Multi Ethnic Literature* 21.2 (1996): 21–33.

Peterson, Nancy J. "History, Postmodernism, and Louise Erdrich's *Tracks*." *PMLA* 109.5 (1994): 982–94.

Pittman, Barbara L. "Cross-cultural Reading and Generic Transformations: The Chronotope of the Road in Erdrich's *Love Medicine*." *American Literature* 67.4 (1995): 777–92.

Purdy, John. "Crossing the Waters to a *Love Medicine* (Louise Erdrich)." *Teaching American Ethnic Literatures: Nineteen Essays*. Ed. John R. Maitino and David R. Peck. Albuquerque: U of New Mexico P, 1996. 83–100.

Rainwater, Catherine. "Reading Between Worlds: Narrativity in the Fiction of Louise Erdrich." *American Literature* 62.3 (1990): 405–22.

Rayson, Ann. "Shifting Identity in the Work of Louise Erdrich and Michael Dorris." *Studies in American Indian Literatures* 3.4 (1991): 27–36.

Ruppert, James. "Mediation and Multiple Narrative in *Love Medicine*." *North Dakota Quarterly* 59.4 (1991): 229–41.

Sarris, Greg. "Reading Louise Erdrich: *Love Medicine* as Home Medicine." *Keeping Slug Woman Alive: A Holistic Approach to American Indian Texts*. Berkeley: U of California P, 1993. 115–45.

Sarve-Gorham, Kristan. "Power Lines: The Motif of Twins and the Medicine Women of *Tracks* and *Love Medicine*." *Bucknell Review* 39.1 (1995): 167–90.

Scheick, William J. "Structures of Belief/Narrative Structures: Mojtabai's *Ordinary Time* and Erdrich's *The Bingo Palace*." *Texas Studies in Literature and Language* 37.4 (1995): 363–75.

Schiavonne, Michelle. "Images of Marginalized Cultures: Intertextuality in Marshall, Morrison, and Erdrich." *Bulletin of the West Virginia Association of College English Teachers* 17 (1995): 41–49.

Schneider, Lissa. "*Love Medicine:* A Metaphor for Forgiveness." *Studies in American Indian Literatures* 4.1 (1992): 1–13.

Schultz, Lydia A. "Fragments and Ojibwe Stories: Narrative Strategies in Louise Erdrich's *Love Medicine*." *College Literature* 18.3 (1991): 80–95.

Schweninger, Lee. "A Skin of Lakeweed: An Ecofeminist Approach to Erdrich and Silko." *Multicultural Literatures through Feminist/Poststructuralist Lenses*. Ed. Barbara Frey Waxman. Knoxville: U of Tennessee P, 1993. 37–56.

Secco, Anna. "The Search for Origins through Storytelling in Native American Literatures: Momaday, Silko, Erdrich." *RSA Journal: Rivista di Studi Nord Americani* 3 (1992): 59–71.

Sergi, Jennifer. "Storytelling: Tradition, and Preservation in Louise Erdrich's *Tracks.*" *World Literature Today* 66.2 (1992): 279–82.

Shaddock, Jennifer. "Mixed Blood Women: The Dynamic of Women's Relations in the Novels of Louise Erdrich and Leslie Silko." *Feminist Nightmares: Women at Odds: Feminism and the Problem of Sisterhood.* Ed. Susan Ostrov Weisser and Jennifer Fleischner. New York: New York UP, 1994. 106–21.

Siegel, Lee. "De Sade's Daughters." *Atlantic Monthly* February 1997: 97–100, 102.

Silberman, Robert. "Opening the Text: *Love Medicine* and the Return of the Native American Woman." *Narrative Chance: Postmodern Discourse on Native American Indian Literatures.* Ed. Gerald Vizenor. Albuquerque: U of New Mexico P, 1989. 101–20.

Silko, Leslie. "Here's an Odd Artifact for the Fairy-Tale Shelf." Rev. of *The Beet Queen* by Louise Erdrich. *Impact/Albuquerque Journal* 8 October 1986: 10–16.

Slack, John S. "The Comic Savior: The Dominance of the Trickster in Louise Erdrich's *Love Medicine.*" *North Dakota Quarterly* 61 (1993): 118–29.

Sloboda, Nicholas. "Beyond the Iconic Subject: Re-Visioning Louise Erdrich's *Tracks.*" *Studies in American Indian Literatures* 8.3 (1996): 63–79.

Smith, Jeanne Rosier. "Transpersonal Selfhood: The Boundaries of Identity in Louise Erdrich's *Love Medicine.*" *Studies in American Indian Literatures* 3.4 (1991): 13–26.

———. *Writing Tricksters: Mythic Gambols in American Ethnic Literature.* Berkeley: U of California P, 1997. 71–110.

Stripes, James D. "The Problem(s) of (Anishinaabe) History in the Fiction of Louise Erdrich: Voices and Contexts." *Wicazo Sa Review* 7.2 (1991): 26–33.

Tharp, Julie. "Women's Community and Survival in the Novels of Louise Erdrich." *Communication and Women's Friendships: Parallels and Intersections in Literature and Life.* Ed. Janet Doubler Ward and JoAnna Stephens Mink. Bowling Green: Bowling Green State UP, 1993. 165–80.

Towery, Margie. "Continuity and Connection: Characters in Louise Erdrich's Fiction." *American Indian Culture and Research Journal* 16.4 (1992): 99–122.

Van Dyke, Annette. "Questions of the Spirit: Bloodlines in Louise Erdrich's Chippewa Landscape." *Studies in American Indian Literatures* 4.1 (1992): 15–27.

Walker, Victoria. "A Note on Narrative Perspective in *Tracks.*" *Studies in American Indian Literatures* 3.4 (1991): 37–40.

Walsh, Dennis M., and Ann Braley. "The Indianness of Louise Erdrich's *The Beet Queen:* Latency as Presence." *American Indian Culture and Research Journal* 18.3 (1994): 1–17.

Wong, Hertha D. "Adoptive Mothers and Thrown-Away Children in the Novels of Louise Erdrich." *Narrating Mothers: Theorizing Maternal Subjectivities.* Ed. Brenda O. Daly and Maureen T. Reddy. Knoxville: U of Tennessee P, 1991. 174–92.

———. "Louise Erdrich's *Love Medicine:* Narrative Communities and the Short Story Sequence." *Modern American Short Story Sequences: Composite Fictions and Fictive Communities.* Ed. J. Gerald Kennedy. Cambridge: Cambridge UP, 1995. 170–93.

Woodward, Pauline G. "Chance in Louise Erdrich's *The Beet Queen:* New Ways to Find a Family." *ARIEL* 26.2 (1995): 109–27.

Zeck, Jeanne-Marie. "Erdrich's *Love Medicine.*" *Explicator* 54.1 (1995): 58–60.

Bibliographies

Burdick, Debra A. "Louise Erdrich's *Love Medicine, The Beet Queen,* and *Tracks:* An Annotated Survey of Criticism through 1994." *American Indian Culture and Research Journal* 20.3 (1996): 137–66.

"Louise Erdrich: A.S.A.I.L. Bibliography #9." *Studies in American Indian Literatures* 9.1 (1985): 37–41.

Pearlman, Mickey. "A Bibliography of Writings about Louise Erdrich." *American Women Writing Fiction.* Ed. Mickey Pearlman. Lexington: UP of Kentucky, 1989. 108–10.

Interviews

Bonetti, Kay. "An Interview with Louise Erdrich and Michael Dorris." *Missouri Review* 11.2 (1988): 79–99.

Chavkin, Allan, and Nancy Feyl Chavkin, eds. *Conversations with Louise Erdrich and Michael Dorris.* Jackson: UP of Mississippi, 1994.

Contributors

Allan Chavkin

Allan Chavkin's publications include *Conversations with Louise Erdrich and Michael Dorris, English Romanticism and Modern Fiction, Conversations with John Gardner,* and more than thirty articles in books and such journals as *Studies in the Novel, Papers on Language and Literature, Philological Quarterly,* and *Comparative Literature Studies.* He is Professor of English at Southwest Texas State University.

Nancy Feyl Chavkin

Nancy Feyl Chavkin is Professor of Social Work at Southwest Texas State University. Her publications include *Conversations with Louise Erdrich and Michael Dorris, Families and Schools in a Pluralistic Society,* and *The Use of Research in Social Work Practice.*

Robert F. Gish

Robert F. Gish is currently Director of Ethnic Studies at California Polytechnic State University, San Luis Obispo. He is the author of *Songs of My Hunter Heart: A Western Kinship, First Horses: Stories of the New West,* and numerous other books and writings about the American West. His *When Coyote Howls: A Lavaland Fable* is forthcoming from the University of New Mexico Press. He is a member of the Cherokee Nation of Oklahoma.

Robert A. Morace

Robert A. Morace is the author of *The Dialogic Novels of Malcolm Bradbury and David Lodge* as well as articles on contemporary and American realist fiction in *Critique, Modern Fiction Studies, Review of Contemporary*

Fiction, Studies in American Fiction, and elsewhere, most recently "Dialogues and Dialogics" (*Modern Language Studies,* 1993) and "Tales from the Crypt(o-autobiography): A User's Guide to John Cheever's Journals" (*The Critical Response to John Cheever,* 1994). He has also compiled *John Gardner: An Annotated Secondary Bibliography* and edited *John Gardner: Critical Perspectives* (with Kathryn VanSpanckeren). He teaches at Daemen College.

NANCY J. PETERSON

Nancy J. Peterson is Associate Professor of English at Purdue University and Assistant Editor of *Modern Fiction Studies.* She recently edited *Toni Morrison: Critical and Theoretical Approaches* (1997), and her book about historical memory and women writers, *Against Amnesia,* is forthcoming.

JOHN PURDY

John Purdy lives in the Northwest and teaches Contemporary American/Native American written literatures at Western Washington University. His works include *Word Ways: The Novels of D'Arcy McNickle* and the forthcoming collection, *D'Arcy McNickle and the Canonization of Native America,* which he edited. He has published numerous articles and reviews on Native American authors, including James Welch, Leslie Marmon Silko, Elizabeth Cook Lynn, and Joseph Bruchac. His articles on Louise Erdrich appear in *The Dictionary of Native American Literature* and the collection *Teaching American Ethnic Literatures.* He also edits *A.S.A.I.L. Notes,* the newsletter for the Association for the Study of Native American Literatures.

CATHERINE RAINWATER

Catherine Rainwater is Associate Professor of English at St. Edward's University in Austin, Texas. She is the author of numerous articles in books and journals and co-editor of two books on women writers. Her works have recently appeared in such journals as *American Literature, Philological Quarterly, American Journal of Semiotics,* and *Texas Studies in Literature and Language.* In 1990 her article on Louise Erdrich, published in

American Literature, was awarded the Norman Foerster Prize by the Modern Language Association. She is also the president of the Ellen Glasgow Society and editor of the *Ellen Glasgow Newsletter.* At the present time, she is nearing completion of a book-length study of contemporary Native American narrative.

A. LAVONNE BROWN RUOFF

A. LaVonne Brown Ruoff is Professor Emerita of English at the University of Illinois at Chicago. She has published extensively on American Indian literatures, including *American Indian Literatures: An Introduction, Bibliographic Review, and Selected Bibliography.* She is series editor for University of Nebraska's Native American Lives and has directed NEH seminars in American Indian literatures.

WILLIAM J. SCHEICK

William J. Scheick is J. R. Millikan Centennial Professor of English and American Literature at the University of Texas at Austin. His most recent books include *The Splintering Frame: The Later Fiction of H. G. Wells* (1984), *Contemporary American Women Writers: Narrative Strategies* (with Catherine Rainwater, 1985), *Fictional Structure and Ethics: The Turn-of-the-Century English Novel* (1990), *Design in Puritan American Literature* (1992), *Paine, Scripture, and Authority* (with Edward Davidson, 1994), and *The Ethos of Romance at the Turn of the Century* (1994).

ANNETTE VAN DYKE

Annette Van Dyke is Assistant Professor of Interdisciplinary Studies and Women's Studies at the University of Illinois at Springfield. She has published articles on Native American women writers in *MELUS* and *Studies in American Indian Literatures* and in a number of books. Her book, *The Search for a Woman-Centered Spirituality,* containing a chapter on Leslie Marmon Silko and Paula Gunn Allen, was published by New York University Press in 1992.

Index